FRENCH for COMMUNICATION

BY

GARY A. MILGROM
John F. Kennedy High School, Bronx, New York

FRANÇOISE SANTALIS, Ph.D
New Rochelle School District, New Rochelle, New York

Editorial Consultant
Jacqueline Lucido Friedman
Horace Mann-Barnard Elementary School (New York)

ISBN 0-941519-14-7

Acknowledgements

Thanks to my consultant and friend, French teacher Jacqueline Lucido Friedman, for her advice and support.

Thanks to Suzanne Cohen, former French teacher at John Adams High School (Queens, NY) for most graciously assisting in the review of this manuscript.

Thanks also to Ralph Santalis, former Principal and teacher of French and Spanish, for his advice and encouragement.

CURRICULUM PRESS, INC.
PO BOX 387
GUILDERLAND, NY 12084

10 9 8 7 6 5

Gary A. Milgom graduated from the City College of New York with a Bachelor of Arts Degree in Spanish. He earned a Masters Degree in Spanish from New York University in Spain at the University of Madrid.

He has taught Spanish at the junior high school, high school and college level and conducts workshops on many aspects of foreign language teaching including Mastery Learning, Cooperative Learning and Student-centered classroom tecniques.

Mr. Milgrom is a Teacher of Spanish at John F. Kennedy High School, Bronx, New York.

Françoise Santalis is a native of Paris, France. After settling in America she earned both B.A. and M.A. degrees from Hunter College and a Ph.D in French literature from the Graduate Center of the City University of New York. Her dissertation was awarded *Le Prix de l'Ambassade de France.*

Dr. Santalis has been President of the New York Metropolitan chapter of the American Association of Teachers of French. She has taught French and Spanish at Hunter College High School, Spanish at SUNY Purchase and bilingual education courses at William Patterson College in New Jersey.

Dr. Santalis is Supervisor of Foreign Languages and ESL for the New Rochelle School District (NY).

Dedication

à mon père, ***Charles Vavasseur***

whose love of the French language and culture
brought joy and meaning to my life

TABLE OF CONTENTS

UNIT I
Qui es-tu? Me voici. (Première partie) ....Page 1

UNIT II
Qui es-tu? Me voici. (Deuxième partie) ....Page 25

UNIT III
Le climat et le temps
Qui êtes-vous? Me voici. ....Page 49

UNIT IV
L'école ....Page 79

UNIT V
La famille ....Page 107

UNIT VI
Révision ....Page 139

UNIT VII
Quelle heure est-il?
La maison et la vie chez soi ....Page 157

UNIT VIII
La santé
Les passe-temps ....Page 187

UNIT IX
La nourriture et la boisson
Dans un restaurant ....Page 213

UNIT X
Les achats ....Page 249

UNIT XI
La France et sa géographie
Une promenade dans Paris
Voyager dans Paris et en Métro
La pendule de 24 heures
Voyager par la SNCF ....Page 275

UNIT XII
Les magasins
Mon quartier
Les métiers / Les professions ....Page 311

UNIT ONE

Qui es-tu? Me voici.

(Première partie)

TOPIC
Personal identification
SITUATION
Interaction with individual peers in the classroom
FUNCTION
Introducing oneself, greeting, leave-taking, exchanging basic information of personal identification
PROFICIENCY
Can comprehend simple questions and respond appropriately with possible need for repetition

AIM I : Each student will be able to introduce himself to a peer and be able to ask "What's your name?"

AIM II: Each student will be able to greet a peer asking "How are you?" and be able to respond

AIM III: Each student will be able to take leave of his peers

AIM IVA: Each student will be able to identify and locate the French-speaking countries of the western hemisphere

AIM IVB: Each student will be able to ask a peer "Where are you from?" and be able to respond

AIM VA: Each student will be able to add and subtract employing numbers 0 - 10

AIM VB: Each student will be able to ask a peer "What's your telephone number?" and be able to respond

AIM VIA: Each student will be able to add and subtract employing numbers 1 - 20

AIM VIB: Each student will be able to ask a peer "How old are you?" and be able to respond

Aim I: *Each student will be able to introduce himself to a peer and be able to ask "What's your name?"*

Exercice oral

1. **Philippe:** Je m'appelle Philippe. Et toi, comment t'appelles-tu?

   Marie: Je m'appelle Marie.

2. **Hélène:** Je m'appelle Hélène. Et toi, comment t'appelles-tu?

   Paul: Je m'appelle Paul.

Conversation

1. Introduce yourself to three other peers near you and after each introduction ask *Et toi, comment t'appelles-tu?* Begin to learn the names of your classmates as you will be speaking French to them throughout this course.

2. Chain drill by rows: The first student introduces himself and then asks the second student in the row, *Et toi, comment t'appelles-tu?* The second student answers the question and then introduces himself to the third student followed by the appropriate question.

Exercice écrit

Write the question you would ask of a peer to find out his name. Then write how you would respond to this question.

What mark is sometimes written over the vowels *"a"* and *"e"* in French? The marks " ´ " or " ` " are called an accent mark. Learn to spell correctly by placing the accent mark, whenever it appears, over the appropriate vowel.

Résumé

1. One or two pairs of students can act out the following roles for the whole class. Note that one or more lines may be missing so that some thought will be required.

2. Pairs of students throughout the class can work together to practice the dialogues.

A. **Christine:** Je m'appelle Christine. Et toi, __________?
Antoine: Je m'appelle Antoine.

B. **Jean:** ____________. Et toi, comment t'appelles-tu?
Anne: Je m'appelle Anne.

C. **Philippe:** Je m'appelle Philippe. Et toi, comment t'appelles-tu?
Michel: ____________.

D. **Odile:**___________. Et toi, comment t'appelles-tu?
Claude:_____________.

Note culturelle

In English when one person addresses another, the person is addressed as "you", regardless of the relationship. In French when a young person addresses a peer, the person is addressed as *"tu"*. Two adults who call each other by their first names also use *"tu"*. *"Tu"* is known as the familiar or informal form of address.

Vocabulaire

Et toi? *And you*
Comment t'appelles-tu? *What's your name?*
Je m'appelle ... *My name is ...*

Antoine *Anthony*
Charles *Charles*
Philippe *Philip*
Joseph *Joseph*
Jean *John*
Michel *Michael*

Anne *Ann*
Christine *Christine*
Hélène *Ellen*
Marie *Mary*
Paul *Paul*
Odile *Odile*

Note Culturelle

Religion has always played a major role in the formation and development of many societies. This is particularly true of France and the many countries to whom it had given its language and culture. In whose honor were the following French names given? *Antoine, Philippe, Jean, Pierre, Vincent, Thérèse...*

Many girls and boys have two first names and quite often one of them is *Marie* in honor of the Virgin Mary: *Marie-Thérèse, Marie-Claude, Marie-France.*

Aim II: *Each student will be able to greet a peer asking "How are you?" and be able to respond*

Exercice oral 1

Je vais bien.

Je vais très bien.

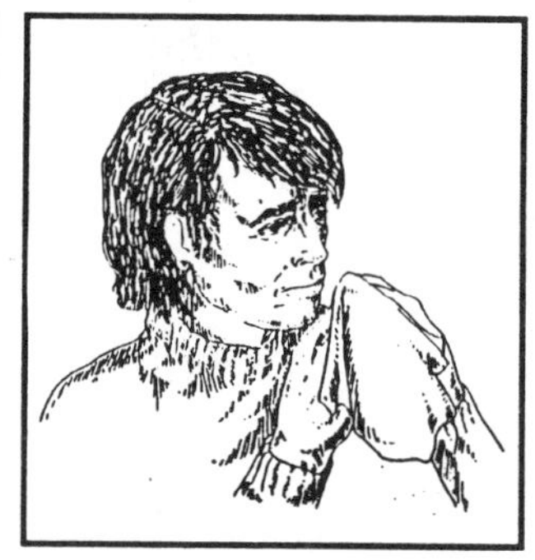

Je suis malade.

Je suis malade.

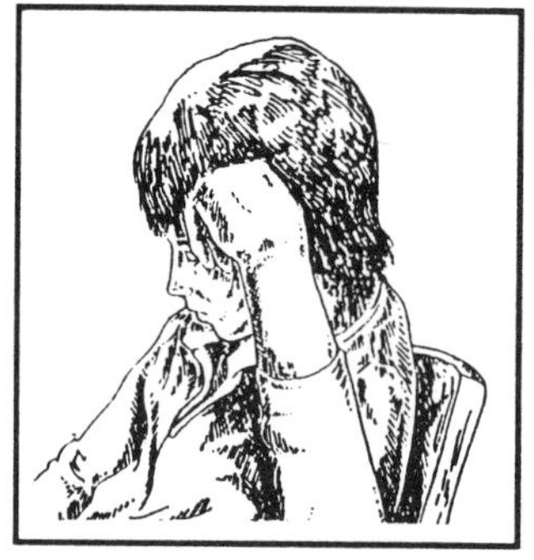

Je suis fatigué.

Je suis fatiguée.

Exercice oral 2

1. **Isabelle:** Bonjour! Ça va?
   Patrick: Ça va bien. Et toi?
   Isabelle: Ça va très bien, merci.

2. **Pierre:** Bonjour! Comment vas-tu?
   Cécile: Ça va bien. Et toi?
   Pierre: Ça va comme ci, comme ça.

3. **Rose:** Comment vas-tu, Paul?
   Paul: Je suis fatigué. Et toi?
   Rose: Ça va très bien, merci.

4. **Jean:** Quoi de neuf, Anne?
   Anne: Je suis très fatiguée. Et toi?
   Jean: Moi aussi.

Réfléchissons

When responding to the question *Comment vas-tu?* or *Quoi de neuf?* if a male answers with an adjective ending in the letter "e", in what letter must the adjective end for a female? From what example did you get your answer? How would a male spell "I'm tired?" How would a female spell it?

Conversation

1. Ask two other peers near you *Comment vas-tu?* and two more *Quoi de neuf?* and listen carefully to each response.

2. Situations: Take turns playing the following roles with your partner.

A. You meet a friend between classes. Ask her how she is. She responds that she is very tired.

B. As you enter the school, you see one of your classmates. Greet him. He responds that he is so-so.

C. After school you call a good friend who was not in class that day. Greet her. Ask her how she is. She responds that she is sick.

Exercice écrit

1. Write a question you would ask of a peer or friend to find out how s/he is. Then write how you would respond.

2. Write the **Conversation** 2, **A, B,** and **C** in dialogue form.

3. Write two original three line dialogues showing how one peer greets another, receives a response, and then asks about the health of the other with an appropriate response. Write the name of each speaker.

Je suis très malade.

Vocabulaire

Bonjour! Comment vas-tu? *Hello! How are you?*
Bonjour! Quoi de neuf? / Ça va? *Hello! How are you?*
Ça va bien. *I am fine. I am well.*
Ça va très bien. / Je vais très bien. *I am very well.*
Ça va comme ci, comme ça. *I am so-so.*
Je suis fatigué(e). *I am tired.*
Je suis malade. *I am sick.*
Quoi de neuf? *What's new? What's up?*
Et toi? *And you?*
Moi aussi. *Me too.*
Merci. *Thank you.*

Claude *Claude*
Isabelle *Isabel*
Paul *Paul*
Pierre *Peter*
Rose *Rose*
Thérèse *Theresa*
Patrick *Patrick*
Vincent *Vincent*

Aim III: *Each student will be able to take leave of his peers*

Exercice oral

1. **Philippe:** Au revoir, Claude.
   Claude: Au revoir, Philippe.

2. **Hélène:** Au revoir, Michel.
   Michel: A plus tard.

3. **Rose:** Au revoir, Charles.
   Charles: A demain, Rose.

4. **Patrick:** Au revoir, Michelle.
   Michelle: A bientôt.

Conversation

1. Situations: Play the following roles with your peer partner.

A. You say goodbye to your friend at the end of class. S/he responds.

B. You are chatting with your friend between classes. The bell rings so you say goodbye. S/he responds that s/he will see you later.

C. At the end of the school day you tell your friend that you will see him/her tomorrow. Your friend responds.

Exercice écrit

1. Write the **Conversation**, 1, **A**, **B**, and **C**.

Résumé

One or two pairs of students can play the roles for the entire class followed by peer practice.

1. **Pierre:** Bonjour! ________.
2. **Isabelle:** Je suis très fatiguée. Et toi?
3. **Pierre:** __________.
4. **Isabelle:** Au revoir, Pierre.
5. **Pierre:** __________.

1. **Anne:** Bonjour! Ça va?
2. **Joseph:** __________. __________.
3. **Anne:** _________ aussi.
4. **Joseph:** __________.
5. **Anne:** A bientôt, Joseph.

Vocabulaire

Au revoir. *Goodbye.*
A plus tard. *See you later. So long.*
A bientôt. *See you later. So long. See you soon.*
A demain. *See you tomorrow.*

Note: Look at the word *bientôt*. What do you notice over the "*ô*"? It is called an *accent circonflexe*. In general it will appear on the vowels "*o*", "*e*" and "*a*" when they appear in front of the letter "*t*".

Aim IVA: *Each student will be able to identify and locate the French-speaking countries of the western hemisphere.*

Exercice oral

Où est-ce qu'on parle français? Individual students come to the wall map to point out the location of the French-speaking countries as the entire class repeats each country's name.

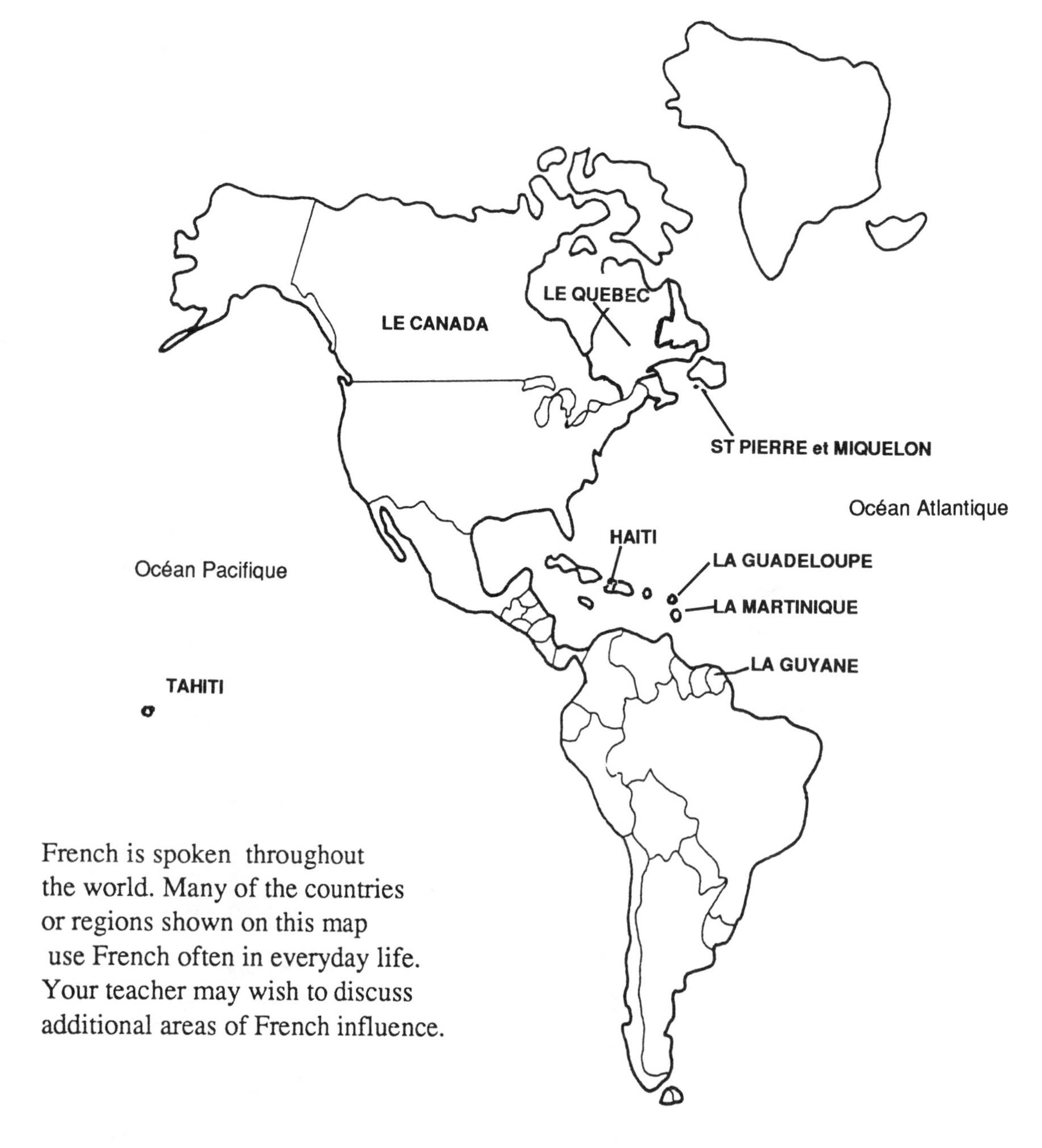

French is spoken throughout the world. Many of the countries or regions shown on this map use French often in everyday life. Your teacher may wish to discuss additional areas of French influence.

Conversation

Peer practice in groups of two.

1. *Où est-ce qu'on parle français? On parle français en____.* One partner asks the question as the other answers pointing to his map. Partners can take turns asking and answering the question until all the countries have been mentioned.

2. *Où est le Canada? **--(le Canada)** est en **Amérique du Nord.***
*Où est la Martinique?--**(La Martinique)** est **dans l'océan Atlantique.***

Partners take turns asking each other in what region each French-speaking country is located.

Réfléchissons

How do we ask where something is located? This phrase is also used to ask where a person is located.

Exercice écrit

1. Write the **Conversation, 2.** Write both the five questions (five countries) and the appropriate answers.

2. Examine once again the geographic regions under study. Write and complete the following statements with the appropriate word or expression.

A. The large peninsula situated in the north-east part of America is_____.
B. The islands which are situated in the Atlantic Ocean near Puerto Rico are _____ and _____.
C. The small country situated in South America surrounded by Brazil and the Atlantic Ocean is _____.
D. The small island situated in the Pacific Ocean which belongs to the Polynesian islands is _____.
E. The islands close to Québec in the Atlantic Ocean are _____ and _____.

Note culturelle

La Guadeloupe is characterized by its diversity; the "Basse Terre" is volcanic and mountainous, while the "Grande Terre" is very flat. The two islands are linked together by a bridge. Their main industries are sugar cane and bananas. The population is highly concentrated in Pointe-à-Pitre.

Résumé

On a blank map write the name of each of the French-speaking countries of the regions under study and the principal bodies of water which surround them.

Vocabulaire

Où parle-t-on français? *Where is French spoken?*
Où est-ce qu'on parle français? *Where is French spoken?*
Dans quel pays parle-t-on français? *In what country is French spoken?*
On parle français en _____. *French is spoken in _____.*

Où est _____? *Where is _____?*
___ est en Amérique du Nord. _____*is in North America.*
Le Canada *Canada*
Québec *Quebec*

____est dans l'océan Atlantique. _____*is in the Atlantic Ocean.*

La Guadeloupe
La Martinique
La Guyane
Saint Pierre
Miquelon

Aim IVB: *Each student will be able to ask a peer "Where are you from?" and be able to respond*

Exercice oral

1. **Antoine:** D'où es-tu?

   Claude: Je suis de la Martinique.

2. **Thérèse:** D'où es-tu?

   Vincent: Je suis des Etats-Unis.

Conversation

1. Each student is given the opportunity to state the country of his birth for the entire class.

2. Ask three students near you *D'où es-tu?* and listen carefully to each response.

3. Chain drill by rows: The first student says *Je suis de*_____ and then asks the next student the appropriate question.

Je suis de Paris.

Exercice écrit

Write the question you would ask of a peer to find out where s/he is from. Then write how you would respond.

Résumé

Two pairs of students can play the roles for the entire class followed by peer practice.

A

1. **Jean:** Bonjour! Je m'appelle Jean. Et toi, _______?
2. **Michelle:** D'où es-tu?
3. **Jean:** ________. Et toi?

B

1. **Odile:** Bonjour!______?
2. **Michel:** Je m'appelle Michel. Et toi?
3. **Odile:** __________.
   __________?

4. **Michelle:** _________.

5. **Jean:** A bientôt, Michelle.

6. **Michelle:** ______, Jean.

4. **Michel:** Je suis de la Guadeloupe. Et toi?

5. **Odile:** ________. A demain.

6. **Michel:** ________ .

Vocabulaire

D'où es-tu? *Where are you from?*
Je suis de_____. *I'm from _____.*
Je suis des Etats-Unis. *I'm from the United States.*

Aim VA: *Each student will be able to add and subtract employing numbers 0 - 10*

Exercice oral

Les numéros de 0 à 10

0 zéro **1** un **2** deux **3** trois **4** quatre **5** cinq

6 six **7** sept **8** huit **9** neuf **10** dix

Conversation

To help us learn numbers 0 - 10, let us learn to add and subtract. We will need to know how to say "plus" and "minus" to tell time.

2 + 5 = ? Deux et cinq font sept.
4 + 6 = ? Quatre et six font dix.
9 - 6 = ? Neuf moins six font trois.
8 - 7 = ? Huit moins sept fait un.

First, partner **A** asks his partner *Combien font____et____?* for a problem of addition or *Combien font ___moins ___?* for a subtraction problem. Partner **B** must repeat the numbers to be added or subtracted and then give the answer. Then Partner **B** asks the other set of problems.

Examples:

Partner A:	3 + 5 = ?	*Combien font trois et cinq?*
Partner B:		*Trois et cinq font huit.*
Partner A:	10 - 4 = ?	*Combien font dix moins quatre?*
Partner B:		*Dix moins quatre font six.*

Partner A	**Partner B**	**Partner A**	**Partner B**
1. 3 + 7 = ?	1. 6 + 3 = ?	5. 8 - 2 = ?	5. 7 - 4 = ?
2. 1 + 8 = ?	2. 2 + 8 = ?	6. 9 - 4 = ?	6. 8 - 3 = ?
3. 2 + 4 = ?	3. 4 + 3 = ?	7. 10 - 3 = ?	7. 10 - 1 = ?
4. 5 + 2 = ?	4. 1 + 4 = ?	8. 6 - 5 = ?	8. 5 - 3 = ?

Exercice écrit

Write in French the answers to the problems of the **Conversation.** (Partner **A** asks #1 - 8 and Partner **B** asks #1 - 8.) Write your answers in complete sentences.

Examples:
A 1. *Trois et sept font dix.* **B** 5. *Sept moins quatre font trois.*

* ***Note:*** In French, instead of using *font* and *fait*, we can use "égal."
Example: Trois et cinq égal huit. Both forms are commonly used.

Aim VB: *Each student will be able to ask a peer "What is your telephone number?" and be able to respond*

Exercice oral

1. **Odile:** Quel est ton numéro de téléphone?
   Antoine: Mon numéro de téléphone est cinq-deux-quatre-sept-zéro trois-huit.

2. **Vincent:** Quel est ton numéro de téléphone?
   Catherine: Mon numéro de téléphone est huit-trois-six-neuf-un-deux-cinq.

Conversation

1. Ask two other students near you *Quel est ton numéro de téléphone?* and listen carefully to each response.

2. Chain drill by rows.

Exercice écrit

1. Write the question you would ask of a peer to find out what his/her telephone number is. Then write how you would respond.

2. Write the telephone numbers in French of ten people who live in Paris, the capital of France. Write both name and number.

Example: Alain Amory, trois-neuf-huit-zéro-quatre-deux-un-six.

ALPHE Claire
12 esplanade Salvador Allendè - - (1)39 61 33 55
ALPHONSE Victoire 11 pl Saint Just (1)34 11 39 91
ALRIC Raymond 76 r Anatole Lucas (1)39 80 31 01
ALSOTEL 174 av Jean Jaurès - - - - (1)39 82 61 05
ALTMAN Philippe
76 r Paul Vaillant Couturier - - - - (1)39 47 01 29
ALTMAYER Bernard 7 r Arras - - (1)34 10 02 46
ALTULOR (SA) 176 rte Pontoise - - (1)39 82 71 43
ALTULOR (S A) 176 rte Pontoise - - (1)39 80 31 13
ALTUNA Francisca 19 r Vigneronde (1)39 61 03 45
ALVARADO José 34bis r Justice - - (1)39 80 87 98
ALVAREZ Antonio 42 r Folie - - - (1)34 10 31 40
» **Antonio**
2 all Wolfang Amadeus Mozart - - (1)34 10 45 48
» **Daniel** 126 r Maurice Rechsteiner (1)39 82 36 49
» **François** 25 r Emile Saloy - - - - (1)39 80 48 77
» **Victor** 13 r Arras - - - - - - - - (1)34 10 72 49
ALVES Abilio 16 r Indes - - - - - - (1)39 81 84 01
» **Adlino** 61 av Parc - - - - - - - (1)34 10 72 82
» **Américo** 81 r Jolival - - - - - - (1)39 82 28 43
» **Antonio** 150 r Rochefort - - - - (1)34 11 36 84
» **Bernard** 164 av Stalingrad - - - (1)39 80 33 12
» **Christian**
13 r Doct Pierre Rouquès - - - - (1)34 10 76 40
» **Daniel** 39 r Aveyron - - - - - - (1)39 82 36 12
» **Ema** 4 all François Villon - - - - (1)39 82 76 09
» **Fatima** 2bis r Treilly - - - - - - (1)39 81 77 42
ALVÈS Françoise 19 r Gibet - - - - (1)34 10 91 15
ALVES Ghislaine 51 r Perreux - - - (1)39 47 24 11
» **Jacques** 4 r Doct Lamaze - - - - (1)39 81 66 33
» **Jean** 2 pl Dessau - - - - - - - - (1)34 11 12 64
» **Joaquim** 20 r Repos - - - - - - (1)39 81 17 33
» **José entrepr maçonn**
138 r Perreux - - - - - - - - - - (1)34 10 45 94
» **Manuel** 11 pl Georges Braque - (1)39 61 80 39
» **Raoul** 20 r Marseillaise - - - - - (1)39 81 86 19
ALVES DA ROCHA Francisc
31 r Porte des Prés - - - - - - - - (1)39 80 79 90
ALVES DACUNHA Manuel
11 pl D'Alembert - - - - - - - - - (1)34 11 14 61
ALVES ENTREPRISE
135 av Jean Jaurès - - - - - - - - (1)39 81 96 30
ALZIEU J 8 sq Michelet - - - - - - - (1)39 61 27 76
ALZIN Joëlle coiff.dames
100 r Paul Vaillant Couturier - - - - (1)39 61 35 69
AM INTERNATIONAL (SA) ZI
r Chanteloup - - - - - - - - - - - (1)39 82 62 11
A.M. INTERNATIONAL
6 r Chanteloup - - - - - - - - - - (1)39 82 57 89
» **Gilles plombier** 236 rte Enghien (1)39 80 55 64
AMMOUCHE Ahcène 1 r Arras - - (1)34 10 61 68
» **Roland chauffeur taxi**
40 r Louis Blanc - - - - - - - - - (1)39 80 73 85
AMMOUR Ahmed 19 r St Quentin - (1)39 81 72 04
AMOKRANE Nadia 40 r Temple - - (1)39 61 08 21
AMORIN Agostinho
48 r Paul Vaillant Couturier - - - - (1)39 47 14 01
AMOROS Colette 4 r Liberté - - - (1)39 47 15 62
AMORY Alain 10 cité Champagne - (1)39 80 42 16
» **M** 30 r Balmont - - - - - - - - - (1)39 82 40 03
» **Paul** 6 pl Saint Just - - - - - - - (1)39 81 10 05
AMOURET Francis
3 all François Villon - - - - - - - - (1)34 10 51 85
AMPADU Élisabeth
24 r Henri Barbusse - - - - - - - - (1)39 47 80 39
AMPONSAH Béatrice
10 esplanade Maurice Thorez - - - (1)39 82 22 10
AMPOSTA François 23 r Lévêque - (1)39 47 19 22
AMRANI Francis 30 r Gibet - - - - (1)39 81 91 24
AMRHEIM A 175 r Courlis - - - - - (1)34 10 31 56
AMRI Hassane 52 av Marcel Cachin (1)39 61 08 52
AMROUCHE Kheddoudja
39 bd Karl Marx - - - - - - - - - (1)39 47 28 81
AMROUNI Mosian
15 all Auguste Renoir - - - - - - - (1)34 10 44 89
A.M.S consultez nous sur Minitel
43 r Ambroise Thomas - - - - - - *(1)30 76 06 06
A.M.S 43 r Ambroise Thomas - - - - (1)30 76 06 06
AMSKER Boujemaa
120 r Ferdinand Berthoud - - - - - (1)39 61 79 59
A.M.S.M 33 r Etienne Chevalier - - - (1)39 61 08 97
AMSTUTZ (Ets) Location Thrifty
184 r Paris RN 328 95320 ST LEU - *(1)39 60 91 80
A.M.U. (Argenteuil Médical Urgence-SARL)
10 résid Bretagne - - - - - - - - (1)34 11 11 14
AMUSAN Jean-Claude
10 r Jean Charcot - - - - - - - - - (1)39 80 49 19
AMY Désiré 17 r Balsamines - - - - (1)39 80 60 31
AMYS René 10 pl Denis Diderot - - (1)34 10 09 77
AMZIAN Nadine 38 r Justice - - - (1)34 11 36 28
AMZIANE Amar
2 all Gustave Courbet - - - - - - - (1)34 10 16 91
ANABITARTE Jean-Marie 4 r Paix (1)39 80 74 52
ANACLETO Joseph
98 r Ferdinand Berthoud - - - - - (1)39 47 24 18
ANAD Amar 30 bd Lénine - - - - - (1)39 82 17 77
ANAMR Brahim
120 r Ferdinand Berthoud - - - - - (1)39 61 12 42
ANASTASIO René 46 r Cloviers - - (1)39 80 90 72

Note: *The French often group phone numbers in groups of two. When you learn higher numbers you will be able to read the numbers above as double digits.*

Exercice de compréhension

You will hear three telephone numbers in French. After the second repetition of each number, write them in Arabic numbers.

Example: sept-quatre-trois-cinq-un-huit-zéro. 743-5180

Vocabulaire

Les numéros 0-10

Combien font____et____? *How much is _____ and _____?*
Combien font____moins____? *How much is _____ minus _____?*

et *and*
moins *minus*

zéro *zero*
un *one*
deux *two*
trois *three*
quatre *four*

cinq *five*
six *six*
sept *seven*
huit *eight*
neuf *nine*
dix *ten*

Quel est ton numéro de téléphone? *What is your telephone number?*
Mon numéro de téléphone est_____. *My telephone number is ____ .*

Aim VIA: *Each student will be able to add and subtract employing numbers 1 - 20*

Exercice oral

Les Numéros 11-20

11 onze **12** douze **13** treize **14** quatorze

15 quinze **16** seize **17** dix-sept **18** dix-huit

19 dix-neuf **20** vingt

Conversation

Partner **A** asks Partner **B** *Combien font ___ et ___?* for a problem in addition or *combien font___moins___?* for a subtraction problem. Partner **B** must repeat the numbers to be added or subtracted and then give the answer. Then Partner **B** asks the other set of problems.

Examples:

Partner A:	12 + 6 = ?	*Combien font douze et six?*
Partner B:		*Douze et six font dix-huit.*
Partner A:	19 - 5 = ?	*Combien font dix-neuf moins cinq?*
Partner B:		*Dix-neuf moins cinq font quatorze.*

Partner A	**Partner B**	**Partner A**	**Partner B**
1. 11 + 6 = ?	1. 9 + 8 = ?	6. 20 - 15 = ?	6. 17 - 5 = ?
2. 3 + 9 = ?	2. 12 + 3 = ?	7. 16 - 7 = ?	7. 13 - 10 = ?
3. 13 + 5 = ?	3. 6 + 7 = ?	8. 12 - 8 = ?	8. 20 - 6 = ?
4. 4 + 14 = ?	4. 9 + 11 = ?	9. 19 - 5 = ?	9. 18 - 7 = ?
5. 8 + 7 = ?	5. 5 + 14 = ?	10. 11 - 4 = ?	10. 15 - 9 = ?

Exercice écrit

Write the answers to the **Conversation** (Partner **B** columns, numbers 1 - 10) in complete sentences. Example from Partner **A**, 1:

11 + 6 = ? *Onze et six font dix-sept.*

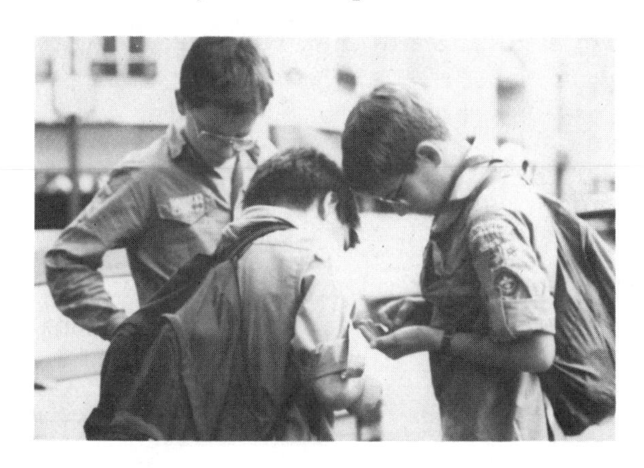

Combien font neuf et six? Neuf et six font quinze.

Aim VIB: *Each student will be able to ask a peer "How old are you?" and be able to respond*

Exercice oral

1. **Pierre:** Quel âge as-tu?
   Hélène: J'ai quatorze ans.

2. **Rose:** Quel âge as-tu?
   Patrick: J'ai seize ans.

Conversation

1. Ask three other students near you *Quel âge as-tu?* and listen carefully to each response.

2. Chain drill by rows: The first student tells his age and then asks the second student how old s/he is.

Exercice écrit

Write the question you would ask of a peer to find out how old s/he is. Then write how you would answer the question.

Exercice de compréhension

You will hear the ages of 5 people. After the second repetition write each age in Arabic numbers.

Résumé

One or two pairs of students can play the roles for the entire class followed by peer practice.

1. **Philippe:** Bonjour! ______ ?
2. **Charles:** Je m'appelle Charles.
   Et toi?
3. **Philippe:** _______ .
   D'où es-tu?

1. **Claude:** Bonjour! _______ ?
2. **Marie:** Ça va bien.
   Et toi?
3. **Claude:** ________ .
   _________?

4. **Charles:** ________ .
Et toi?

5. **Philippe:**________ .
Quel âge as-tu?

6. **Charles**: ________ .
Et toi?

7. **Philippe:** ________ .
Quel est ton numéro de téléphone?

8. **Charles:**________ .

9. **Philippe:** Au revoir, Charles.

10. **Charles:** ________ , Philippe.

4. **Marie:** J'ai quatorze ans.

5. **Claude:** ________ ?

6. **Marie:** Je suis de Paris.

7. **Claude:** ________ ?

8. **Marie:** Mon numéro de téléphone est 703-6495.

9. **Claude:** A bientôt, Marie.

10. **Marie:**________ , Claude.

Vocabulaire

onze	*eleven*	seize	*sixteen*
douze	*twelve*	dix-sept	*seventeen*
treize	*thirteen*	dix-huit	*eighteen*
quatorze	*fourteen*	dix-neuf	*nineteen*
quinze	*fifteen*	vingt	*twenty*

Quel âge as-tu? *How old are you?*
J'ai____ans. *I am ___ years old.*

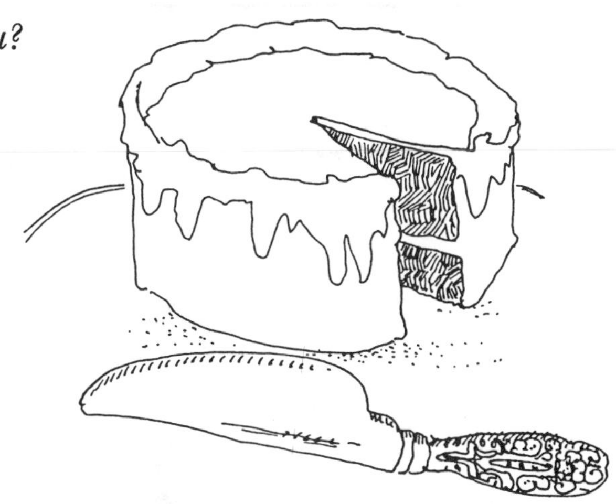

Situation

You meet a French-speaking peer in one of your classes and you decide to get to know him or her. Do the following:

1. Greet the person
2. Ask this person's name
3. Ask where the person is from
4. Ask this person's age
5. Ask this person for his/her telephone number
6. Take leave of the person

This role-play can be done two times with **different partners** to enable each student to do it successfully and experience the satisfaction of mastery. Partners can change roles each time.

J'ai trois ans.

UNIT TWO

Qui es-tu? Me voici.

(Deuxième partie)

TOPIC

Personal Identification

SITUATION

Interaction with individual peers in the classroom

FUNCTION

Introducing oneself, greeting, leave taking, exchanging basic information of personal identification

PROFICIENCY

Listening and speaking: Can comprehend simple questions and respond appropriately with possible need for repetition
Can ask questions appropriate to the communicative situation
Writing: Can write an informal note to a classmate

AIM IA: Each student will be able to ask "What's today's date?" and be able to respond

AIM IB: Each student will be able to ask a peer "When is your birthday?" and be able to respond

AIM II: Each student will be able to ask a peer "In what year were you born?" and be able to respond

AIM III: Each student will be able to ask a peer "Where do you live?" and be able to respond

AIM IV: Each student will be able to ask a peer "What are you like?" and be able to respond

AIM V: Each student will be able to ask a peer "What do you like to do?" and "What don't you like to do?" and be able to respond

Partner A asks:

9 **septembre**

lundi	mardi	mercredi	jeudi	vendredi	samedi	dimanche
				1	2	3
4	5	6	7	8	9	10
11	12	13	14	15	16	17
18	19	20	21	22	23	24
25	26	27	28	29	30	

10 **octobre**

lundi	mardi	mercredi	jeudi	vendredi	samedi	dimanche
						1
2	3	4	5	6	7	8
9	10	11	12	13	14	15
16	17	18	19	20	21	22
23/30	24/31	25	26	27	28	29

11 **novembre**

lundi	mardi	mercredi	jeudi	vendredi	samedi	dimanche
		1	2	3	4	5
6	7	8	9	10	11	12
13	14	15	16	17	18	19
20	21	22	23	24	25	26
27	28	29	30			

12 **décembre**

lundi	mardi	mercredi	jeudi	vendredi	samedi	dimanche
				1	2	3
4	5	6	7	8	9	10
11	12	13	14	15	16	17
18	19	20	21	22	23	24
25	26	27	28	29	30	31

Partner B asks:

9 **septembre**

lundi	mardi	mercredi	jeudi	vendredi	samedi	dimanche
				1	2	3
4	5	6	7	8	9	10
11	12	13	14	15	16	17
18	19	20	21	22	23	24
25	26	27	28	29	30	

10 **octobre**

lundi	mardi	mercredi	jeudi	vendredi	samedi	dimanche
						1
2	3	4	5	6	7	8
9	10	11	12	13	14	15
16	17	18	19	20	21	22
23/30	24/31	25	26	27	28	29

11 **novembre**

lundi	mardi	mercredi	jeudi	vendredi	samedi	dimanche
		1	2	3	4	5
6	7	8	9	10	11	12
13	14	15	16	17	18	19
20	21	22	23	24	25	26
27	28	29	30			

12 **décembre**

lundi	mardi	mercredi	jeudi	vendredi	samedi	dimanche
				1	2	3
4	5	6	7	8	9	10
11	12	13	14	15	16	17
18	19	20	21	22	23	24
25	26	27	28	29	30	31

Aim IA: *Each student will be able to ask "What's today's date?" and be able to respond*

Exercice oral 1

21 (vingt-et-un)	24 (vingt-quatre)	27 (vingt-sept)
22 (vingt-deux)	25 (vingt-cinq)	28 (vingt-huit)
23 (vingt-trois)	26 (vingt-six)	29 (vingt-neuf)
		30 (trente)

Réfléchissons

1. What numbers do we need to know to be able to state any date?
2. If we know numbers 21-30, what other numbers can we figure out?
3. How do we say in French 31, 34, 37, 39?

Exercice oral 2

What months of the year do you recognize as you repeat them after your teacher? *Les mois de l'année: janvier, février, mars, avril, mai, juin, juillet, août, septembre, octobre, novembre, décembre.*

Exercice oral 3

As your teacher states a few dates in French see how many you can recognize. ***Examples:*** *1. Le 14 novembre. 2. Le 31 juillet. 3. Le 6 avril. 4. Le 27 février. 5. Le 19 août. 6. Le 11 décembre.*

Note the exception: The first of each month of the year is expressed by *le premier:* June 1 *le premier juin*

Réfléchissons

1. Are the months of the year capitalized in French when used in a sentence?
2. What does the word *"Le"* mean in the **Exercice oral 3**?
3. To state a date in French , which comes first, the number or the month?

Exercice oral 4

1. **Anne:** Quelle est la date aujourd'hui?
   Jean: Aujourd'hui, c'est le 13 septembre.
2. **Jacques:** Quelle est la date aujourd'hui?
   Hélène: Aujourd'hui, c'est le 24 février.

Conversation

1. Ask two classmates near you *Quelle est la date aujourd'hui?*
2. Peer partners take turns asking the question and answering according to the dates circled on each calendar.

Examples:

May 4 ("the fourth of May") - *Aujourd'hui c'est le 4 mai.*
July 12 ("the twelfth of July") - *Aujourd'hui c'est le 12 juillet.*
October 1 ("the first of October") - *Aujourd'hui c'est le premier octobre.*

Partner A asks:

1 janvier

lundi	mardi	mercredi	jeudi	vendredi	samedi	dimanche
						1
2	3	4	5	6	7	8
9	10	11	12	13	14	15
16	**17**	18	19	20	21	22
23/30	24/31	25	26	27	28	29

2 février

lundi	mardi	mercredi	jeudi	vendredi	samedi	dimanche
		1	2	3	4	5
6	7	8	9	10	11	12
13	14	15	16	17	18	19
20	21	22	23	24	25	**26**
27	28					

3 mars

lundi	mardi	mercredi	jeudi	vendredi	samedi	dimanche
		1	2	3	4	5
6	7	8	**9**	10	11	12
13	14	15	16	17	18	19
20	21	22	23	24	25	26
27	28	29	30	31		

Partner B asks:

1 janvier

lundi	mardi	mercredi	jeudi	vendredi	samedi	dimanche
						1
2	3	4	5	6	7	8
9	10	11	**12**	13	14	15
16	17	18	19	20	21	22
23/30	24/31	25	26	27	28	29

2 février

lundi	mardi	mercredi	jeudi	vendredi	samedi	dimanche
		1	2	3	4	5
6	7	8	9	10	11	12
13	14	15	16	17	18	19
20	21	22	23	**24**	25	26
27	28					

3 mars

lundi	mardi	mercredi	jeudi	vendredi	samedi	dimanche
		1	2	3	4	5
6	7	8	9	10	11	12
13	14	15	16	17	18	**19**
20	21	22	23	24	25	26
27	28	29	30	31		

Partner A asks:

4 avril

lundi	mardi	mercredi	jeudi	vendredi	samedi	dimanche
					1	2
3	4	5	6	7	8	9
10	11	12	13	**14**	15	16
17	18	19	20	21	22	23
24	25	26	27	28	29	30

5 mai

lundi	mardi	mercredi	jeudi	vendredi	samedi	dimanche
1	2	3	4	5	6	7
8	9	10	11	12	13	14
15	16	17	18	19	20	21
22	23	24	25	26	27	28
29	30	31				

6 juin

lundi	mardi	mercredi	jeudi	vendredi	samedi	dimanche
			1	2	3	4
5	6	7	8	9	10	11
12	13	14	15	16	17	18
19	20	21	22	23	24	25
26	27	28	29	**30**		

7 juillet

lundi	mardi	mercredi	jeudi	vendredi	samedi	dimanche
					1	2
3	4	5	6	7	8	9
10	11	12	13	14	15	16
17	18	19	20	21	22	**23**
24/31	25	26	27	28	29	30

8 août

lundi	mardi	mercredi	jeudi	vendredi	samedi	dimanche
	1	2	3	4	5	6
7	8	9	10	11	12	13
14	15	16	17	**18**	19	20
21	22	23	24	25	26	27
28	29	30	31			

Partner B asks:

4 avril

lundi	mardi	mercredi	jeudi	vendredi	samedi	dimanche
					1	2
3	**4**	5	6	7	8	9
10	11	12	13	14	15	16
17	18	19	20	21	22	23
24	25	26	27	28	29	30

5 mai

lundi	mardi	mercredi	jeudi	vendredi	samedi	dimanche
1	2	3	4	5	6	7
8	9	10	11	12	13	14
15	16	17	18	19	20	21
22	23	24	25	26	27	28
29	30	**31**				

6 juin

lundi	mardi	mercredi	jeudi	vendredi	samedi	dimanche
			1	2	3	4
5	6	7	8	9	10	11
12	13	14	**15**	16	17	18
19	20	21	22	23	24	25
26	27	28	29	30		

7 juillet

lundi	mardi	mercredi	jeudi	vendredi	samedi	dimanche
					1	2
3	4	5	6	7	8	9
10	11	12	13	14	15	16
17	18	19	20	21	22	23
24/31	25	26	27	28	29	30

8 août

lundi	mardi	mercredi	jeudi	vendredi	samedi	dimanche
	1	2	3	4	5	6
7	8	9	10	11	12	13
14	15	16	17	18	19	20
21	22	23	24	25	26	**27**
28	29	30	31			

Exercice écrit

1. Write the question you would ask of another person to find out what today's date is. Then respond to this question.
2. Write the following dates in French: ***Example:*** July 3 - *le trois juillet.*

1. May 5	4. April 30	7. September 1	10. July 31
2. March 24	5. August 15	8. February 28	11. December 14
3. June 16	6. January 17	9. November 12	12. October 29

Exercice de compréhension

You will hear five dates in French. After the second repetition, write the date you hear in Arabic numbers. ***Example:*** le vingt-et-un mars - *March 21*

Vocabulaire

trente *thirty* le premier *the first of any month*

les mois de l'année *the months of the year*

janvier	*January*	mai	*May*	septembre	*September*
février	*February*	juin	*June*	octobre	*October*
mars	*March*	juillet	*July*	novembre	*November*
avril	*April*	août	*August*	décembre	*December*

Quelle est la date aujourd'hui? *What is today's date?*
Aujourd'hui, c'est le ___ ___. *Today is* ______.
C'est le ___ ___. *It's*____________.

Aim IB: *Each student will be able to ask a peer "When is your birthday?" and be able to respond*

Exercice oral

1. **Jean:** Quand est ton anniversaire?
   Anne: Mon anniversaire est le 13 août.

2. **Hélène:** Quand est ton anniversaire?
   Thomas: Mon anniversaire est le premier décembre.

Conversation

1. Ask four students near you *Quand est ton anniversaire?* and listen carefully to each response. Next, ask the four students the same question again only this time record each response in your notebook to be able to do the **Exercice écrit** which follows.

Exercice écrit

1. Write the question you would ask of a peer to find out his or her birthday. Then respond to this question.
2. Write the birthdays of four of your classmates. ***Example:*** John's birthday - January 30 *L'anniversaire de Jean est le trente janvier.*

Note culturelle

Many French-speaking people not only celebrate their birthday but also their saint's day. Due to the influence of the Catholic Church in daily life in the French-speaking countries, many of their calendars have a name of a saint for every day of the year. If your name is Joseph, your saint's day is March 19; if Thérèse, it's October 15; if Françoise, it's March 9.

Vocabulaire

Quand est ton anniversaire? *When is your birthday?*
Mon anniversaire est le ___ _____. *My birthday is ___.*

Mon anniversaire? Mon anniversaire est le huit janvier.

Aim II: *Each student will be able to ask a peer "In what year were you born?" and be able to respond*

Exercice oral 1

Les numéros 40 - 90

40 *quarante*	50 *cinquante*	60 *soixante*
70 *soixante-dix*	80 *quatre-vingt*s	90 *quatre-vingt-dix*

Conversation 1

1. Partner **A** states the first group of numbers in French to partner **B**. Then partner **B** states the second group of numbers to partner **A**.

Examples:

47 quarante-sept	86 quatre-vingt-six	79 soixante-dix-neuf
64 soixante-quatre	51 cinquante et un	95 quatre-vingt-quinze

Partner **A** states:
57, 49, 98, 72, 65, 84, 21, 16, 33

Partner **B** states:
83, 59, 91, 65, 46, 74, 37, 18, 22

Exercice oral 2

1. **Paul:** En quelle année es-tu née?
   Odile: Je suis née en 1952. (mille neuf cent cinquante-deux)

2. **Vincent:** En quelle année es-tu née?
   Chantal: Je suis née en 1971. (mille neuf cent soixante et onze)

3. **Hélène:** En quelle année es-tu né?
Michel: Je suis né en 1952. (mille neuf cent cinquante-deux)

4. **Isabelle:** En quelle année es-tu né?
Pierre: Je suis né en 1971. (mille neuf cent soixante et onze)

Note: Paul asked Odile: *En quelle année es-tu **née**? (F)*
Isabelle asked Pierre: *En quelle année es-tu **né**?(M)*

Conversation 2

1. Ask three classmates near you *En quelle année es-tu né (née)?* and listen carefully to each response.
2. Partner **A** states: 1953, 1979, 1946, 1987, 1931, 1964, 1995
   Partner **B** states: 1972, 1945, 1994, 1968, 1936, 1951, 1989

Exercice écrit

1. Write the question you would ask of a peer to find out in what year s/he was born. Then respond to this question.
2. Write the years of the **Conversation 2.**

Example: 1946 - *mille neuf cent quarante-six.*

Exercice de compréhension

Listen carefully as your teacher states a few years of the twentieth century in French. After the second repetition, write the year you hear in Arabic numbers.

Examples:

mille neuf cent cinquante-huit - *1958*
mille neuf cent vingt-quatre - *1924*

Vocabulaire

En quelle année es-tu né(née)? *In what year were you born?*
Je suis né(née) en ____. *I was born in ____.*
mille *one thousand* neuf-cent *nine hundred*

Les numéros 40 - 90:

quarante	*forty*	soixante	*sixty*	quatre-vingts*	*eighty*
cinquante	*fifty*	soixante-dix	*seventy*	quatre-vingt-dix*	*ninety*

*When followed by a number, *vingt* is singular. When multiplied by a number, it is plural. See also page 245.

Aim III: *Each student will be able to ask a peer "Where do you live?" and be able to respond*

Exercice oral 1

1. **Françoise:** Où habites-tu?
   Philippe: J'habite à Paris dans le 17ème.

2. **Jacques:** Où habites-tu?
   Chantal: J'habite à Tours en Touraine.

Exercice oral 2

1. Ask two peers near you *Où habites-tu?* and listen carefully to each response.
2. Chain drill by rows.

Exercice écrit

Write the question you would ask of a peer to find out where he or she lives. Then write how you would answer this question.

Où habites-tu? J'habite à Paris.

Résumé

One or two pairs of students can play the roles for the entire class followed by peer practice.

A

1. **Vincent:** __________?
2. **Thérèse:** J'habite à Plattsburg dans l'état de New York. Et toi?
3. **Vincent:** __________. __________?
4. **Thérèse:** Mon anniversaire est le 12 mars.
5. **Vincent:** __________?
6. **Thérèse:** Je suis née en 1972. Et toi?
7. **Vincent:** __________. A demain, Thérèse.
8. **Thérèse:**______ , Vincent.

B

1. **Rose:** Quand est ton anniversaire?
   Jean: __________.
3. **Rose:** Et en quelle année es-tu né?
4. **Jean:** __________. Et toi?
5. **Rose:** __________. Où habites-tu?
6. **Jean:** __________. Et toi?
7. **Rose:** __________. _______ , Jean.
8. **Jean:** A bientôt, Rose.

Vocabulaire

Où habites-tu? *Where do you live?*
J'habite à ____. *I live in ____.*
la ville *the city*
la ville de New York
the City of New York or New York City
l'état *the state*
l'état de Californie
the state of California

Aim IV: *Each student will be able to ask a peer "What are you like?" and be able to respond*

Exercice oral 1

The following people are describing themselves. Can you figure out what they are saying?

Je suis grand. Je suis petit.

Je suis gros. Je suis maigre.

Je suis vieux. Je suis jeune.

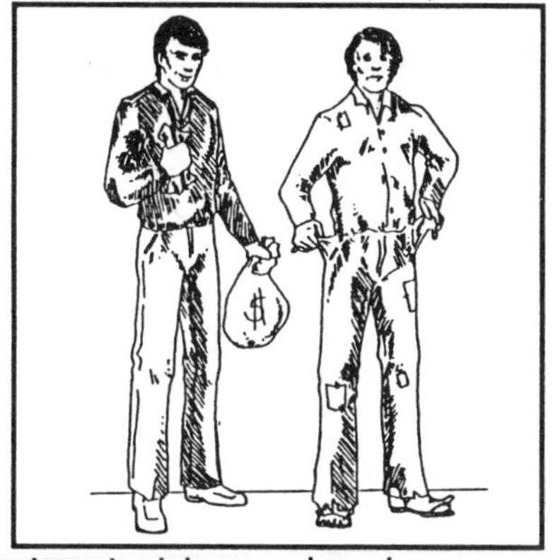

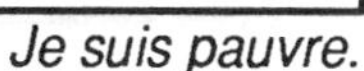

Je suis riche. Je suis pauvre.

Je suis fort. Je suis faible.

Je suis laid. Je suis beau.

Exercice oral 2

1. **Rose:** Comment es-tu?
   Pierre: Je suis grand, jeune et fort.

2. **Charles:** Comment es-tu?
   Isabelle: Je suis grande, jeune et forte.

3. **Marie:** Comment es-tu?
   Antoine: Je suis petit, maigre et beau.

4. **Vincent:** Comment es-tu?
   Catherine: Je suis petite, maigre et belle.

Réfléchissons

1. Every adjective must agree in gender and number with the noun it modifies. Most adjectives add *"e"* to the masculine form to form the feminine. The final consonant sound is heard in the feminine form but not in the masculine form.

Examples: *il est grand (m.), elle est grande (f.)*
il est petit (m.), elle est petite (f.)

2. Certain adjectives sound the same in the masculine and feminine forms. When an adjective ends in a vowel or a pronounced consonant such as *"r"* or *"l"*, we form the feminine by adding *"e"*.

Examples: *Je suis fatigué. (m.).*
Je suis fatiguée. (f.)
Je suis joli. (m.)
Je suis jolie. (f.)

3. When the adjective ends with a mute *"e"*, the written and oral forms are the same for the masculine and feminine forms.

Examples:

Pierre est stupide. (m.)
Claire est stupide. (f.)
Jean est sympathique. (m.)
Claudine est sympathique. (f.)

Vincent est jeune. (m.)
Françoise est jeune. (f.)
Jean est riche. (m.)
Laure est riche. (f.)

4. Adjectives ending in *"el"*, *"eil"*, *"il"*, *"en"*, *"on"*, *"et"* and *"s"* in the masculine double the final consonant before the *"e"* to form the feminine.

Examples:

Masculine	**Feminine**
gentil	*gentille*
bon	*bonne*
ancien	*ancienne*
parisien	*parisienne*
gros	*grosse*
épais	*épaisse*

5. Adjectives ending in *"er"* change to *"ère"* in the feminine form:

Examples:

Masculine	**Feminine**
cher	*chère*
léger	*légère*
premier	*première*
étranger	*étrangère*

Note: The characteristics in **Exercice oral 1 and 2** are called descriptive adjectives because they describe people.

6. Many useful adjectives have been presented above that follow spelling rules; however, there are some irregularities:

Masculine	**Feminine**
faux	fausse
attentif	attentive
neuf	neuve
favori	favorite
blanc	blanche
vieux	vieille
beau	belle

Conversation 1

1. Partners take turns asking each other *"Comment es-tu?"* while pointing to each picture of the appropriate gender. Each partner must answer as if he or she were the person in the picture.

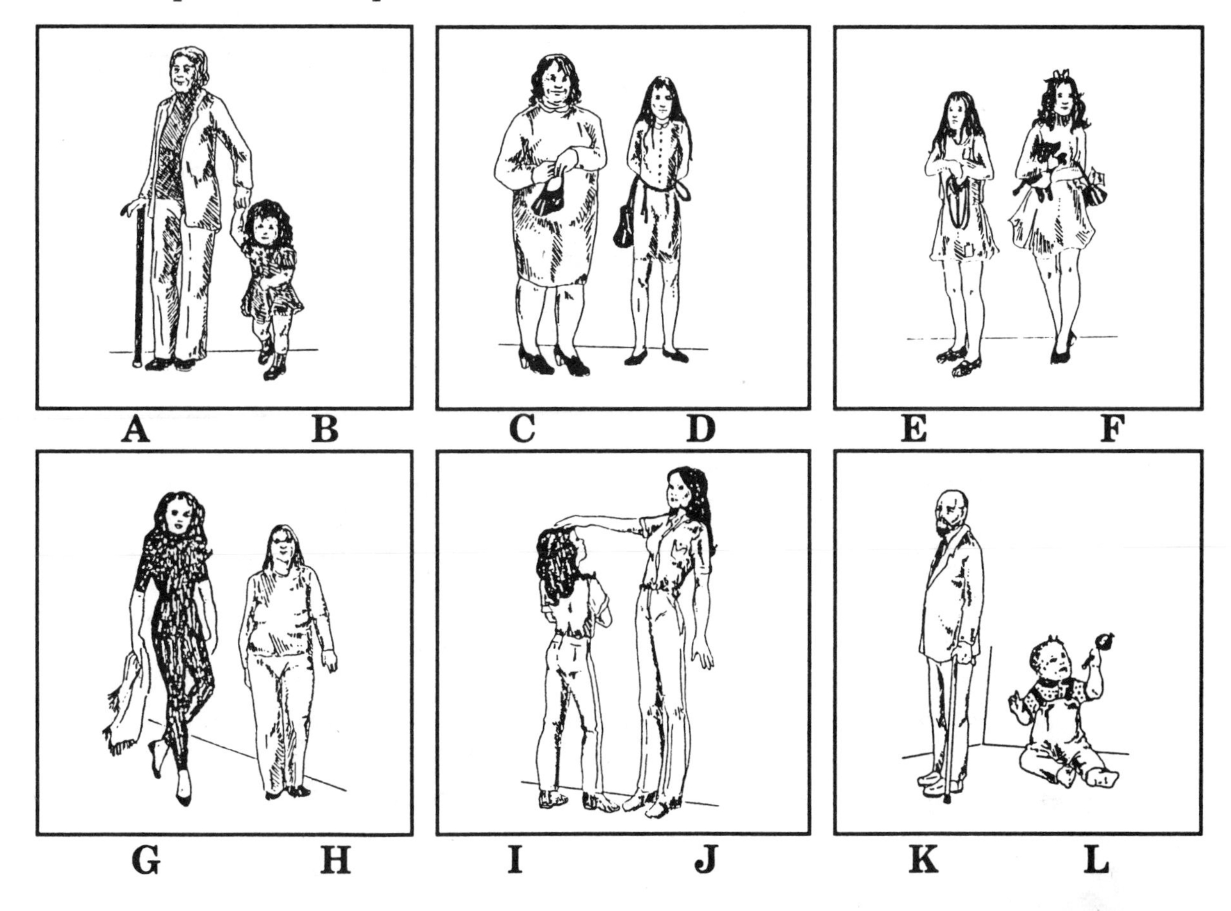

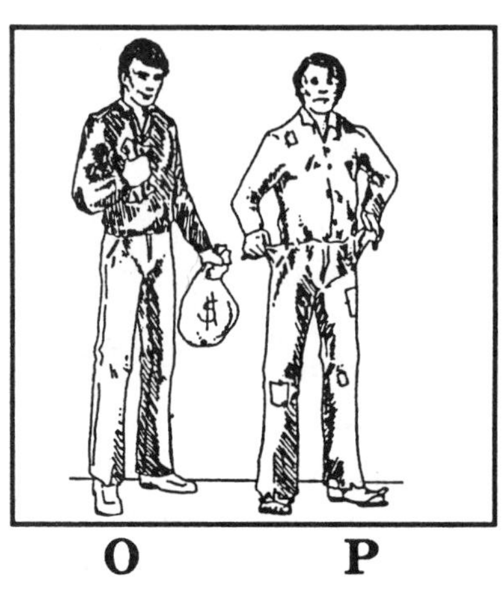

M **N** **O** **P** **Q** **R**

2. Ask two classmates near you *Comment es-tu?* and listen to each response. Describe yourself using 3 or 4 adjectives.

Exercice écrit

1. Write the question you would ask of a peer to find out what s/he is like. Then write how you would respond.
2. Write the antonym of the underlined words to complete each sentence. Column A for boys and column B for girls.

	A		B
1.	Je ne suis pas grand, je suis ___.	1.	Je ne suis pas grande, je suis ___.
2.	Je ne suis pas gros, je suis ___.	2.	Je ne suis pas grosse, je suis ___.
3.	Je ne suis pas vieux, je suis ___.	3.	Je ne suis pas vieille, je suis ___.
4.	Je ne suis pas pauvre, je suis ___.	4.	Je ne suis pas pauvre, je suis ___.
5.	Je ne suis pas faible, je suis ___.	5.	Je ne suis pas faible, je suis ___.
6.	Je ne suis pas laid, je suis ___.	6.	Je ne suis pas laide, je suis ___.

Réfléchissons

To make a sentence negative, what words do we place before and after the verb *"suis"* ?

Exercice de compréhension

You will hear several statements describing the people in the **Conversation 1.** After the second repetition, choose the letter which represents the characteristic you hear.

Exercice oral 3

In **Exercice oral 1** we learned some physical characteristics. Now we are going to learn some psychological characteristics (adjectives which describe character and personality). Can you guess some of them because of their similarity to English?

1. **Chantal:** Comment es-tu?
   Philippe: Je suis sympathique, intelligent, sincère, généreux et bon.

2. **Paul:** Comment es-tu?
   Hélène: Je suis sympathique, intelligente, sincère, généreuse et bonne.

Conversation 2

1. Ask two classmates near you *Comment es-tu?"* and listen carefully to each response. Include both physical and personality traits.
2. Chain drill by rows.

Exercice écrit 2

Write the antonym of the underlined words (descriptive adjectives) to complete the sentence. Column **A** for the boys and column **B** for the girls.

A

1. Je ne suis pas **stupide,** je suis ___.
2. Je ne suis pas **antipathique,** je suis ___.
3. Je ne suis pas **mauvais,** je suis ___.

B

1. Je ne suis pas **stupide,** je suis ___.
2. Je ne suis pas **antipathique,** je suis ___.
3. Je ne suis pas **mauvaise,** je suis ___.

Activité

Draw or bring 4 or 5 pictures from magazines of people who possess characteristics we have learned. Within groups of three or four, class members take turns showing a picture to the others, pretending that s/he is the person represented by the picture, and states what s/he is like. Add the qualifier *"très"* to each of your statements. **Example:** *Je suis très forte.*

Vocabulaire

antipathique *unfriendly*
athlétique *athletic*
beau, belle *handsome*
bon, bonne *good*
faible *weak*
fort, forte *strong*
généreux, généreuse *generous*
grand, grande *tall*
gros, grosse *fat*
intelligent, intelligente *intelligent*
jeune *young*

laid, laide *ugly*
maigre *thin, skinny*
mauvais, mauvaise *bad*
pauvre *poor*
petit, petite *short*
riche *rich*
sincère *sincere*
sympathique *friendly*
stupide *stupid*
vieux, vieille *old*

(masculine and feminine forms are listed above)
Comment es-tu? *What are you like?*
  Je suis ___. *I am ___.*
  Je ne suis pas ___. *I am not ___.*
  Je suis très ___. *I am very ___.*

Aim V: *Each student will be able to ask a peer "What do you like to do?" and "What don't you like to do?" and be able to respond*

Exercice oral 1

Qu'est-ce-que tu aimes faire?
  J'aime ...

Qu'est-ce que tu n'aimes pas faire?
  Je n'aime pas ...

écouter la radio

regarder la télévision

parler au téléphone

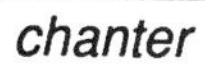
chanter

danser

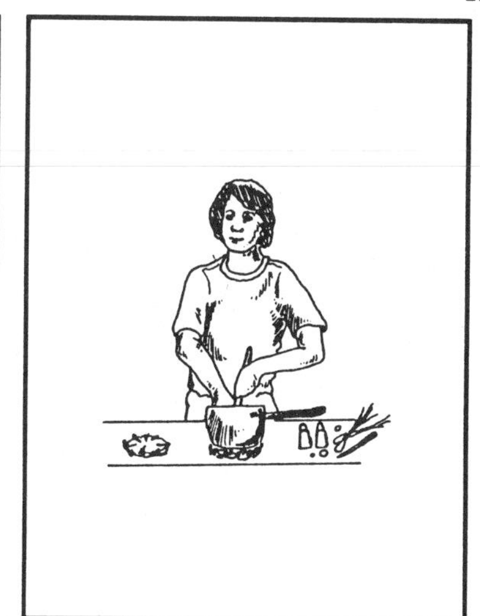
faire la cuisine

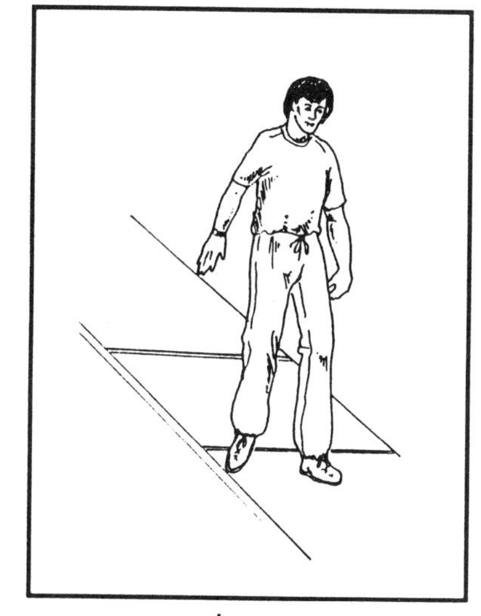
marcher

travailler

donner des cadeaux

nager

voyager

jouer de la guitare

acheter de la nourriture
faire des courses

jouer au baseball

jouer au football

Exercice oral 2

1. **Anne:** Quel est ton passe-temps?
   Jacques: J'aime écouter la radio, danser, nager et jouer au football.

2. **Jean:** Qu'est-ce que tu aimes faire?
   Marie: J'aime voyager, jouer de la guitare, marcher, donnez des cadeaux et parler au téléphone.

3. **Michel:** Qu'est-ce que tu n'aimes pas faire?
   Chantal: Je n'aime ni acheter de la nourriture ni travailler.

4. **Rose:** Qu'est-ce que tu n'aimes pas faire?
   Thomas: Je n'aime ni chanter ni faire la cuisine.

Conversation

1. Ask two classmates near you *"Qu'est-ce que tu aimes faire"?* and *"Qu'est-ce que tu n'aimes pas faire?"* and listen to each response.

2a. One partner asks the other *"Qu'est-ce que tu aimes faire?"* The partner whose turn it is to respond points to each action he or she likes to do and says *"J'aime ...."* Then the second partner asks the questions and the other responds.

2b. One partner now asks *"Qu'est-ce que tu n'aimes pas faire?"* and the second partner points to each action s/he does not like to do and says *"Je n'aime pas ...."* or *"Je n'aime ni ... ni."* Then reverse roles and continue the exercise.

3. Peer partner practice with another partner:

Partners take turns (every other picture) asking each other *"Est-ce que tu aimes?"* followed by the activity represented in the picture. Partners respond *"J'aime ...."* if they like or *"Je n'aime pas ..."* if they don't like to do the activity. After completing one round, the other partner begins the second round.

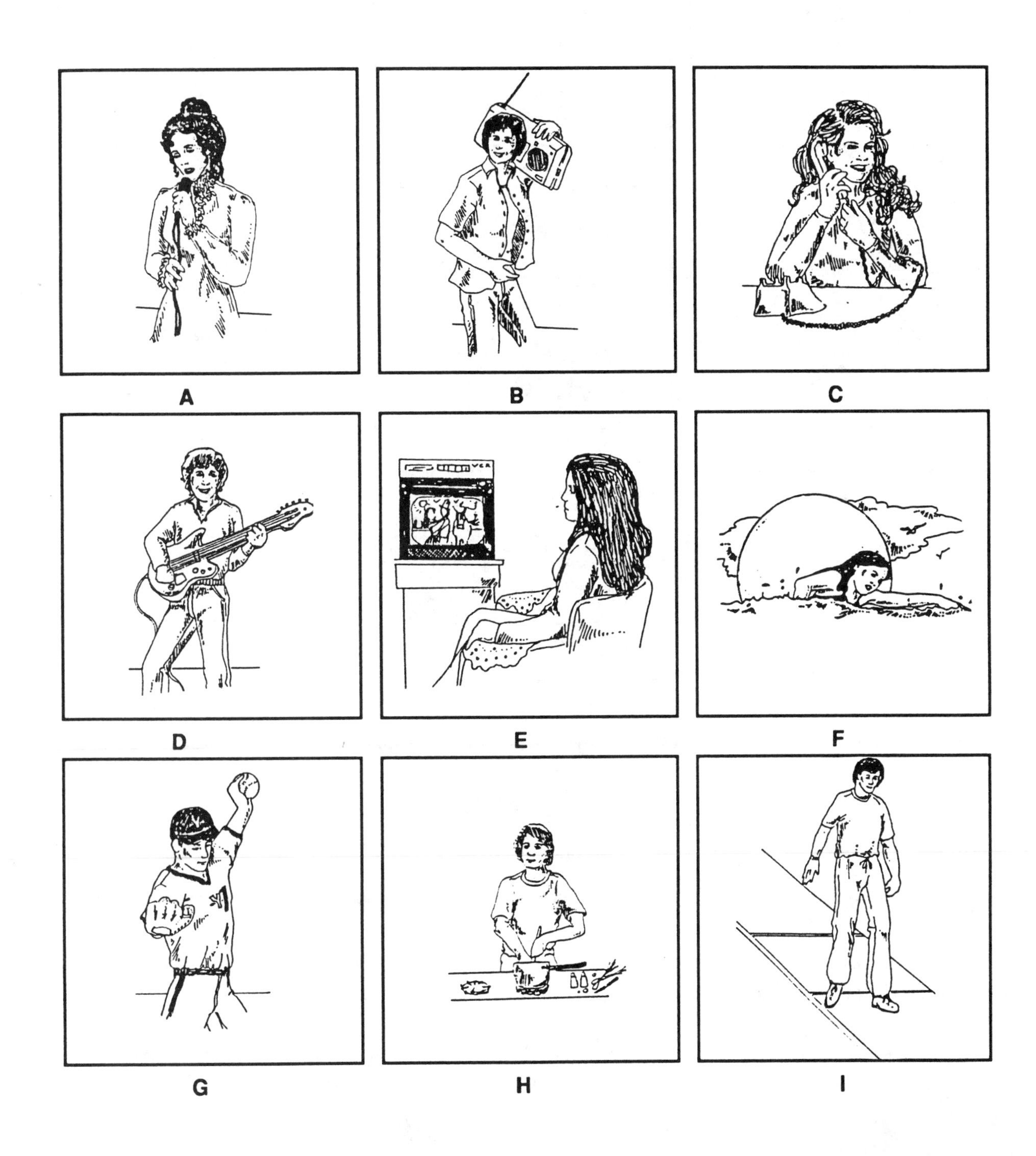

J K L

M N O

Exercice écrit

1. Write the questions you would ask of a peer to find out what s/he likes to do and doesn't like to do. Then respond to each question with 3 or 4 activities.

2. Write whether you like to do or don't like to do each activity in the **Conversation,** 3. **Example:** D. *J'aime chanter.* or *Je n'aime pas chanter.*

Exercice de compréhension

You will hear a few statements indicating whether the people in the **Conversation,** 3, like to do or don't like to do a certain activity. After the second repetition, choose the picture which represents the activity you hear in each statement.

Résumé

Pairs of students can play the roles for the entire class followed by peer practice.

1. **Antoine:** Bonjour, Ça va?
2. **Catherine:** _____. Et toi?
3. **Antoine:** _____. Quand est ton anniversaire?
4. **Catherine:** _____.
5. **Antoine:** En quelle année es-tu née?
6. **Catherine:** _____.
7. **Antoine:** Comment vas-tu?
8. **Catherine:** _____.
9. **Antoine:** Quel est ton passe-temps?
10. **Catherine:** _____.
11. **Antoine:** Quel est ton numéro de téléphone?
12. **Catherine:** _____.
13. **Antoine:** Au revoir, Catherine.
14. **Catherine:** _____, Antoine.

1. **Thérèse**: Bonjour, _____?
2. **Charles:** Je m'appelle Charles. Et toi?
3. **Thérèse:** _____. _____?
4. **Charles:** Je suis de Paris.
5. **Thérèse:** _____?
6. **Charles:** J'habite à Evreux en Normandie.
7. **Thérèse:** _____?
8. **Charles:** J'ai seize ans.
9. **Thérèse:** _____?
10. **Charles:** Mon anniversaire est le 13 décembre.
11. **Thérèse:** _____?
12. **Charles:** J'aime jouer au football, jouer de la guitare et nager.
13. **Thérèse:** _____, Charles.
14. **Antoine:** A bientôt, Thérèse.

Vocabulaire

acheter *to buy*
de la nourriture *...food*
chanter *to sing*
danser *to dance*
écouter la radio
to listen to the radio
faire la cuisine *to cook*
jouer *to play*
de la guitare *the guitar*
au football *soccer*
au basket *basketball*

donner des cadeaux
to give gifts
marcher *to walk*
nager *to swim*
parler au téléphone
to speak on the telephone
regarder la télévision (télé)
to look at (watch) television
travailler *to work*
voyager *to travel*

Quel est ton passe-temps? *What do you like to do?*
J'aime ... *I like to ...*
Je n'aime pas ... *I don't like to ...*
Je n'aime ni ... ni ... *I don't like to ... or ...*
Est-ce que tu aimes ... ? *Do you like to ...?*

J'aime jouer au basket.

Situation

1. At the end of the school day you see a French-speaking peer whom you recognize from one of your classes. You decide to introduce yourself and to get to know him/her. Do the following:

1. Greet the person
2. Introduce yourself
3. Ask the person his/her name
4. Ask the person where s/he is from
5. Ask the person his/her age
6. Ask the person his/her telephone number
7. Ask the person where s/he lives
8. Ask the person when is his/her birthday
9. Ask the person in what year s/he was born
10. Ask the person what s/he is like
11. Ask the person what s/he likes to do
12. Take leave of the person

This role play can be done two or three different times with **different partners.** Partners can change roles each time.

2. *Une note pour un (une) camarade de classe* (A note to a classmate)

Write a note to a French-speaking peer in one of your classes whom you would like to get to know. Tell him/her about yourself and then ask some questions. Include in your note all the information you have learned to communicate.

Glimpses of France

UNIT THREE

Le climat et le temps

Qui êtes-vous? Me voici.

TOPIC

A. Climate and weather B. Personal identification

SITUATION

Interaction with teachers and other adults

FUNCTION

Introducing oneself, greeting, leave taking,
exchanging basic information of personal identification

PROFICIENCY

Can comprehend simple questions and
respond appropriately with possible need for repetition
Can ask questions appropriate to the communicative situation

AIM IA: Each student will be able to ask "What's the temperature?" and be able to respond

AIM IB: Each student will be able to ask "What's the weather like?" and be able to respond

AIM II: Each student will be able to ask "What is your favorite season?" and "Why?" and be able to respond

AIM III: Each student will be able to identify the French-speaking countries of the eastern hemisphere

AIM IV: Each student will be able to greet the teacher or other adult at different times of the day, ask "How are you?" and be able to respond

AIM V: Each student will be able to ask an adult or stranger "What do you like to do?" and "Do you like to...?" and be able to respond

AIM VI: Each student will be able to ask an adult or stranger the basic questions of personal identification and be able to respond

Aim IA: *Each student will be able to ask "What's the temperature?" and be able to respond*

Exercice oral

1. **Jean:** Quelle est la température?
   Marie: 39 degrés.

2. **Anne:** Quelle est la température?
   Paul: 68 degrés.

Conversation

1. Ask two classmates near you *Quelle est la température?* and listen carefully to each response.

2. Peer partners take turns asking *Quelle est la température?* and respond accordingly.

Partner A	Partner B
1. 45 degrés	1. 73 degrés
2. 19	2. 26
3. 82	3. 91
4. 37	4. 58
5. 61	5. 15

Partner A	Partner B
6. 94 degrés	6. 64 degrés
7. 78	7. 89
8. 53	8. 30
9. 26	9. 17
10. 14	10. 42

Exercice écrit

Write in French the temperature stated by Partner B in the **Conversation,** 2, numbers 1 - 10.

Quelle est la température?

Note culturelle

In France and all of the French-speaking countries, Centigrade, not Fahrenheit, is used to state the temperature. Centigrade is part of the metric system. Examine the following table of equivalents of Fahrenheit (F°) and Centigrade (C°).

F°	C°	F°	C°
212	100	68	20
(boiling point)		59	15
100	38	50	10
98.6	36.9	41	5
(body temp.)		32	0
86	30	(freezing point)	

The following are average afternoon temperatures in Centigrade of Paris, France, and their equivalents in Fahrenheit. When it is 11 degrees in February, what is the equivalent temperature in Fahrenheit? When it is 31 degrees in July, what is the equivalent temperature in Fahrenheit?

	Jan.	Feb.	Mar.	Apr.	May	June	July	Aug.	Sept.	Oct.	Nov.	Dec.
C°	8	11	14	18	22	27	31	30	25	19	12	9
F°	47	51	57	64	71	80	87	86	77	66	54	48

Vocabulaire

Quelle est la température? *What is the temperature?*
degrés *degrees*

Aim IB: *Each student will be able to ask "What's the weather like?" and be able to respond*

Exercice oral

Quel temps fait-il?

Il fait froid.

Il fait chaud.

Il ne fait ni froid ni chaud.
Il fait frais.

Il fait du soleil.

Il fait du vent

Il fait nuageux.

Il pleut.

Il neige.

Il fait mauvais.

Conversation

1. Ask two classmates near you *Quel temps fait-il?* and listen to each response.

2. Peer partners take turns asking each other *Quel temps fait-il?* while pointing to each picture. Both partners have an opportunity to state all the weather conditions.

3. Peer partners take turns asking each other the following questions about today's weather.....*Quel temps fait-il aujourd'hui?*

Examples:

1. **Jean:** Est-ce qu'il fait chaud?
   Marie: Oui, il fait chaud.
2. **Christine:** Est-ce qu'il fait froid?
   Antoine: Non, il ne fait pas froid.
3. **Anne:** Est-ce qu'il pleut?
   Paul: Oui, il pleut.
4. **Thomas:** Est-ce qu'il neige?
   Rose: Non, il ne neige pas.

1. Est-ce qu'il fait du vent?
2. Est-ce qu'il fait du soleil?
3. Est-ce qu'il fait froid?
4. Est-ce qu'il fait chaud?
5. Est-ce qu'il fait frais?
6. Est-ce qu'il fait beau?
7. Est-ce qu'il fait mauvais?
8. Est-ce qu'il fait nuageux?
9. Est-ce qu'il pleut?
10. Est-ce qu'il neige?

Exercice écrit

1. Write how you would ask another person "What's the weather like?" and respond to the question.

2. Write the questions and answers of the **Conversation 3,** numbers 1 - 10.

Exercice de compréhension

You will hear a few statements indicating a weather condition. After the second repetition, choose the picture which corresponds to what you hear. Refer to the **Conversation 2** for the pictures.

Note: To state "It snows", we say *Il neige.*
To state "It rains", we say *Il pleut.*
To state "very..." before the nouns in the **Exercice oral** numbers 1 - 5, we say *très: Il fait très froid, il fait très chaud, il fait très frais.*
Or we may say *beaucoup: Il fait beaucoup de soleil, il fait beaucoup de vent.*

Résumé

A

1. **Pierre:** _______ ?
2. **Hélène:** Il fait très chaud.
3. **Pierre:** Quelle est la température?
4. **Hélène:** _______ .

B

1. **Anne:** Quel temps fait-il?
2. **Jean:** _______.
3. **Anne:** _______ ?
4. **Jean:** Quinze degrés.

C

1. **Jean:**_______ ?
2. **Rose:** Il fait très frais.
3. **Jean:** _______ ?
4. **Rose:** 45 degrés.

D

1. **Christine:** Quel temps fait-il?
2. **Thomas:** _______ .
3. **Christine:** _______ ?
4. **Thomas:** 70 degrés.

Quel temps fait-il

Vocabulaire

Weather expressions using "il"+*verb:*

Il fait beau. *The weather is good / It's nice weather.*
Il fait mauvais. *The weather is bad / It's bad weather.*
Il fait froid. *It's cold.*
Il fait chaud. *It's hot.*
Il fait frais *It's cool.*
Il pleut. *It's raining.*
Il neige. *It's snowing.*
Il fait nuageux. *It's cloudy.*
Il fait du vent. *It's windy.*
Il fait du soleil. *It's sunny.*

To indicate a certain condition is not present:

Non, il ne fait pas nuageux. *It is not cloudy.*
Non, il ne fait pas de vent. *It is not windy.*
Il ne fait ni chaud ni froid. *It's not hot or cold.*
Il ne pleut pas. *It's not raining.*

Questions referring to the weather:

Quelle est la température? *What's the temperature?*
Quel temps fait-il? *What's the weather like? / How's the weather?*
Est-ce qu'il fait...? *Is it....?*
Est-ce qu'il fait chaud? *Is it hot?*
Est-ce qu'il pleut? *Is it raining?*

Il fait ... *It is ...*
Il fait beaucoup de vent. *It's very windy.*
Il fait très chaud. *It's very hot.*

oui *yes*
non *no, not*

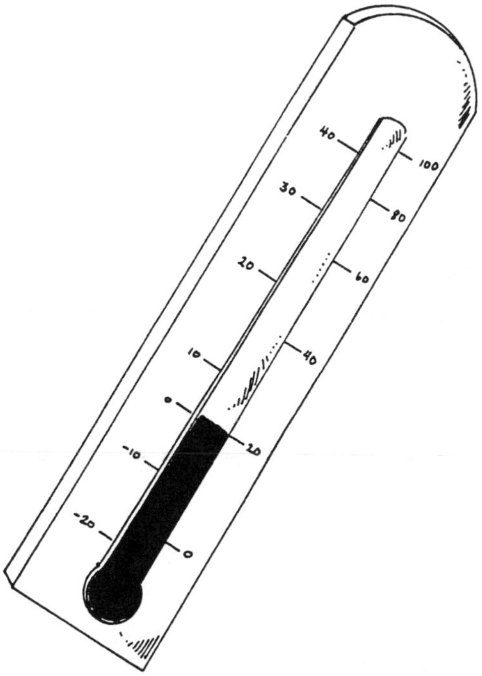

Est-çe qu'il fait froid ou chaud?

Aim II: *Each student will be able to ask "What is your favorite season?" and "Why?" and be able to respond*

Exercice oral 1

Quelles sont les saisons de l'année?

Les saisons de l'année sont...

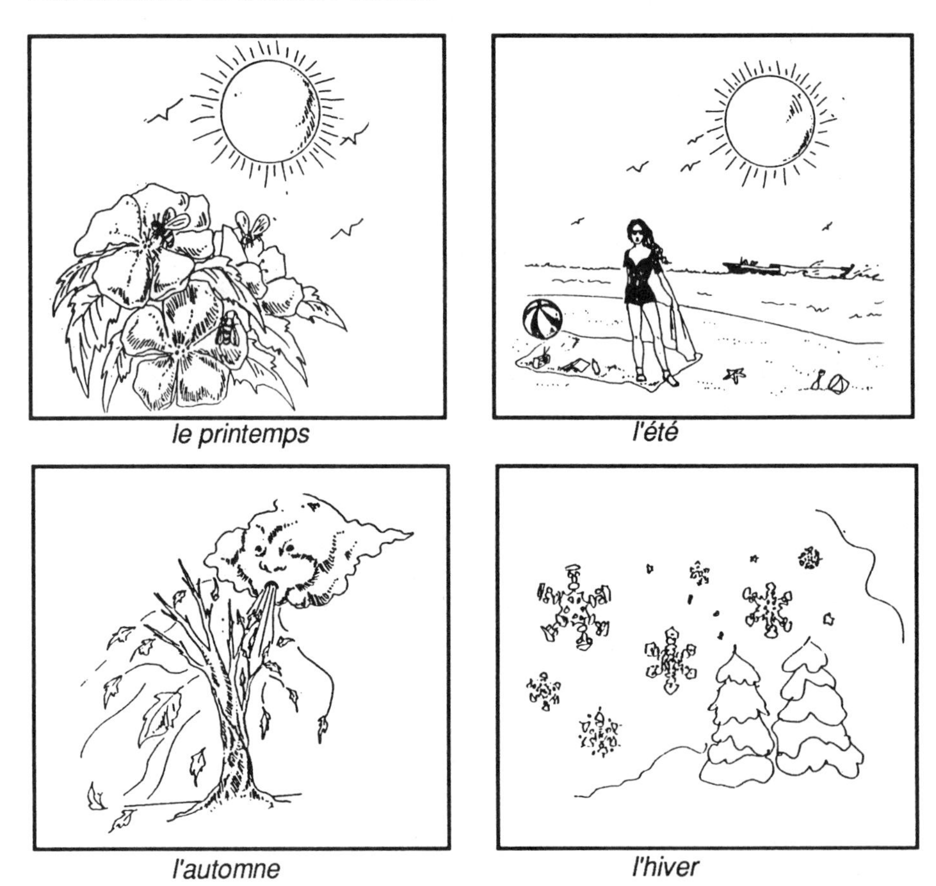

le printemps *l'été*

l'automne *l'hiver*

Conversation 1

Partners take turns asking the questions.

A

Example: **Isabelle:** En quelle saison fait-il mauvais?

Philippe: Il fait mauvais en hiver.

1. En quelle saison fait-il très froid?
2. En quelle saison fait-il très chaud?
3 En quelle saison fait-il frais?
4. En quelle saison pleut-il beaucoup?
5. En quelle saison neige-t-il beaucoup?

B

Example: **Michel:** Quel temps fait-il en automne?
Laure: Il fait frais en automne.

6. Quel temps fait-il au printemps?
7. Quel temps fait-il en hiver?
8. Quel temps fait-il en été?
9. Quel temps fait-il en automne?

Exercice écrit 1

Write the questions and answers of **Conversation 1,** numbers 1 - 9.

Exercice oral 2

1. **Rose:** Quelle est ta saison favorite? Pourquoi?
   Thomas: Ma saison favorite est l'été parce que j'aime nager, me bronzer, et jouer au volley-ball.

2. **Vincent:** Quelle est ta saison favorite? Pourquoi?
   Laure: Ma saison favorite est l'hiver parce que j'aime faire du ski et faire du patin à glace.

3. **Thérèse:** Quelle est ta saison favorite? Pourquoi?
   Michelle: Ma saison favorite est le printemps parce que je n'aime ni le froid ni la chaleur. J'aime regarder les fleurs.

4. **Monsieur Vavasseur:** Quelle est votre saison favorite? Pourquoi?
   Madame Vial: Ma saison favorite est l'automne parce qu'il fait frais et j'aime regarder les feuilles.

Réfléchissons

1. How do we say "your..." when talking to a peer?
2. How do we say "your..." when talking to an adult?

Conversation 2

Ask two classmates near you *Quelle est ta saison favorite? Pourquoi?*

Exercice écrit 2

1. Write the question you would ask of a peer to find out what his/her favorite season is. Then respond to the question.

2. Write the same question, but ask it of an adult. Then respond to the question.

Note culturelle

Around the center of the earth is an imaginary line called the equator which divides the earth into equal hemispheres - the northern hemisphere and the southern hemisphere. The seasons of the year are opposite in the northern and southern hemispheres. When it is winter in the north it is summer in the south, and when it is spring in the northern hemisphere it is fall in the southern one.

French is spoken as far north as Québec and in the south it is spoken in French Guiana in South America.

Vocabulaire

Quelles sont les saisons de l'année?
What are the seasons of the year?
Les saisons de l'année sont.....
The seasons of the year are.....
l'été *the summer* l'hiver *the winter*
l'automne *the fall, autumn* le printemps *the spring*
En quelle saison...? *In what season.....?*
En quelle saison fait-il ...? *In what season is it ...?*
En quelle saison pleut-il beaucoup? *In what season does it rain a lot?*
en été *in summer* en hiver *in winter*
en automne *in autumn* au printemps *in spring*
Quelle est ta saison favorite? *What is your favorite season?*
Quelle est votre saison favorite? *What is your favorite season?*
Ma saison favorite est... *My favorite season is...*

Pourquoi? *Why?*
...parce que... *...because...*
...J'aime faire du patin à glace. *...I like to iceskate.*
...J'aime me bronzer sur la plage. *...I like to sunbathe on the beach.*

...J'aime faire du ski. *...I like to ski.*
...J'aime regarder les fleurs. *...I like to look at the flowers.*
...J'aime regarder les feuilles. *...I like to look at the leaves.*
...Je n'aime ni le froid ni la chaleur. *...I don't like the cold or the heat.*

Ma saison favorite est l'hiver.

AIM III: *Each student will be able to identify and locate the French-speaking countries of the eastern hemisphere.*

Exercice oral

Où est-ce qu'on parle français? Individual students come to the wall map to point out the location of the French-speaking countries as the entire class repeats each country's name.

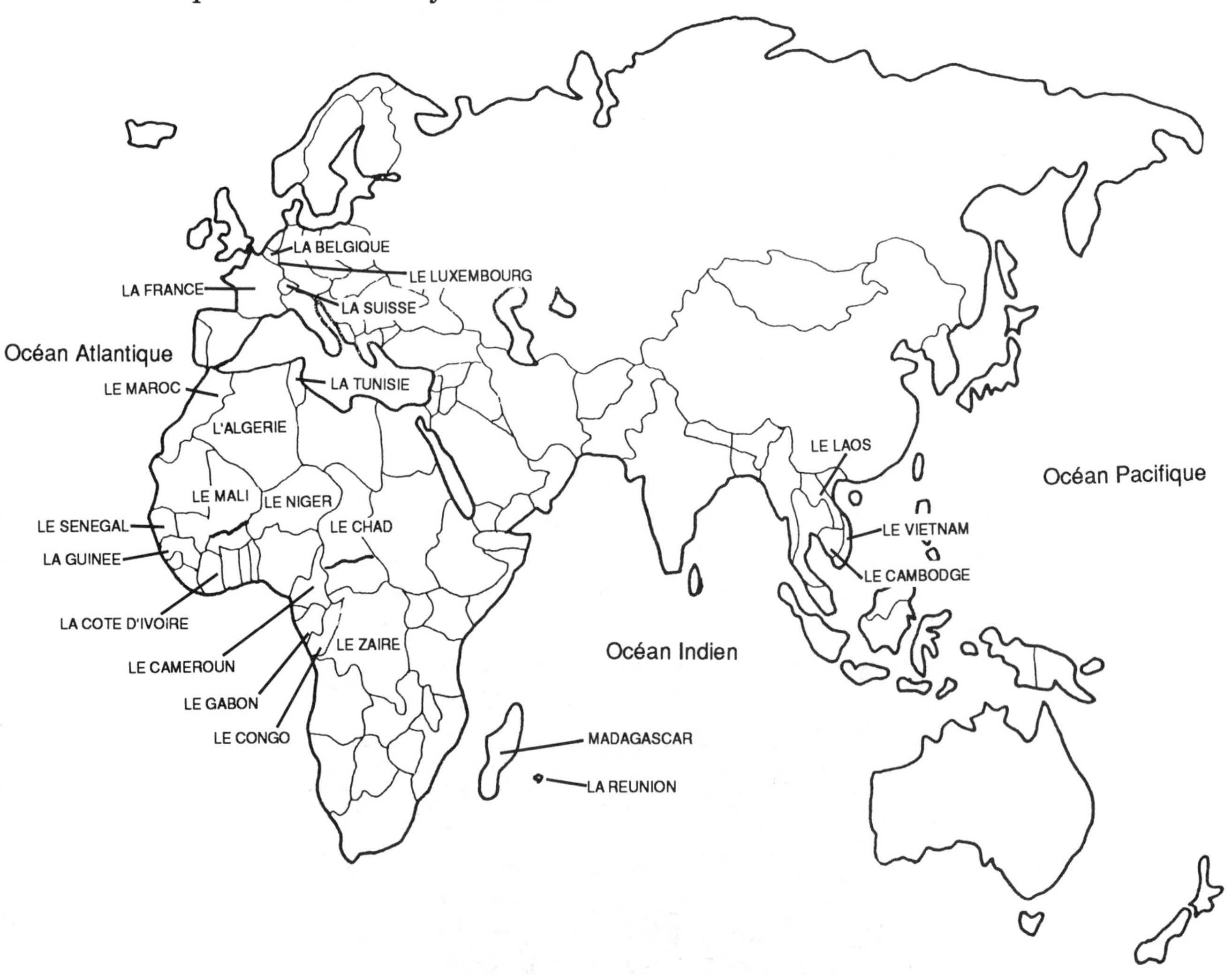

French is spoken throughout the world. Many of the countries shown on this map speak French today because of former French colonial influence. Notice that this extended to Southeast Asia as well.
Your teacher may wish to discuss additional areas of French influence.

Conversation

1. *Dans quels pays parle-t-on français? On parle français en(au) ______.*

One partner asks the question as the other answers, pointing to the map. Partners can take turns asking and answering the question until all the countries have been mentioned.

2. *Où est la Guadeloupe? La Guadeloupe est dans l'océan Atlantique.*

Partners take turns asking each other where each of the French-speaking countries are located.

Exercice écrit

1. Write the **Conversation,** 2.

2. Examine the map on page 62 and an atlas to answer the following questions.

a. The large island situated in the Indian Ocean is _______.

b. The european country bordering France, famous for its beautiful mountains, and where French is spoken along with two other major languages is _______.

c. The southeast-asian country in which both the French and Americans fought major wars is _____.

d. The French-speaking country bordering France and which is surrounded by Holland and Germany is _______.

e. The French-speaking country between Belgium and Switzerland is _______.

f. France, Belgium, Luxembourg and Switzerland are on the continent of _______.

Résumé

On a blank map write the name of the French-speaking countries of the Western Hemisphere.

Vocabulaire

Où est ...? *Where is ...?*
... est en Europe.
... est en Afrique.
... est dans l'océan Atlantique
... est dans l'océan Pacifique

Où parle-t-on français?
Liste des pays principaux où l'on parle français:

la France
la Belgique
la Suisse

la Réunion
le Luxembourg

le Québec
la Martinique

la Guyane
la Guadeloupe

On parle français en (au) (à la) ___.

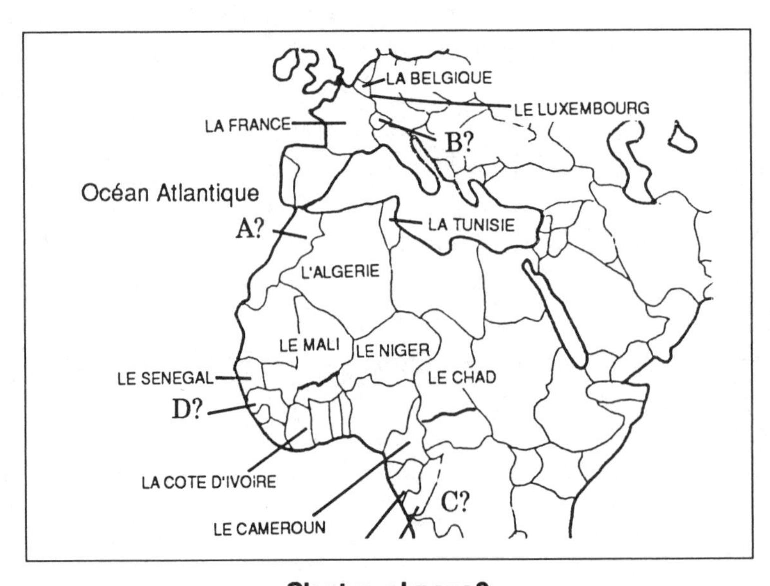

C'est quel pays?

AIM IV: *Each student will be able to greet the teacher or other adult at different times of the day, ask "How are you?" and be able to respond*

Exercice oral

1. **Il est huit heures du matin (8:00 A.M.):**
   Jean: Bonjour, Madame Dubois. Comment allez-vous?
   Mme Dubois: Ça va très bien, merci. Et toi?
   Jean: Comme ci, comme ça.

2. **Il est une heure et demie de l'après-midi (1:30 P.M.):**
   Laure: Bonjour, M. Dupont. Comment allez-vous?
   M. Dupont: Ça va. Et toi?
   Laure: Ça va bien, merci.

3. **Il est sept heures et demie (7:30) P.M.:**
   M. Durand: Bonsoir, Mlle. Valois. Comment allez-vous?
   Mlle Valois: Je suis un peu fatiguée. Et vous?
   M. Durand: Ça va très bien, merci.

Conversation

1. Ask two "adults" near you *Comment allez-vous?* and listen carefully to each response.

2. Peer partners play the roles of student and teacher or adult. Partners take turns greeting each other properly according to the time of day indicated.

Note:

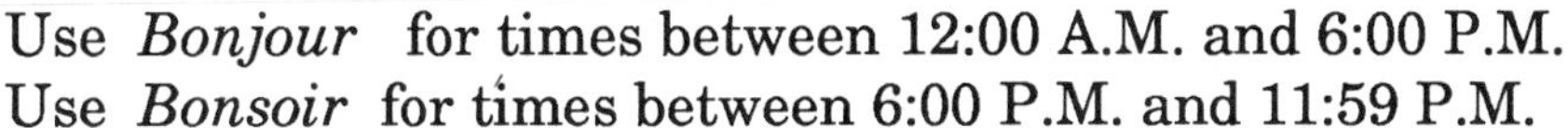

Use *Bonjour* for times between 12:00 A.M. and 6:00 P.M.
Use *Bonsoir* for times between 6:00 P.M. and 11:59 P.M.

Examples:

9:00 A.M. - Bonjour, M. (Mme) (Mlle)... Comment allez-vous?
8:30 P.M. - Bonsoir, M. (Mme) (Mlle)... Comment allez-vous?

1. 4:00 P.M.
2. 7:15 A.M.
3. 9:30 P.M.
4. 8:45 A.M.
5. 2:30 P.M.
6. 10:00 P.M.
7. 6:15 A.M.
8. 3:45 P.M.
9. 11:15 A.M.
10. 9:45 P.M.
11. 12:30 P.M.
12. 7:00 P.M.

3. Situations:
Take turns playing the following roles with your partners:

a. You meet your teacher in the morning. Greet him/her. The teacher responds that s/he is a little tired.
b. At an evening performance of the theater you see your friend's father. Greet him. He responds that he is fine.
c. You see your teacher in the afternoon. Greet him/her. The teacher responds that s/he is so-so.

Exercice écrit

1. Write the question you would ask of a teacher or other adult to find out how s/he is. Then write how you would respond.

2. Write **Conversation** and **Situations** (both roles).

Résumé

1. 9:00 A. M.

Jean: _______ , Mme Nédélec. _______ ?

Mme Nédélec: Ça va très bien, merci. Et toi?

Jean: _______ . Au revoir, Mme Nédélec.

Mme Nédélec: _______ , Jean.

2. 7:30 P.M.

M. Dupont: _______ , Mme Valois. _______ ?

Mme Valois: Je suis un peu______. Et vous?

M. Dupont: Je suis fatigué _______ . A bientôt.

Mme Valois: _______.

Note culturelle

In French when a young person addresses an adult or a stranger, the person is addressed as *vous.* Adults who do not call each other by their first names use *vous.* This is known as the polite or formal form of address.

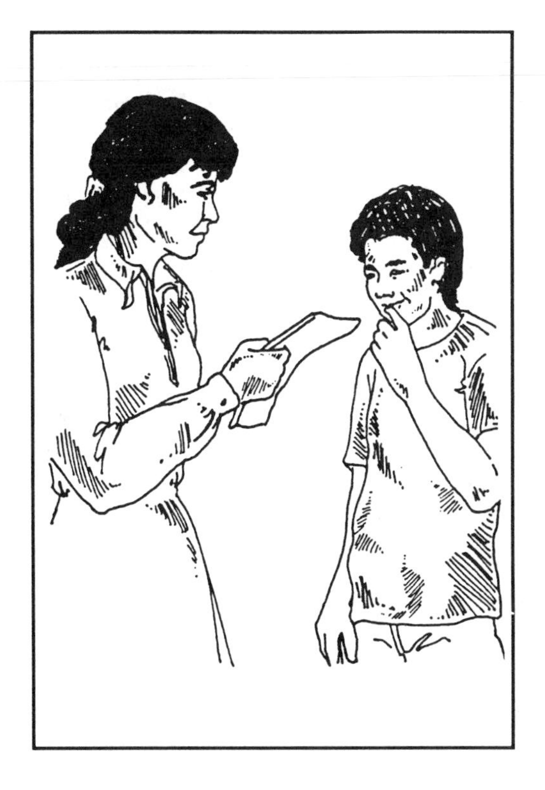

Vocabulaire

Bonjour. *Good morning. (Hello)*
Bonsoir. *Good evening. Good night.*

vous *you*
Et vous? *And you?*
Comment allez-vous? *How are you?*
Je suis un peu... *I'm a little...*

Monsieur *Mr. (often abbreviated as* M.*)*
Mademoiselle *Miss (often abbreviated as* Mlle*)*
Madame *Mrs. (often abbreviated as* Mme*)*

Note: In French, "bonjour" is used at any time of the day or evening, simply meaning "hello." "Bonsoir" is used after 5:59 P.M. meaning "good evening".

Aim V: *Each student will be able to ask an adult or stranger "What do you like to do?" and "Do you like to...?" and be able to respond*

Exercice oral 1

Quel est votre passe-temps?
J'aime....

Est-ce que vous aimez ...?
Oui, j'aime.../ Non, je n'aime pas...

lire le journal

courir

manger

faire des exercices

aller à des parties

aller au cinéma

aller à la plage

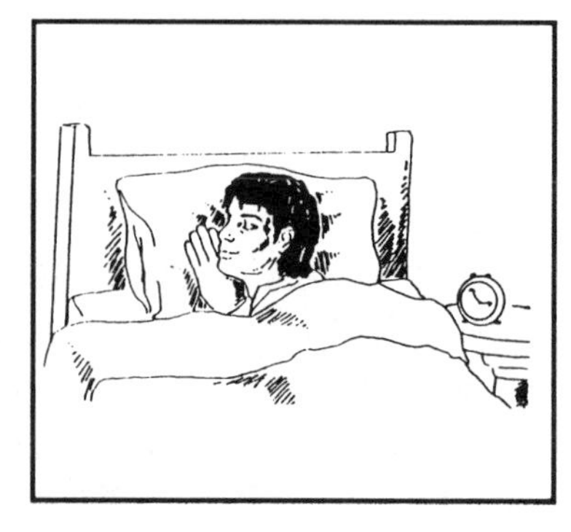

dormir

sortir avec mon ami (amie).

écrire des lettres

Note: The form of a verb as it is listed in the dictionary is called the "infinitive". Infinitives in French end in *"er", "ir", "re",* or *"oir".* The expressions *J'aime..* and *Je n'aime pas...* are followed by the infinitive when you wish to indicate an action you like or don't like to do. In English the infinitive begins with "to": to sing, to eat.

Exercice oral 2

1. **Jean:** Qu'est-ce que vous aimez faire?
   Mme Rousseau: J'aime lire le journal, jouer de la guitare, aller à des parties, sortir avec mes amis et faire des exercices.

2. **Anne:** Est-ce que vous aimez travailler?
   M. Sorel: Oui, j'aime travailler.
   Anne: Est-ce que vous aimez dormir?
   M. Sorel: Non, je n'aime pas dormir.

Réfléchissons

1. How do you ask an adult "What do you like to do?"

2. How does this differ from the way we ask a peer the same question?

Conversation

1. Ask two "adults" near you *Qu'est-ce que vous aimez faire* and listen to each response.

2. One partner asks the other *Qu'est-ce que vous aimez faire ?* The

partner whose turn it is to respond points to each action s/he likes to do and says *J'aime...* Then the second partner asks the question and the other responds.

3. Partners take turns (every other picture) asking each other *Est-ce que vous aimez...?* followed by the activity represented in the picture. Partners respond *Oui, j'aime...* or *Non, je n'aime pas...* stating the activity they like or don't like to do. After one round the second partner begins the next one.

Exercice écrit

1. Write the question you would ask of an adult to find out what s/he likes to do. Then respond with three or four activities.

2. Write whether you like to do or don't like to do each activity in the **Conversation,** 3, A - J.

Exercice de compréhension

You will hear a few statements indicating whether the people in the **Conversation** 3, A - J like to do or don't like to do a certain activity. After the second repetition, choose the picture by letter which represents the activity you hear.

Vocabulaire

manger *to eat*
courir *to run*
dormir *to sleep*
écrire *to write*
  des lettres *letters*
travailler *to work*
faire *to do*
  des exercices *exercises*
aller *to go*
  au cinéma *to the movies*
  à des parties *to parties*
  à la plage *to the beach*
lire *to read*
  le journal *the newspaper*
sortir *to go out*
  avec un ami *with a friend*
  avec une amie *with a friend*

Qu'est-ce que vous aimez faire? *What do you like to do?*
Est-ce que vous aimez ...? *Do you like to ...?*
Aimez-vous ...? *Do you like to ...?*

Activité

Discovery Game

1. Each partner will write five activities s/he likes to do chosen from the Discovery Game sheet given to you.

2. Partners will take turns asking their opponent *Est-ce que vous aimez...?*

3. Partners will answer according to what they have written on their papers: *Oui, j'aime...* or *Non, je n'aime pas....*

4. The partner who asks the question will write his/her partner's *Oui* or *Non* in the space on the sheet next to the appropriate activity.

5. When one partner has guessed all five of the other's answers, that partner wins the game.

Do not write on this sample activity sheet. Use the copy given to you.

Choose five activities you like to do from the list below.

1. ________ 4. ________
2. ________ 5. ________
3. ________

Oui or *Non* is to be recorded before each activity according to your partner's answers.

_____ aller à la plage
_____ voyager
_____ lire un journal
_____ écouter la radio
_____ nager
_____ faire des exercices
_____ marcher
_____ dormir
_____ jouer au baseball
_____ aller au cinéma
_____ jouer de la guitare
_____ sortir avec un ami (ou une amie)
_____ regarder la télévision
_____ manger
_____ travailler
_____ écrire des lettres
_____ jouer au football
_____ chanter
_____ aller à des parties
_____ parler au téléphone
_____ acheter de la nourriture
_____ danser
_____ courir
_____ faire la cuisine

Aim VI: *Each student will be able to ask an adult or stranger the basic questions of personal identification and be able to respond*

Conversation

Mr. Dubois, Vice President of "La Société Générale" bank in New York, grants an interview to John, a student taking French. John decides to take advantage of this opportunity to practice the questions of personal identification.

1. **Jean:** Comment allez-vous?

2. **M. Dubois:** Très bien, merci. Et toi?

3. **Jean:** Ça va, merci. Comment vous appelez-vous?

4. **M. Dubois:** Je m'appelle M. Dubois.

5. **Jean:** D'où êtes-vous?

6. **M. Dubois:** Je suis de Paris, la capitale de la France.

7. **Jean:** Depuis combien de temps est-ce que vous travaillez ici?

8. **M. Dubois:** Je travaille ici depuis vingt ans.

9. **Jean:** Quand est votre anniversaire?

10. **M. Dubois:** Mon anniversaire est le 31 janvier.

11. **Jean:** En quelle année êtes-vous né?

12. **M. Dubois:** Je suis né en 1940.

13. **Jean:** Où habitez-vous?

14. **M. Dubois:** J'habite à Paris. Quand je suis à New York j'habite à Manhattan.

15. **Jean:** Quel est votre numéro de téléphone?

16. **M. Dubois:** Mon numéro de téléphone est 962-3807 à Manhattan et 83-64-18-32 à Paris.

17. **Jean:** Qu'est-ce que vous aimez faire pendant votre temps libre?

18. **M. Dubois:** Pendant mon temps libre, j'aime jouer au tennis, aller au cinéma et courir.

19. **Jean:** Merci beaucoup M. Dubois, j'aime parler français avec vous.

20. **M. Dubois:** Avec plaisir, Jean.

Vrai ou faux (True or false):

If the statement about the dialogue is true, state *Vrai* and read the statement as is; if the statement is false, state *Faux* and correct the bold part of the statement to make it true.

1. M. Dubois est **fatigué.**

2. M. Dubois est de Paris, la capitale de **la France.**

3. M. Dubois travaille à New York depuis **20 ans.**

4. L'anniversaire de M. Dubois **est le 30 janvier.**

5. Quand M. Dubois est à New York, il habite à **Manhattan.**

6. M. Dubois aime **jouer au football, aller à la plage, et chanter.**

Conversation

One peer partner plays the role of the adult who is being interviewed by the young person and then partners change roles.

1. Comment allez-vous?
2. Comment vous appelez-vous?
3. D'où êtes-vous?
4. Quel âge avez-vous?
5. Quand est votre anniversaire?
6. En quelle année êtes-vous né?
7. Où habitez-vous?
8. Quel est votre numéro de téléphone?
9. Qu'est-ce que vous aimez faire pendant votre temps libre?

Exercice écrit

Write and answer the questions of the **Conversation,** 1 - 9.

Vocabulaire

tu / vous *you*
Comment allez-vous? *How are you?*
Comment vous appelez-vous? *What's your name?*
D'où êtes-vous? *Where are you from?*
Quel âge avez-vous? *How old are you?*
Quand est votre anniversaire? *When is your birthday?*
En quelle année êtes-vous né? *In what year were you born?*
Où habitez-vous? *Where do you live?*
Quel est votre numéro de téléphone? *What is your telephone number?*
Qu'est-ce que vous aimez faire pendant votre temps libre?
What do you like to do during your free time?
Quand je suis à..... *When I'm in.....*
Avec plaisir. *At your service. With pleasure.*
avec vous *with you*

Depuis combien de temps est-ce que vous travaillez ici?
How long have you been working here?
Je travaille ici depuis vingt ans.
I have been working here for twenty years.

Nouveau vocabulaire du résumé

J'apprends le français au lycée.
I study French in high school.

J'aimerais vous poser quelques questions personnelles.
I would like to ask you a few personal questions.

s'il vous plaît *please*
avec plaisir *gladly, with much pleasure*

Je travaille depuis six heures du matin.
I have been working since six o'clock in the morning.

Résumé

One or two pairs of students can play the roles for the entire class followed by peer practice.

Your assignment is to interview a French-speaking person in your community. Your name is Philip. You decide to interview the owner of a grocery store in the neighborhood. It is 5:00 P.M.

1. **Philippe:**__________Philippe Johnson. J'étudie le français au lycée. J'aimerais vous poser quelques questions personnelles, s'il vous plaît.

2. **M. Vaux:** Avec plaisir, Philippe.

3. **Philippe:** _______ ?

4. **M. Vaux:** Je m'appelle Vincent Vaux.

5. **Philippe:** _______ ?

6. **M. Vaux:** Je suis fatigué parce que je travaille depuis six heures du matin.

7. **Philippe:** _______ ?

8. **M. Vaux:** Je suis du Québec, de la capitale, qui s'appelle Québec.

9. **Philippe:**_______ ?

10. **M. Vaux:** J'ai trente-sept ans.

11. **Philippe:** _______ ?

12. **M. Vaux:** Mon anniversaire est le 9 juillet.

13. **Philippe** _______ ?

14. **M. Vaux:** Je suis né en 1955.

15. **Philippe:**_______ ?

16. **M. Vaux:** J'habite dans la ville de New York, à Queens.

17. **Philippe:**_______ ?

18. **M. Vaux:** Pendant mon temps libre, j'aime regarder le jeu de football à la télévision, lire le journal et dormir.

19. **Philippe:** Merci beaucoup, M. Vaux. J'aime parler français avec vous.

20. **M. Vaux:** Avec plaisir. Au revoir, Philippe.

21. **Philippe:** ________, M. Vaux. Et merci beaucoup.

Glimpses of France

UNIT FOUR

L'école

TOPIC
School
SITUATION
Interaction with individual peers and adults
FUNCTION
Socializing
Providing and obtaining information about school
Expressing personal feelings about school
PROFICIENCY
Can comprehend simple statements and questions
and can respond appropriately with possible need for repetition
Can ask questions appropriate to the commiunicative situation

AIM I: Each student will be able to identify objects and materials commonly found in the classroom and be able to ask "Do you have...?" and "Will you lend me...?" and be able to respond

AIM IIA: Each student will be able to state a few activities each person usually does in the classroom

AIM IIB: Each student will be able to ask a peer and an adult if he/she does certain activities in school and after work

AIM IIC: Each student will be able to do a *Résumé de grammaire:* (a grammatical summary): the use of the singular subject pronouns with regular -ER verbs in the present tense

AIM III: Each student will be able to ask "Are there classes...?" on any particular day of the week and be able to respond

AIM IV: Each student will be able to ask a peer questions about the subjects he/she studies in school and be able to respond

Aim IA: *Each student will be able to identify objects and materials commonly encountered in the classroom and be able to ask* "Do you have...? *and* "Will you lend me ...? *and be able to respond*

Exercice oral

Dans la classe

Le maître: Qu'est-ce que c'est?
Marie: C'est un ...
C'est une ...

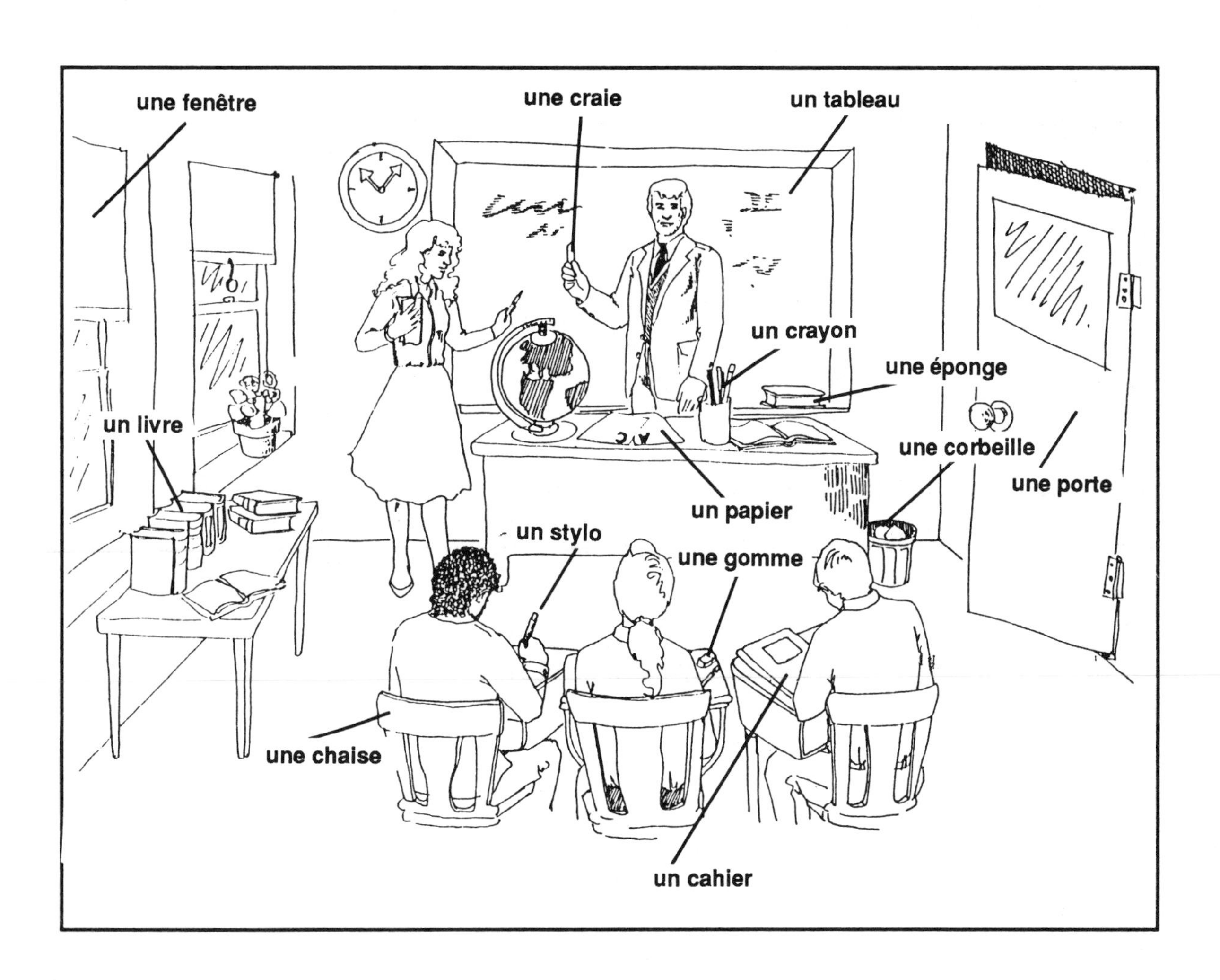

Réfléchissons

Nouns have gender in French, that is, all nouns are either masculine or feminine. Gender is indicated by the marker or "article" preceding the noun:

Example: *un livre* a book
une chaise a chair

It is very important to learn every noun with the appropriate article in order to determine gender.

Now look at the classroom picture on the preceding page.

1. How do we express "a" or "an" before a masculine noun?
2. How do we express "a" or "an" before a feminine noun?

Conversation

1. Each partner asks the other if s/he has the following objects. Partners take turns asking the questions. **Example:**

Jacques: As-tu un crayon?
Rose: Oui, j'ai un crayon.

Laure: As-tu un stylo?
Michel: Non, je n'ai pas de stylo.

1. un livre
2. un crayon
3. un stylo
4. un papier
5. une gomme

2. Each partner asks the other if s/he will lend him/her the following objects. Partners take turns asking the questions. **Example:**

Véronique: Tu me prêtes un crayon?
Isabelle: Oui, avec plaisir.

Raymond: Tu me prêtes un stylo?
Claire: Je suis navrée. J'ai besoin du stylo.

1. un papier
2. un crayon
3. un livre
4. une gomme
5. un stylo

Exercice écrit

Write both the questions and answers of the **Conversation 1,** numbers 1 - 3 and the **Conversation 2**, numbers 4 - 6.

Exercice de compréhension

You will hear a few statements, questions, or commands, each indicating the presence of an object or material found in the classroom. After the second repetition, identify each by letter in the following picture.

Vocabulaire

Dans la classe *in the classroom*
Qu'est-ce que c'est? *What is this?*
C'est ... *It is ...*

un stylo *a pen*
une éponge *a blackboard eraser*
une corbeille *a wastepaper basket*
un cahier *a notebook*
une gomme *an eraser*
un crayon *a pencil*
un livre *a book*
un papier *a paper*
un tableau *a blackboard*
une porte *a door*
une chaise *a chair*
une craie *a chalk*
une fenêtre *a window*

As-tu un(une) ...? *Do you have a ...?*
Oui, j'ai un(une) ... *Yes, I have a ....*
Non, je n'ai pas **de** ....

Tu me prêtes un(une) ...? *Will you lend me a ...?*
Oui, avec plaisir. *Yes, gladly. Yes, with pleasure.*
Je suis navré(e). J'ai besoin de.... *I'm sorry. I need ....*

Aim IIA: *Each student will be able to state a few activities each person usually does in the classroom*

Exercice oral

Que fait ... dans la classe?

1. Que fait le maître?

Le maître enseigne la leçon.
Il enseigne la leçon.

2. Que fait la maîtresse?

La maîtresse enseigne la leçon.
Elle enseigne la leçon.

3. Que fait l'élève?

L'élève parle français.
Il parle français.

4. Que fait l'élève?

L'élève parle français.
Elle parle français.

5. Que fait le garçon?

Le garçon étudie l'anglais.
Il étudie l'anglais.

6. Que fait la fille?

La fille étudie beaucoup.
Elle étudie beaucoup.

7. Que fait le garçon?

Le garçon travaille beaucoup.
Il travaille beaucoup .

8. Que fait la fille?

La fille travaille beaucoup.
Elle travaille beaucoup.

9. Que fait Robert?

Robert passe un examen.
Il passe un examen.

10. Que fait Alice?

Alice passe un examen d'espagnol.
Elle passe un examen d'espagnol.

11. Que fait Jean?

Jean écoute bien la leçon.
Il écoute bien la leçon.

12. Que fait Marie?

Marie écoute bien la leçon.
Elle écoute bien la leçon.

Conversation

Peer partners take turns asking one another *Que fait ... dans la classe?* while pointing to each picture. The partner whose turn it is to respond begins each answer with the appropriate subject pronoun (*"Il"* or *"Elle"*).

Example:

Partner 1: Que fait Robert dans la classe?
Partner 2: Il parle français dans la classe.

A.	...Robert...	E.	...Laure...	I.	...Françoise...
B.	...L'élève...	F.	...la fille...	J.	...le maître...
C.	...le garçon...	G.	...Jean...	K.	...Marie...
D.	...la maîtresse...	H.	...Pierre...	L.	...le garçon...

J

K

L

Exercice écrit

Write the questions and answers of the **Conversation.**

Exercice de compréhension

You will hear a few statements indicating what each person does in the classroom. After the second repetition, choose the picture which corresponds to what you hear. Refer to the **Conversation.** Write only the letter.

Vocabulaire

Que fait ... dans la classe?
What does ... do in the classroom?
Le maître (La maîtresse) enseigne la leçon.
The teacher teaches the lesson.
L'élève parle français.
The student speaks French.
Le garçon étudie l'anglais.
The boy studies English.
La fille travaille beaucoup.
The girl works a lot
Robert (Laure) passe un examen de français.
Robert (Laure) takes a French test.

Note: Teachers in elementary and middle school are called *le maître (la maîtresse.)* In high school they are called *le professeur* (no f. form)

Jean (Marie) écoute bien la leçon.
John (Mary) listens to the lesson well.
Il *He*
Elle She

Aim IIB: *Each student will be able to ask a peer and an adult if s/he does certain activities in school and after work*

Exercice oral

A. A l'école

1. **Christine:** Parles-tu français?
2. **Pierre:** Oui, je parle français.

3. **Christine:** Où étudies-tu?
4. **Pierre:** J'étudie à la bibliothèque de l'école. Et toi?

5. **Christine:** J'étudie à la maison. Est-ce que tu travailles beaucoup en mathématiques?
6. **Pierre:** Non, je ne travaille pas beaucoup en mathématiques. Je travaille beaucoup en histoire et en sciences.

B. Après le travail

1. **Anne:** Vous parlez beaucoup au téléphone?
2. **Mlle Jolia:** Oui, je parle beaucoup au téléphone.

3. **Anne:** Où achetez-vous la nourriture?
4. **Mlle Jolia:** J'achète la nourriture au supermarché.

5. **Anne:** Regardez-vous la télévision après le travail?
6. **Mlle Jolia:** Non, je ne regarde pas la télévision. A la maison j'écoute la radio, je joue de la guitare et je me repose.

Réfléchissons

1. Is the individual who asks the question in **Exercice oral, A** a peer (or friend) or stranger (or adult) to the person who answers the question? What part of the verb in each question of **Exercice oral A** tells us the relationship of the speaker to the person who is being addressed? When you talk to a peer, in what letter does the -ER verb end? What is the subject of the verb?

2. Is the individual who asks the question in **Exercice oral, B** a peer (or friend) or stranger (or adult) to the person who answers the question? Explain your answer. When you talk to an adult or stranger, in what letter does the -ER verb end? What is the subject of the verb?

3. Can you state what the word *"je"* means?

4. How do we answer a question negatively ("no")? Explain.

5. Are you able to state what each question and answer of the **Exercice oral** means?

Conversation 1

A l'école

Peer partners take turns asking each other the following questions.

1. Est-ce que tu parles anglais?

2. Est-ce que tu étudies le français?

3. Est-ce que tu travailles beaucoup dans la classe de français?

4. Est-ce que tu enseignes la leçon de français?

5. Est-ce que tu passes beaucoup d'examens dans la classe de français?

6. Est-ce que tu écoutes bien la leçon?

Exercice oral 2

Aux cours du soir.

One partner interviews an adult (the second partner) who attends a French class in the evening.

1. Parlez-vous beaucoup français?
2. Travaillez-vous beaucoup dans la classe?
3. Etudiez-vous beaucoup?
4. Est-ce que vous passez beaucoup d'examens?
5. Est-ce que vous écoutez bien la leçon?
6. Est-ce que vous enseignez la leçon?

Exercice oral 3

Après les cours

1. Est-ce que tu travailles dans un supermarché après les cours?
2. Regardes-tu la télévision?
3. Ecoutes-tu la radio?
4. Est-ce que tu joues de la guitare?
5. Est-ce que tu joues au basketball?

J'écoute bien la leçon.

Exercice oral 4

Après le travail

1. Est-ce que vous vous reposez après le travail?
2. Est-ce que vous marchez beaucoup?
3. Est-ce que vous achetez de la nourriture?
4. Regardez-vous la télévision?
5. Parlez-vous au téléphone?

Exercice écrit

1. Write both the questions and the answers of the **Exercice oral 1,** numbers 1 - 6 and the **Exercice oral 2,** numbers 1 - 6.

2. Write both the questions and the answers of the **Exercice oral 3,** numbers 1 - 5 and the **Exercice oral 4,** numbers 1 - 5.

Résumé 1

1. **Hélène:** Bonjour! Comment ça va?
2. **Charles:** _____ Et toi?
3. **Hélène:** _____. Qu'est-ce que tu fais après les cours?
4. **Charles:** Après les cours je _____ et _____. Et toi?
5. **Hélène:** Après les cours je _____ et _____. Tu travailles dans _____?
6. **Charles:** Oui, _____. A bientôt, Hélène.
7. **Hélène:** _____, Charles.

Résumé 2

1. **Joseph:** Bonjour, _____?
2. **M. Dupont:** Je suis fatigué. _____?
3. **Joseph:** Comme ci, comme ça, merci. Que faites-vous après le travail?
4. **M. Dupont:** Après le travail je _____ et _____.
5. **Joseph:** _____ vous au téléphone?
6. **M. Dupont:** Non, je ne _____ au téléphone à la maison parce que je parle beaucoup au téléphone au travail.
7. **Joseph:** _____, M. Dupont.
8. **M. Dupont:** Au revoir, Joseph.

Vocabulaire

le français *French:* le cours de français *the French class*
l'anglais *English:* la leçon d'anglais *the English lesson*
l'italien *Italian:* l'examen d'italien *the Italian test*
l'espagnol *Spanish:* le maître d'espagnol *the Spanish teacher*
à l'école *at school:* les cours du soir *night school*
dans la classe *in the classroom*
à la bibliothèque *in the library*
au travail *at work*
au supermarché *in the supermarket*
à la maison *at home*
après les cours *after classes*
après le travail *after work*
le cours *the course*
marcher *to walk*
Passez-vous beaucoup d'examens? / Passes-tu beaucoup d'examens?
Do you take many tests?
Oui, je passe beaucoup d'examens. *Yes, I take many exams.*
Non, je ne passe pas beaucoup d'examens. *No, I don't take many exams.*

Note: Questions in French can be formulated in two ways:
1. Parles-tu français?
2. Est-ce que tu parles français?

Aim IIC: Each student will be able to do a "Résumé de grammaire": *the use of the singular subject pronouns with regular -ER verbs in the present tense*

parler français	**regarder** la télévision
je parle ...	je regarde ...
tu parles ...	tu regardes ...
il/elle parle...	il/elle regarde ...

Note: In French the subject pronoun *'vous"* ("you") has two meanings:
1. It is the formal way to address someone (singular). The teacher asks Jean, *Jean, est-ce que vous parlez français?*
2. It is the general way to speak to a group (implying plural). The teacher asks her class, *Est-ce que vous regardez la télévision à la maison?*

Exercice écrit

A. Choose the correct form of the following -ER verbs.

1. Le maître _____ le français.
   a. enseigne b. enseignes c. enseignez

2. Laure _____ beaucoup d'examens.
   a. passez b. passes c. passe

3. Je _____ la télévision après les cours.
   a. regardez b. regardes c. regarde

4. M. Dubois, _____-vous français?
   a. parles b. parlez c. parle

5. Thérèse _____ -tu à la bibliothèque?
   a. étudies b. étudie c. étudiez

B. Write the appropriate subject pronoun.

6. ___ nage en été.
7. ___ danses à la discothèque.
8. ___ achète la nourriture.
9. ___ écoutez la radio.
10. ___ regardes la télévision.

C. Write the correct form of the -ER infinitive in parenthesis.

11. (marcher) Mon ami _____ beaucoup après les cours.
12. (chanter) Je ne _____ pas bien.
13. (enseigner) Mlle Jolia, _____ -vous les cours du soir?
14. (voyager) Mon amie _____ au Mexique en été.
15. (jouer) Antoine, est-ce que tu _____ de la guitare?
16. (regarder) Je _____ la télévision après le travail.
17. (travailler) Marie _____ dans un supermarché.

Vocabulaire

Singular subject pronouns

je	*I*
tu	*you - (family or friend)*
il	*he*
elle	*she*
vous	*you - (formal - see note, page 94)*

Aim III: Each student will be able to ask " Are there classes ...?" and be able to respond

Exercice oral 1

Le 5 janvier est un lundi.
Le 6 janvier est un mardi.
Le 7 janvier est un mercredi.
Le 8 janvier est un jeudi.
Le 9 janvier est un vendredi.
Le 10 janvier est un samedi.
Le 11 janvier est un dimanche.

janvier

lundi	mardi	mercredi	jeudi	vendredi	samedi	dimanche
			1	2	3	4
5	6	7	8	9	10	11
12	13	14	15	16	17	18
19	20	21	22	23	24	25
26	27	28	29	30	31	

Note culturelle

What is the first day of the week on a French calendar?

Exercice oral 2

1. **Hélène:** Quel jour sommes-nous aujourd'hui?
   Laure: Aujourd'hui c'est vendredi.

2. **Anne:** Quel jour sommes-nous aujourd'hui?
   Raymond: C'est mercredi.

Conversation 1

1. Ask two classmates *Quel jour sommes-nous aujourd'hui?*

2. One peer partner asks the other *Quel jour de la semaine est le premier janvier?* The other partner responds according to the French calendar: *Le premier janvier est vendredi.* One partner asks the **A** column questions and the other partner asks the **B** column.

A		B	
1.	le 1er janvier	8.	le 3 janvier
2.	le 5 janvier	9.	le 4 janvier
3.	le 11 janvier	10.	le 12 janvier
4.	le 14 janvier	11.	le 15 janvier
5.	le 16 janvier	12.	le 7 janvier
6.	le 20 janvier	13.	le 28 janvier
7.	le 31 janvier	14.	le 30 janvier

janvier

lundi	mardi	mercredi	jeudi	vendredi	samedi	dimanche
			1	2	3	4
5	6	7	8	9	10	11
12	13	14	15	16	17	18
19	20	21	22	23	24	25
26	27	28	29	30	31	

Exercice écrit 1

1. Write the question you would ask of another person to find out what day of the week today is. Respond to the question.

2. Write the Column **A** answers of the **Conversation 1,** number 2.

Conversation 2

Each partner asks the other if there are classes tomorrow or on any particular day of this week or next week.

Example:

1. **Jean:** Est-ce qu'il y a des cours demain?
   Anne: Oui, il y a des cours demain.

2. **Antoine:** Est-ce qu'il y a des cours le jeudi?
   Laure: Non, il n'y a pas de cours le jeudi.

3. **Louise:** Est-ce qu'il y a des cours lundi prochain?
   Jules: Oui, il y a des cours lundi prochain.

1. Est-ce qu'il y a des cours demain?
2. Est-ce qu'il y a des cours lundi?
3. Est-ce qu'il y a des cours mercredi?
4. Est-ce qu'il y a des cours jeudi?
5 Est-ce qu'il y a des cours dimanche?
6. Est-ce qu'il y a des cours mardi prochain?
7. Est-ce qu'il y a des cours jeudi prochain?
8. Est-ce qu'il y a des cours samedi prochain?

Réfléchissons

1. What does the expression*"Est-ce qu'il y a...?"* mean in a question?

2. What does the expression*"il y a...?"* mean in a statement?

3. Where is the negative "ne...pas" placed when used with *"il y a"* in a statement?

Note: *"Est-ce qu'il y a...?"* can also mean "Is there ...?" when talking about one subject. *(Est-ce qu'il y a un cours d'anglais maintenant?) "Il y a ...* can also mean "There is ..." *(Oui, il y a un cours d'anglais maintenant.*

Exercice écrit

Write the questions and answers of the **Conversation 2,** numbers 1 - 8.

Vocabulaire

les jours de la semaine ***the days of the week***

lundi *Monday*
mardi *Tuesday*
mercredi *Wednesday*
jeudi *Thursday*
vendredi Friday
samedi *Satuday*
dimanche *Sunday*

...prochain *next ...*
jeudi prochain *next Thursday*
samedi prochain *next Saturday*

le mardi *on Tuesday*
le dimanche *on Sunday*

Quel jour de la semaine est-ce aujourd'hui?
What day of the week is today?
Aujourd'hui c'est ... *Today is ...*

Est-ce qu'il y a des cours demain? *Are there classes tomorrow?*
Oui, il y a des cours demain. *Yes, there are classes tomorrow.*
Non, il n'y a pas de cours demain. *No, there are no classes tomorrow.*

Aim IIIB: *Each student will be able to ask a peer questions about the subjects s/he studies in school and be able to respond*

Exercice oral 1

1. **Raoul:** Qu'est-ce que tu étudies à l'école?
   Anne: J'étudie l'anglais, le français, l'histoire, les sciences, les mathématiques, l'art et l'éducation physique.

2. **Marie:** Qu'est-ce que tu étudies à l'école?
   Jean: J'étudie le latin, l'informatique, l'économie, la musique, la littérature et l'éducation physique.

Conversation 1

Ask two classmates near you *"Qu'est-ce que tu étudies à l'école?"* and listen carefully to each response.

Exercice écrit 1

Write the question you would ask of a peer to find out what s/he studies in school. Then respond to the question.

Exercice oral 2

A

1. **Raoul:** Quel est ton sujet préféré?
   Anne: Mon sujet préféré est les mathématiques

2. **Raoul:** Qui est ton professeur de mathématiques?
   Anne: Mon professeur de mathématiques est M. Plomb.

3. **Raoul:** Où est M. Plomb?
   Anne: M. Plomb est dans la salle n° 147.

4. **Raoul:** Combien d'élèves y-a-t-il dans la classe?
   Anne: Il y a trente et un élèves dans la classe.

5. **Raoul:** Comment est ta classe d'anglais?
   Anne: Ma classe d'anglais est bonne, intéressante et facile.

B

1. **Marie:** Quel est ton cours préféré?
   Jean: Mon cours préféré est la littérature.

2. **Marie:** Qui est ton professeur de littérature?
   Jean: Mon professeur de littérature est Mme Cantin.

3. **Marie:** Où est Mme Cantin?
   Jean: Mme Cantin est absente.

4. **Marie:** Combien d'élèves y-a-t-il dans la classe?
   Jean: Il y a vingt-neuf élèves dans la classe.

5. **Marie:** Comment est ta classe d'économie?
   Jean: Ma classe d'économie est mauvaise, ennuyeuse et difficile.

6. **Raoul:** Quand est ton examen de sciences?
   Anne: Mon examen de sciences est mardi prochain.

7. **Raoul:** Est-ce que tu aimes le cours d'histoire?
   Anne: Non, je n'aime pas le cours d'histoire.
   Raoul: Pourquoi ne l'aimes-tu pas?
   Anne: Je ne l'aime pas parce qu'il y a trop d'examens et je reçois de mauvaises notes.

8. **Raoul:** Est-ce que tu as beaucoup de devoirs dans la classe?
   Anne: Non, je n'ai pas beaucoup de devoirs dans la classe.

6. **Marie:** Quand est ton examen d'ordinateur?
   Jean: Mon examen d'ordinateur est demain.

7. **Marie:** Est-ce que tu aimes le cours de latin?
   Jean: Oui, j'aime le cours de latin.
   Marie: Pourquoi l'aimes-tu?
   Jean: Je l'aime parce-que le professeur enseigne bien et je reçois de bonnes notes.

8. **Marie:** As-tu beaucoup de devoirs dans la classe?
   Jean: Oui, j'ai toujours beaucoup de devoirs dans la classe.

Conversation

Peer partners take turns asking one another the following questions.

1 Qu'est-ce que tu étudies à l'école?
2. Quel est ton sujet préféré?
3. Qui est ton professeur de ...?(#2, above)
4. Où est ton professeur de ...? (#2)
5. Est-ce que tu as beaucoup de devoirs dans la classe de ...?(#2)
6. Comment est ta classe de ...?
7. Quand est ton examen de ...? (#6)
8. Combien d'élèves y-a-t-il dans la classe de ...? (#6)
9. Est-ce que tu aimes la classe de ...? (#6)
10. Pourquoi est-ce que tu ne l'aimes pas?

Exercice écrit 2

Write both the questions and answers to the **Exercice oral 2.**

Exercice de compréhension

You will hear a few questions related to the subjects you study in school; after the second repetition, write the answer to each question with a complete sentence in French.

Activité

Mon programme de cours ***My program card***

Write your program in French listing the days of the week and the periods you have each class. Include your lunch period *(déjeuner)*. Partners ask one another the following questions to find out each other's program.

Example:
Thomas: Quels cours as-tu le lundi?
Julie: Le lundi j'ai les mathématiques, l'art, l'éducation physique, le déjeuner, l'histoire, le français, l'anglais et les sciences.
Thomas: Quels cours as-tu le mardi?
Julie: J'ai le même programme tous les jours.

Résumé

1. **Philippe:** ______________________?
2. **Rachel:** J'étudie l'anglais, la biologie, l'algèbre, l'histoire, le français, l'art et l'éducation physique.

3. **Philippe:** ______________________?
4. **Rachel:** Mon sujet préféré est l'histoire.

5. **Philippe:** ______________________?
6. **Rachel:** Mon professeur d'histoire c'est Mlle Périgaud.

7. **Philippe:** ______________________?
8. **Rachel:** Mlle Périgaud est dans la classe n° 264.

9. **Philippe:** ______________________?
10. **Rachel:** Il y a trente et un élèves dans ma classe d'histoire.

11. **Philippe:** ______________________?
12. **Rachel:** Ma classe de biologie est intéressante et difficile.

13. **Philippe:** ______________________?
14. **Rachel:** Mon examen de biologie est mardi prochain.

15. **Philippe:** ______________________?
16. **Rachel:** J'aime la classe de français parce que le professeur enseigne bien et je parle beaucoup français dans la classe.

Vocabulaire

Qu'est-ce que tu étudies à l'école? *What do you study in school?*
J'étudie ... *I study ...*

l'algèbre *algebra*
l'art *art*
l'anglais *English*
la biologie *biology*
la chimie *chemistry*
la dactylo *typewriting*
l'économie *economics*
l'éducation physique *physical education*
le français *French*
la géométrie *geometry*
l'histoire *history*
la littérature *literature*
les mathématiques *mathematics*
l'informatique *computers*
les sciences *science*
la physique *physics*

Quel est ton cours préféré? *What is your favorite subject?*
Qui est ton professeur? *Who is your teacher?*
Mon ... est M. ... / Mme ... / Mlle ...
Où est ton professeur de ...? *Where is your ... teacher?*
... est dans ... *... is in ...* ... est absent(e) *... is absent*
Combien d'élèves y-a-t-il dans ...? *How many students are there in ...?*
Quand est ton examen de ...? *When is your ... test?*
aujourd'hui *today* demain *tomorrow* vendredi *on Friday*
Comment est ta classe de ...? *What is your ... class like?*
bonne *good* intéressante *interesting*
difficile *difficult* mauvaise *bad*
facile *easy* ennuyeux(euse) *boring*
Pourquoi l'aimes-tu? / Pourquoi ne l'aimes-tu pas?
Why do you like / don/t like it?
Je l'aime parce que ... / Je ne l'aime pas parce que...
I like it because ... / I don't like it because...
...parce qu'il y a trop d'examens. *...because there are too many tests.*
...parce que je reçois de mauvaises notes.
...because I receive bad grades.
...parce que je reçois de bonnes notes.
...because I receive good grades.
Est-ce que tu as beaucoup de devoirs dans la classe...?
As-tu beaucoup de devoirs dans la classe...?
Do you have a lot of homework in ...
J'ai toujours beaucoup de devoirs... *I always have a lot of homework ...*
Je n'ai pas beaucoup de devoirs... *I don't have a lot of homework*
Quels cours as-tu le lundi? *What classes do you have on Mondays?*
J'ai le même programme tous les jours
I have the same program every day.

UNIT FIVE

La famille

TOPIC

The family

SITUATION

Interaction with individual peers and adults

FUNCTION

Socializing, providing and exchanging information about one's family

PROFICIENCY

Can comprehend simple questions and respond appropriately with possible need for repetition
Can ask questions appropriate to the communicative situation

AIM I: Given a French family tree, each student will be able to state the relationship of one member of a French family to another

AIM II: Each student will be able to ask a peer how many people there are in his/her family and who they are and be able to respond

AIM III: Each student will be able to ask a peer the names of the members of his/her family and be able to respond

AIM IV: Each student will be able to ask a peer the ages of the members of his/her family and be able to respond

AIM V: Each student will be able to ask a peer what each member of his/her family is like and be able to respond

AIM VI: Each student will be able to ask a peer where each member of his/her family is from and be able to respond

AIM VII: Each student will be able to ask a peer what he/she does with each member of the family

AIM VIII Each student will be able to ask a peer what activities each member of the family does and what two or more family members do together and be able to respond

AIM IX: Each student will be able to do a *"Résumé de grammaire"*:: the use of singular and plural subject pronouns with regular -ER verbs

Aim I: *Given a French family tree, each student will be able to state the relationship of one member of a French family to another*

Exercice oral 1

Une famille française

Françoise Baudoin (38 ans)

Jean Baudoin (43 ans)

Isabelle Baudoin (11 ans)

Thomas Baudoin (9 ans)

Thérèse Baudoin (13 ans)

Can you figure out the relationship of one member of this French family to the other?

1. Françoise Baudoin est **la femme** de Jean Baudoin.
2. Jean Baudoin est **le mari** de Françoise Baudoin.
3. Thomas Baudoin est **le fils** de Jean et de Françoise.
4. Isabelle Baudoin est **la fille** de Jean et de Françoise.

5. Thérèse Baudoin est **la fille** de Jean et de Françoise.

6. Jean Baudoin est **le père** d'Isabelle, de Thomas et de Thérèse.

7. Françoise Baudoin est **la mère** d'Isabelle, de Thomas et de Thérèse.

8. Thomas est **le frère** d'Isabelle et de Thérèse.

9. Isabelle est **la soeur** de Thomas et de Thérèse.

10. Thérèse est **la soeur** d' Isabelle et de Thomas.

Conversation 1

Peer partners take turns asking and answering the following questions about the relationships of the French family pictured on the preceding page.

Example: - Comment s'appelle le mari de Françoise?
Le mari de Françoise s'appelle Jean.

1. Comment s'appelle le père de Thérèse, d'Isabelle et de Thomas?

2. Comment s'appelle la mère de Thérèse, d'Isabelle et de Thomas?

3. Comment s'appelle le frère d'Isabelle et de Thérèse?

4. Comment s'appelle une des soeurs de Thomas?

5. Comment s'appelle l'autre soeur de Thomas?

6. Comment s'appelle une des filles de Jean?

7. Comment s'appelle l'autre fille de Jean?

8. Comment s'appelle le fils de Françoise?

9. Comment s'appelle le mari de Françoise?

10. Comment s'appelle la femme de Jean?

Exercice écrit

Write the questions and answers of the **Conversation 1.**

Exercice oral 2

Une autre famille française

Jacqueline Vautrin
(45 ans)

Marcel Vautrin
(57ans)

Robert Vautrin
(21 ans)

Hélène Vautrin
(17 ans)

Réfléchissons 1

1. How do we say “the” before a noun which refers to a male?
2. How do we say “the” before a noun which refers to a female?

State the relationship of one member of this French family to another by completing the following statements correctly.

1. Jacqueline Vautrin est_____de Robert et d' Hélène.
2. Marcel Vautrin est_____de Robert et d' Hélène.
3. Robert est_____d'Hélène.
4. Hélène est_____de Robert.
5. Jacqueline Vautrin est______de Marcel Vautrin.
6. Marcel Vautrin est______de Jacqueline Vautrin.
7. Hélène Vautrin est______de Marcel Vautrin.
8. Robert Vautrin est______de Jacqueline Vautrin.

Conversation 2

Peer partners take turns asking and answering the following questions about the relationships of the French family in **Exercice oral 2.**

Example: Qui est la mère de Robert?
La mère de Robert est Jacqueline.

1. Qui est le fils de Jacqueline?
2. Qui est la soeur de Robert?
3. Qui est le mari de Jacqueline?
4. Qui est le père d'Hélène?
5. Qui est la femme de Marcel?
6. Qui est le frère d'Hélène?
7. Qui est la fille de Marcel?
8. Qui est la mère de Robert?

Exercice écrit 2

Write the questions and answers of the **Conversation 2.**

La mère d'Hélène est Jacqueline.

Exercice oral 3

Marie Baudoin
(63 ans)

Charles Baudoin
(72 ans)

Françoise Baudoin
(38 ans)

Jean Baudoin
(43 ans)

Jacqueline Vautrin
(45 ans)

Marcel Vautrin
(51 ans)

Isabelle Baudoin
(11 ans)

Thomas Baudoin
(9 ans)

Thérèse Baudoin
(13 ans)

Robert Vautrin
(21 ans)

Hélène Vautrin
(17 ans)

Can you figure out the relationship of one member to the other in these two French families?

1. Charles Baudoin est **le mari** de Marie Baudoin.

2. Jean Baudoin est **le fils** de Marie et de Charles.

3. Marie Baudoin est **la mère** de Jacqueline Vautrin.

4. Jacqueline Vautrin est **la soeur** de Jean Baudoin.

5. Charles Baudoin est **le grand-père** d'Isabelle et de Robert.

6. Marie Baudoin est **la grand-mère** de Thomas et de Thérèse.

7. Marcel Vautrin est **l'oncle** de Thomas et de Thérèse.

8. Françoise Baudoin est **la tante** de Robert et d'Hélène.

9. Robert est **le cousin** de Thérèse et de Thomas.

10. Isabelle est **la cousine** de Robert et d'Hélène.

11. Robert est **le neveu** de Jean Baudoin.

12. Thérèse est **la petite-fille** de Marie Baudoin.

Conversation 3

Peer partners take turns asking and answering the following questions about the relationships of the French families pictured in the **Exercice oral 3.**

1. Comment s'appelle la femme de Charles?

2. Comment s'appelle la fille de Charles et de Marie?

3. Comment s'appelle le père de Jean?

4. Comment s'appelle le frère de Jacqueline?

5. Comment s'appelle la grand-mère d'Isabelle, de Thomas et de Thérèse?

6. Qui est l'oncle de Robert et d' Hélène?

7. Qui est la cousine d'Isabelle, de Thomas et de Thérèse?

8. Qui est le grand-père de Robert et d'Hélène?

9. Qui est la tante d'Isabelle, de Thomas et de Thérèse?

10. Qui est le cousin de Robert et d'Hélène?

11. Qui est la nièce de Jean Baudoin?

12. Qui est un des petit-fils de Charles Baudoin?

Charles est le grand-père de Robert et d'Hélène.

Exercice écrit 3

Write the questions and answers of the **Conversation 3.**

Exercice de compréhension

You will hear several family relationships. Write the name of the person who corresponds to the relationship you hear. Refer to the French family tree in the **Exercice oral 3.**

Example: Le mari de Françoise Baudoin s'appelle _______ .

Exercice oral 4

Can you figure out the relationships of the two members of these French families to the others? Refer to the family tree in the **Exercice oral 3.**

1. Marie et Charles sont **les parents** de Jean et de Jacqueline.

2. Jean et Jacqueline sont **les enfants** de Marie et de Charles.

3. Marie et Charles sont **les grands-parents** d'Isabelle, de Thomas, de Thérèse, de Robert et d'Hélène.

4. Isabelle, Thomas, Thérèse, Robert et Hélène sont **les petits-enfants** de Marie et de Charles.

5. Isabelle et Thérèse sont **les soeurs** de Thomas.

6. Thomas et Isabelle sont **le frère et la soeur** de Thérèse.

7. Marcel et Jacqueline sont **l'oncle et la tante** d'Isabelle, de Thomas et de Thérèse.

Une autre famille

8. Isabelle, Thérèse et Thomas sont **les nièces et le neveu** de Jacqueline et de Marcel.

9. Isabelle et Thérèse sont **les cousins** de Robert et d'Hélène.

10. Robert et Hélène sont **le cousin et la cousine** d'Isabelle, de Thomas et de Thérèse.

Marie est la mère de Françoise.

Réfléchissons 2

1. How do we say "the" before a plural noun?

2. What letter or letters do we add to form the plural of nouns?

Conversation 4

Example: Comment s'appellent les parents de Robert et d'Hélène?
Les parents de Robert et d'Hélène s'appellent Jacqueline et Marcel.

1. Comment s'appellent les enfants de Jacqueline et de Marcel?

2. Comment s'appellent les grands-parents d'Isabelle, de Thomas et de Thérèse?

3. Comment s'appellent les soeurs de Thomas?

4. Comment s'appellent les oncles de Robert et d'Hélène?

5. Comment s'appellent les cousins d'Isabelle, de Thomas et de Thérèse?

6. Comment s'appellent les petits-enfants de Marie et de Charles?

7. Comment s'appellent les neveux de Jacqueline et de Marcel?

8. Comment s'appellent les parents de Robert et d'Hélène?

Exercice écrit 4

Write the **Conversation 4.**

Françoise Baudoin

Réfléchissons 3

How is possession expressed in French?

1. What does *le frère de Jacqueline* mean?
   What does *la grand-mère d'Antoine* mean?
2. What word is used to express possession in French?
3. How do we express possession in English?

Exercice:

Say the following phrases in French indicating possession.

Example: Joseph's niece *la nièce de Joseph.*
Rose's grandson *le petit-fils de Rose*

1. John's sister
2. Mary's son
3. Ann's husband
4. Michael's aunt
5. Ellen's grandfather
6. Peter's cousin (female)
7. Carmen's father
8. Robert's daughters
9. Teresa's brothers
10. Paul's aunt and uncle

Vocabulaire

la famille ***the family***

le père *the father*
la mère *the mother*
les parents *the parents*

le mari *the husband*
la femme *the wife*
les époux *the husband and wife*

le frère *the brother*
la soeur *the sister*

le grand-père *the grandfather*
la grand-mère *the grandmother*
les grands-parents *the grandparents*

le fils *the son*
la fille *the daughter*
les enfants *children*
le petit-fils *the grandson*
la petite-fille *the granddaughter*
les petits-enfants *the grandchildren*

l'oncle *the uncle*
la tante *the aunt*
les oncles *aunt and uncle*

le neveu *the nephew*
la nièce *the niece*

le cousin *the cousin (male)*
la cousine *the cousin (female)*
les cousins *male and female cousins*

Comment s'appelle...? *What is ... name?*
Qui est...? *Who is...?*
Comment s'appellent...? *What are...names?*
Une des... *one of the...(feminine)*
Un des... *one of the...(masculine)*
l'autre... *the other*

Aim II: *Each student will be able to ask a peer how many people there are in his / her family and who they are and be able to respond*

Exercice oral

1. **Michel:** Combien de personnes y-a-t-il dans ta famille?
   Catherine: Il y a trois personnes dans ma famille.
   Michel: Qui sont-elles?
   Catherine: Il y a ma mère, mon frère et moi.

2. **Laure:** Combien de personnes y-a-t-il dans ta famille?
   Antoine: Il y a cinq personnes dans ma famille.
   Laure: Qui sont-elles?
   Antoine: Il y a mes parents, mes deux soeurs et moi.

3. **Paul:** Combien de personnes y-a-t-il dans ta famille?
   Paulette: Il y a neuf personnes dans ma famille.
   Paul: Qui sont-elles?
   Paulette: Il y a ma mère, mon père, ma grand-mère, mes trois soeurs, mes deux frères et moi.

Conversation

Each student asks two other peers *Combien de personnes y-a-t-il dans ta famille?* After receiving a response, s/he then asks *Qui sont-elles?* Listen carefully to each response.

Exercice écrit

Write the questions that a peer would ask you to find out how many people there are in your family and who they are. Then respond to each question.

Vocabulaire

Combien de personnes y-a-t-il dans ta famille?
How many people are there in your family?
Il y a...personnes dans ma famille.
There are...people in my family.
Qui sont-elles?
Who are they?
Il y a...et moi.
We are........and I. (**Note:** *The French use* "Il y a ..." for this expression)

le père *the father*
la mère *the mother*

mon père *my father*
ma mère *my mother*
mes parents *my parents*

Aim III: *Each student will be able to ask a peer the names of the members of his / her family and be able to respond*

Exerçice oral

1. **Claire:** Comment s'appelle ta mère?
   Thomas: Ma mère s'appelle Laure.

2. **Rose:** Comment s'appelle ton père?
   Jean: Mon père s'appelle Pierre.

3. **Joseph:** Comment s'appelle ton frère?
   Louis: Il s'appelle Paul.

4. **Anne:** Comment s'appelle ta soeur?
   Raoul: Elle s'appelle Anne.

5. **Jules:** Comment s'appellent tes frères?
   Philippe: Ils s'appellent Vincent et Henri.

6. **Victoire:** Comment s'appellent tes soeurs?
   Julie: Elles s'appellent Sylvie et Marguerite.

Réfléchissons

1. What does *Ils* mean in **Exercice oral,** 5?
2. What does *Elles* mean in **Exercice oral,** 6?
3. To whom do each of these subjects refer?

Conversation

One peer partner asks the other *Combien de personnes y-a-t-il dans ta famille?* followed by *Qui sont-elles?* ; then based on the information given,s/he asks the names of the family members of his/her partner. Then the other partner asks the questions.

Example:

1. **Louis:** Combien de personnes y-a-t-il dans ta famille?
2. **Claire:** Il y a cinq personnes dans ma famille.
3. **Louis:** Qui sont-elles?
4. **Claire:** Il y a ma mère, mes deux frères, ma soeur et moi.
5. **Louis:** Comment s'appelle ta mère?
6. **Claire:** Elle s'appelle Victoire.
7. **Louis:** Comment s'appellent tes frères?
8. **Claire:** Ils s'appellent Antoine et Robert.
9. **Louis:** Comment s'appelle ta soeur?
10. **Claire:** Elle s'appelle Marguerite.

Marguerite est la mère de Claire.

Exercice écrit

Write the following in dialogue form using your own name and the name of a friend. Refer to the example in the preceding dialogue.

1. First write the questions that a friend would ask you to find out how many people there are in your family and who they are . Respond to each question.
2. Write the questions that s/he would ask you to find out the names of each of your family members and respond to each question.

Vocabulaire

Comment s'appelle...? *What is...name?*
...s'appelle... *...name is...*
Comment s'appellent...? *What are...names?*
...s'appellent... *...names are...*

Henri *Henry*
Louis *Lewis*
Jules *Julio*
Raymond *Raymond*
Raoul *Raul*
Robert *Robert*

Claire *Clara*
Victoire *Victoria*
Julie *Julia*
Louise *Louise*
Marguerite *Margaret*
Rachelle *Rachel*
Sylvie *Sylvia*

ils *they (males or males and females)*
elles *they (females only)*

Aim IV: *Each student will be able to ask a peer the ages of the members of his/her family and be able to respond*

Exercice oral

1. **Henri:** Quel âge a ta mère?
   Julie: Elle a quarante et un ans.

2. **Sylvie:** Quel âge a ton frère?
   Raymond: Il a dix-neuf ans.

3. **Julie:** Quel âge a ta soeur?
   Louise: Ma soeur Isabelle a quinze ans.

4. **Victoire:** Quel âge ont tes grands-parents?
   Jules: Mon grand-père Thomas a soixante-huit ans et ma grand-mère Marie a soixante-quatre ans. Je ne sais pas l'âge de mes autres grands-parents.

Conversation

One peer partner asks the other *Combien de personnes y-a-t-il dans ta famille?* followed by *Qui sont elles?* Based on the information given, s/he asks the ages of the family members of his/her partner. Then the other partner asks the questions.

Example:

1. **Thérèse:** Combien de personnes y-a-t-il dans ta famille?
2. **Michel:** Il y a six personnes dans ma famille.
3. **Thérèse:** Qui sont-elles?
4. **Michel:** Il y a mes parents, mes deux soeurs, mon frère et moi.
5. **Thérèse:** Quel âge ont tes parents?
6. **Michel:** Mon père a quarante deux ans et ma mère a trente-sept ans.
7. **Thérèse:** Quel âge ont tes soeurs?
8. **Michel:** Ma soeur Claire a douze ans et ma soeur Louise a quatorze ans.
9. **Thérèse:** Quel âge a ton frère?
10. **Michel:** Il a seize ans.

Exercice écrit

Write the following in dialogue form using your own name and the name of a peer. Refer to the **Conversation** dialogue.

1. Write the questions that a peer would ask you to find out how many people there are in your family and who they are. Respond to each question.
2. Write the questions that s/he would ask you to find out the ages of each of your family members and respond to each question.
3. Write the names and ages in words of all the members of the two French families in **Exercice oral 3**, *(Aim I)*

Vocabulaire

Quel âge a...? *How old is...?*
...a...ans. *...is...years old.*
Quel âge ont... *How old are...?*
...ont...ans. *...are...years old.*
Je ne sais pas. *I don't know.*
Je ne sais pas quel âge a... *I don't know how old ... is.*
mon autre... *my other...*

Aim V: *Each student will be able to ask a peer what each member of his/her family is like and be able to respond*

Exercice oral

1. **Sylvie:** Comment est ton père?
   Raymond: Mon père est grand, mince, fort et sympatique.

2. **Raoul:** Comment est ta mère?
   Louis: Ma mère est petite, grosse, intelligente et bonne.

3. **Julie:** Comment est ton frère?
   Joseph: Il est méchant, laid, antipathique et stupide.

4. **Claire:** Comment est ta grand-mère?
   Victoire: Elle est belle, vieille, sincère et généreuse.

5. **Henri:** Comment sont tes frères et soeurs?
   Marguerite: Mon frère Robert est petit, jeune, créatif et drôle et ma soeur Sylvie est grande, romantique, paresseuse et forte.

Conversation 1

One peer partner asks the other *Combien de personnes y-a-t-il dans ta famille?* followed by *Qui sont-elles?* Based on the information given s/he asks what each member of the other partner's family is like. Then the other partner asks the questions.

Example:

1. **Jean:** Combien de personnes y-a-t-il dans ta famille?
2. **Anne:** Il y a cinq personnes dans ma famille.
3. **Jean:** Qui sont-elles?
4. **Anne:** Il y a ma mère, mon frère, mes deux soeurs et moi.
5. **Jean:** Comment est ta mère?
6. **Anne:** Elle est grande, sympatique, forte et généreuse.
7. **Jean:** Comment est ton frère?
8. **Anne:** Il est mince, drôle, paresseux et beau.
9. **Jean:** Comment sont tes soeurs?
10. **Anne:** Ma soeur Hélène est grosse, bonne, créative et généreuse et ma soeur Louise est mince, jolie, intelligente et drôle.

Conversation 2

Partners take turns asking and answering the following questions. Answer with at least three characteristics for each person.

1. Comment est ton cousin?
2. Comment est ta cousine?
3. Comment est ton grand-père?
4. Comment est ta grand-mère?
5. Comment est ton meilleur ami?
6. Comment est ta meilleure amie?

Thomas est drôle.

Exercice écrit

Write the following in dialogue form using your own name and the name of a peer. Refer to the **Conversation 1.**

1. Write the questions that a peer would ask to find out how many people there are in your family and who they are. Respond to each question.
2. Then write the questions s/he would ask you to find out what each member of your family is like and respond.
3. Write the questions and answers of the **Conversation 2,** numbers 1 - 6.

Vocabulaire

Comment est...? *What is...like?*
Comment sont...? *What are...like?*

beau/belle *handsome*
joli/jolie *pretty*
créatif/créative *creative*
drôle *funny*
paresseux/paresseuse *lazy*
romantique *romantic*
méchant/méchante *nasty*
fort / forte *strong*

Mon grand-père est mort.
..is no longer living.

mon meilleur ami *my best friend*
ma meilleure amie *my best friend*
bon/bonne *kind*
mince *slender*

Aim VI: *Each student will be able to ask a peer where each member of his/her family is from and be able to respond*

Exercice oral

1. **Hélène:** D'où est ton grand-père?
   Pierre: Il est de Belgique.

2. **Joseph:** D'où est ta grand-mère?
   Claire: Je ne sais pas d'où est ma grand-mère.

3. **Michel:** D'où sont tes oncles?
   Isabelle: Ils sont des Etats-Unis.

4. **Rachelle:** D'où sont tes grands-parents?
   Philippe: Ma grand-mère est du Luxembourg et mon grand-père est d'Italie.

être ***to be (irregular)***

je suis	nous sommes
tu es	vous êtes
il est	ils sont
elle est	elles sont

Conversation

One peer partner asks the other *Combien de personnes y-a-t-il dans ta famille?* followed by *Qui sont-elles?* Based on the information given, he/she asks where each member of his/her partner's family is from. Then the other partner asks the questions.

Example:

1. **Julie:** Combien de personnes y-a-t-il dans ta famille?
2. **Louis:** Il y a six personnes dans ma famille.
3. **Julie:** Qui sont-elles?
4. **Louis:** Il y a mes parents, mes grands-parents, ma soeur et moi.
5. **Julie:** D'où sont tes parents?
6. **Louis:** Ils sont des Etats-Unis.
7. **Julie:** D'où sont tes grands-parents?
8. **Louis:** Ils sont de la Martinique.
9. **Julie:** D'où est ta soeur?
10. **Louis:** Elle est des Etats-Unis.

Exercice écrit

Write the following in dialogue form using your own name and the name of a friend.

1. Write the questions a peer would ask you to find out how many people there are in your family and who they are. Respond to each question.
2. Then write the questions s/he would ask you to find out where each member of your family is from and respond.
3. Write the question s/he would ask you to find out where your grand-parents are from and respond to the question.

Exercice de compréhension

You will hear a few oral questions in French about your family; after the second repetition, write the answer to each question with a complete sentence in French.

Les grands-parents

Aim VII: *Each student will be able to ask a peer what activities s/he does with each member of the family and be able to respond*

Exercice oral

1. **Pierre:** Que faites-vous toi et ton père? (Que font-ils?)
   Paul: Mon père et moi nous jouons au tennis, nous achetons la nourriture, nous voyageons et nous nageons l'été.

2. **Sylvie:** Que faites-vous, toi et ta mère? (Que font-elles?)
   Marie: Ma mère et moi nous parlons beaucoup, nous nettoyons la maison et nous faisons la cuisine.

3. **Hélène:** Que faites-vous, toi et ton frère? (Que font-ils?)
   Carlos: Mon frère et moi nous regardons la télévision, nous travaillons après l'école et nous jouons aux jeux de vidéo.

4. **Louis:** Que faites-vous, toi et ta soeur? (Que font-elles)
   Rose: Ma soeur et moi nous étudions, nous écoutons la musique, chantons et dansons dans les parties.

5. **Joseph:** Que faites-vous, toi et ton cousin (Que font-ils?)
   Jean: Mon cousin et moi nous allons au cinéma le dimanche, nous allons à la plage en été, nous faisons beaucoup de promenades au printemps et nous jouons au football en automne.

Refléchissons

1. What does the word ***nous*** mean? To whom does it refer?

2. When the subject of a sentence is ***nous*** or an equivalent *(mon amie et moi / mon frère et moi)*, in what letters does the verb end?

Conversation

A. One peer partner asks the other *Combien de personnes y-a-t-il dans ta famille?* followed by *Qui sont-elles?* Based on the information given, s/he asks what s/he does with each member of the family.

Example:

1. **Raymond:** Combien de personnes y-a-t-il dans ta famille?
2. **Louis:** Il y a trois personnes dans ma famille.
3. **Raymond:** Qui sont-elles?
4. **Louis:** Il y a ma mère, mon frère et moi.
5. **Raymond:** Que faites-vous, toi et ta mère?
6. **Louis:** Nous parlons beaucoup, faisons la cuisine, allons au cinéma et nous jouons au tennis.
7. **Raymond:** Que faites-vous, toi et ta soeur?
8. **Louis:** Nous achetons la nourriture, nettoyons la maison, lavons la vaisselle et jouons de la guitare.

B. Partners ask one another the following questions.

1. Que faites-vous toi et ton meilleur ami?
2. Que faites-vous toi et ta meilleure amie?
3. Que faites-vous toi et ton cousin?
4. Que faites-vous toi et ta grand-mère?

Vocabulaire

faire une promenade *to take a walk*
laver / faire la vaisselle *to wash the dishes*
faire le ménage *to clean the house*
jouer aux jeux de vidéo *to play video games*
travailler dans un magasin *to work in a store*
nous *we* vous *you (two or more peers or adults)*

faire ***to do, to make (irregular)***

je **fais**	nous **faisons**
tu **fais**	vous **faites**
il **fait**	ils **font**
elle **fait**	elles **font**

Aim VIII: *Each student will be able to ask a peer what each member of the family does and what two or more family members do together*

Exercice oral

1. **Rachelle:** Combien de personnes y-a-t-il dans ta famille?
2. **Thomas:** Il y a sept personnes dans ma famille.
3. **Rachelle:** Qui sont-elles?
4. **Thomas:** Il y a mes parents, mes deux soeurs, mon frère, ma grand-mère et moi.
5. **Rachelle:** Que font tes parents?
6. **Thomas:** Ils travaillent dans un magasin, écoutent la musique, font beaucoup de promenades et voyagent pendant l'été.
7. **Rachelle:** Que font tes soeurs?
8. **Thomas:** Elles regardent la télévision, nettoient la maison, jouent de la guitare, vont au cinéma et jouent au tennis.
9. **Rachelle:** Que fait ton frère?
10. **Thomas:** Il écoute la radio, danse dans les discothèques, joue au basketball et va beaucoup au cinéma.
11. **Rachelle:** Que fait ta grand-mère?
12. **Thomas:** Elle fait la cuisine et la vaisselle, parle au téléphone et elle regarde la télévision.

Refléchissons

1. When a person talks about two or more people, in what letter(s) does an *-ER* verb end?
2. When a person talks about one person, in what letter does an *-ER* verb end?

aller ***to go (irregular)***

je **vais**	nous allons
tu **vas**	vous allez
il **va**	ils **vont**
elle **va**	elles **vont**

Conversation

1. Ask the appropriate questions to find out how many people there are in your friend's family and who they are. Then find out what each member of the family does and what two or more members do together.

2. Partners ask one another the following questions.

   A. Que font tes amis?
   B. Que font tes amies?
   C. Que font tes cousins?
   D. Que font tes grands-parents?

Exercice écrit

1. Write the appropriate questions a peer partner would ask you to find out how many people there are in your family and who they are. Then respond to each question.

2. Write the questions s/he would ask you to find out what each member of the family does and what two or more members do together and respond.

Résumé

One or two pairs of students can play the roles for the entire class followed by peer practice.

1. **Marie:** ___________________ ?
2. **Hélène:** Il y a cinq personnes dans ma famille.

3. **Marie:** ___________________ ?
4. **Hélène:** Il y a ma mère, mon frère, mes deux soeurs et moi.

5. **Marie:** ___________________ ?
6. **Hélène:** Ma mère s'appelle Rose.

7. **Marie:** ___________________ ?
8. **Hélène:** Elle a trente-sept ans.

9. **Marie:** ___________________ ?
10. **Hélène:** Elle est intelligente, belle, sympathique, mince et athlétique.

11. **Marie:** ____________________ ?
12. **Hélène:** Elle est de Paris.

13. **Marie:** ____________________ ?
14. **Hélène:** Ma mère et moi nous parlons beaucoup, nous allons au supermarché, faisons la cuisine, et nous allons au cinéma.

15. **Marie:** ____________________ ?
16. **Hélène:** Mon frère regarde la télévision, joue au baseball et étudie beaucoup.
17. **Marie:** ____________________ ?
18. **Hélène:** Mes soeurs nettoient la maison, lavent la vaisselle, vont à beaucoup de parties, dansent et jouent au volleyball.

Jacqueline regarde la télévision.

Aim IX: Each student will be able to do a "Résumé de grammaire: the use of singular and plural subject pronouns with regular -ER verbs

parler français		**regarder** le télévision	
je parl**e**...	nous parl**ons**...	je regard**e**..	nous regard**ons**...
tu parl**es**...	vous parl**ez**...	tu regard**es**...	vous regard**ez**...
il parl**e**...	ils parl**ent**...	il regard**e**...	ils regard**ent**...
elle parl**e**...	elles parl**ent**...	elle regard**e**...	elles regard**ent**...

Exercice écrit

A. Choose the correct form of the following *-ER* verbs.

1. Mes frères________beaucoup la radio.
   a. écoutes b. écoutons c. écoutent d. écoute

2. Mon amie et moi ______ beaucoup le dimanche.
   a. marchent b. marche c. marches d. marchons

3. Je________la maison le samedi.
   a. lave b. lavent c. laves d. lavons

4. Monsieur Valois, ________-vous la télé après le travail?
   a. regarde b. regardent c. regardez d. regardes

5. Robert,________-tu dans un magasin après les classes?
   a. travaille b. travaillent c. travailles d. travaillons

B. Write any appropriate subject pronoun:

6. ________regardes la télévision.

7. ________ chantons très bien.

8. ________ lave la vaisselle.

9. ________ voyagent à Bruxelles.

10. ________ nage pendant l'été.

C. Write the correct form of the verb in parenthesis.

11. (danser) Ma meilleure amie et moi______beaucoup aux parties.
12. (jouer) Mon frère______du piano et de la guitare.
13. (aimer) Mes soeurs_______ les bonnes notes.
14. (parler) Henri, tu______très bien français.
15. (étudier) Caroline et Anne, où______-vous?
16. (marcher) Je______beaucoup quand il fait beau.
17. (acheter) Madame Dupont, quand______-vous la nourriture?

Vocabulaire

Subject pronouns:

Singular		**Plural**	
je	*I*	nous	*we*
tu	*you (familiar)*	vous	*you*
il	*he*	ils	*they (males or males and females*
elle	*she*	elles	*they (females)*

Note: Refer back to the note on page 94 for an explanation of *"vous"*, formal singular.

Situation

1. You meet a French-speaking peer at a party. After s/he asks you about your family, you also want to know about his/her family. Find out:

a. How many people there are in the family
b. Who they are
c. The name of each member of the family
d. The age of each member of the family
e. What each member of the family is like
f. Where each member of the family is from
g. What s/he does with each member of the family
h. What each member of the family does
i. What two or more members of the family do together

This role play can be done two times with different partners. Partners can change roles each time.

Réfléchissons

If you had to interview a French-speaking adult about his/her family as part of your job, how would you ask each of the questions of the **Situation?**

Charles parle à Marcel.

Résumé

Une lettre à un(e) ami(e) pour correspondre
(A letter to a pen pal)

You are given an opportunity to write a letter to a French-speaking pen pal. In the first paragraph of your letter do the following:

1. Greet him/her
2. Tell him/her your name
3. Tell him/her your age
4. Tell him/her where you live
5. Tell him/her what you are like
6. Tell him/her what you like to do
7. Ask him/her how old he/she is
8. Ask him/her when his/her birthday is
9. Ask him/her what s/he is like
10. Ask him/her what s/he likes to do

In the second paragraph of your letter tell him/her about your family. Give all the information outlined in the **Situation**, letters a - g on the previous page.

In the third paragraph, ask him/her five questions about his/her family. Ask questions that you have learned.

Use the following format to indicate your city, the date, the salutation and the farewell.

New York le 10 mai 19__

Cher ami (name),
or
Chère amie (name),

____
____
____
____
____
____

A bientôt,
(Your name)

Vocabulaire

cher/chère *dear*

embrasser *to hug, to kiss*

UNIT SIX

Révision

A. Qui es-tu? Qui êtes-vous? Me voici.
B. L'école
C. La famille

TOPIC

A. Personal Identification B. School C. Family

SITUATION

Interaction with individual peers in the classroom
and adults in the community

FUNCTION

Providing and obtaining basic information of personal identification
Providing and obtaining basic information about school and family
Introducing oneself, greeting, leave-taking

PROFICIENCY

Listening and speaking:
Can comprehend simple questions and respond appropriately
with possible need for repetition
Can ask questions appropriate to the communicative situation
Can initiate and carry on a simple face-to-face conversation
Writing:
Can write a letter to a French-speaking penpal

AIM I: Each student will be able to read with comprehension a dialogue between two teenagers who meet in France

AIM II: Each student will be able to ask a peer if s/he likes to do each of the following activities and be able to respond

AIM III: Each student will be able to ask a peer some basic questions of personal identification about the family and school and be able to respond

AIM IV: Each student will be able to ask an adult some basic questions of personal identification about the family and school and be able to respond

AIM V: Each student will be able to initiate and carry on a face-to-face conversation with both a peer and an adult

Aim I: *Each student will be able to read with comprehension a dialogue between two teenagers who meet in France.*

Lecture: Première partie

Anne, une fille sympathique rencontre Jacques, un beau garçon, dans un café à Paris.

1. **Jacques:** Bonjour, je m'appelle Jacques. Et toi, comment t'appelles-tu?

2. **Anne:** Je m'appelle Anne.

3. **Jacques:** D'où es-tu?

4. **Anne:** Je suis des Etats-Unis. Et toi?

5. **Jacques:** Je suis de France.
   Quel âge as-tu, Anne?

6. **Anne:** J'ai seize ans. Et toi, Jacques?

7. **Jacques:** J'ai dix-sept ans.
   Quand est ton anniversaire?

8. **Anne:** Mon anniversaire est le treize août. Et le tien?

9. **Jacques:** C'est le trente janvier. Où habites-tu?

10. **Anne:** J'habite à Manhattan.

11. **Jacques:** J'habite ici à Paris.
    Qu'est-ce que tu aimes faire pendant ton temps libre?

12. **Anne:** J'aime écouter la musique, parler au téléphone avec mes amis, lire des romans, jouer au tennis et danser. Et toi?

13. **Jacques:** J'aime sortir avec mes amis, aller au cinéma, aller à la plage et jouer au football.

Compréhension de lecture:

If the statement is true, state *vrai.* If the statement is false, state *faux* and **correct the bold portion.**

1. Anne rencontre Jacques à **New York.**

2. Anne est **antipathique** et Jacques est **laid.**

3. Anne est **des Etats-Unis.**

4. Jacques a **dix-huit** ans.

5. L'anniversaire de Jacques est **le vingt** février.

6. Anne habite en **Floride à Miami.**

7. Anne aime **parler au téléphone et lire des romans.**

8. Jacques aime **aller aux discothèques et jouer au tennis.**

Vocabulaire de la lecture:

...rencontrer... *to meet*
8. Et le tien? *And yours? (when used with* "ton anniversaire"*)*
11. ici *here*
12. Et toi? *And you?*

Lecture: Deuxième partie

14. **Jacques:** Combien de personnes y-a-t-il dans ta famille?

15. **Anne:** Il y a cinq personnes dans ma famille.

16. **Jacques:** Qui sont-elles?

17. **Anne:** Il y a mes parents, mon frère, ma soeur et moi. Et combien de personnes y-a-t-il dans ta famille?

18. **Jacques:** Il y a huit personnes dans ma famille. Il y a mes parents, mes deux soeurs, mon frère, mes grands-parents et moi. A quelle école vas-tu?

19. **Anne:** Je vais au lycée. Et toi?

20. **Jacques:** Je vais au cours Balzac*. Qu'est-ce que tu étudies à l'école?

21. **Anne:** J'étudie l'anglais, les mathématiques, le français, la musique, les sciences, l'histoire, l'éducation physique et l'emploi des ordinateurs. Et toi?

22. **Jacques:** J'étudie le français, l'anglais, la biologie, les mathématiques, la physique et la chimie. Quel est ton sujet favori?

23. **Anne:** Mon sujet favori est la musique. Et toi?

24. **Jacques:** Mon sujet favori est l'anglais.

25. **Anne:** Il est tard. Parlons ici demain.

26. **Jacques:** D'accord. A demain, Anne.

27. **Anne:** A demain, Jacques.

****Note:*** High schools in France are often named after famous people, including writers and educators. Cours Balzac is a school in Paris.

Compréhension de lecture:

If the statement is true, state *vrai.* If the statement is false, state *faux and* ***correct the bold portion.***

9. Il y a **six** personnes dans la famille d'Anne.

10. **Les grands-parents** de Jacques habitent avec la famille de Jacques.

11. Anne étudie dans **un lycée.**

12. Jacques étudie dans **un institut.**

13. Anne étudie deux langues: **l'italien et le français.**

14. Jacques étudie **la physique et la chimie.**

15. Le sujet favori d'Anne est **l'anglais.**

Vocabulaire de la lecture:

21. l'emploi *usage, how to use*
25. Il est tard. *It is late.*
26. D'accord. *Okay.*
    Allons... *let's..., let's go...*
27. A demain *Until tomorrow.*
    la langue *language*

Mon sujet favori est l'anglais.

Résumé

Write five sentences indicating what you learned about Anne and five about Jacques.

Révision de Vocabulaire

1. Comment t'appelles-tu?/Comment vous appelez-vous?
   What's your name?
   Je m'apppelle... *My name is...*

2. D'où es-tu?/D'où êtes-vous? *Where are you from?*
   Je suis de... *I'm from...(place of birth)*

3. Quel âge as-tu?/Quel âge avez-vous? *How old are you?*
   J'ai...ans. *I'm ...years old.*

Les numéros 1-20

un	1	six	6	onze	11	seize	16
deux	2	sept	7	douze	12	dix-sept	17
trois	3	huit	8	treize	13	dix-huit	18
quatre	4	neuf	9	quatorze	14	dix-neuf	19
cinq	5	dix	10	quinze	15	vingt	20

4. Quand est ton anniversaire? *When is your birthday?*
   Quand est votre anniversaire? *When is your birthday?*
   Mon anniversaire est le ... *My birthday is the ...(day / month)*
   Note: *Exception* - le premier.... *the first day of ..... (any month)*

Les mois de l'année

janvier	avril	juillet	octobre
février	mai	août	novembre
mars	juin	septembre	décembre

5. En quelle année es-tu né(e)? En quelle année êtes-vous né(e)?
   In what year were you born?
   Je suis né(e) en 19...
   I was born in 19...

les numéros 30-90

trente 30 quarante 40 cinquante 50 soixante 60
soixante-dix 70 quatre-vingts 80 quatre-vingt-dix 90

6. Où habites-tu?/Où habitez-vous? *Where do you live?*
   J'habite à ... *I live in ... (city or state)*

7. Quel est (ton / votre) numéro de téléphone?
   What is your telephone number?
   Mon numéro de téléphone est ..... *My telephone number is.....*
   sept-huit-un-cinq-trois-six-zéro *781-5360*

8. Qu'est-ce que (tu aimes / vous aimez) faire pendant (ton/ votre) temps libre? *What do you like to do in your free time?*

   J'aime... ***I like to...***

acheter de la nourriture *to buy food*
acheter des vêtements *to buy clothes*
acheter des livres *to buy books*
chanter *to sing*
danser *to dance*
donner des cadeaux *to give presents*
écouter la radio *to listen to the radio*
faire la cuisine *to cook*
faire de l'exercice *to do exercises*
faire le ménage *to clean the house*
faire du sport *to play sports*
jouer au basket *to play basketball*
jouer au football *to play soccer*
jouer de la guitare *to play the guitar*
jouer aux jeux de vidéo *to play video games*
manger *to eat*
marcher *to walk*
nager *to swim*
parler au téléphone *to speak on the telephone*
regarder la télévision *to watch television*
sortir avec un/une amie *to go out with a friend*
travailler *to walk*
voyager *to travel*
aller au cinéma *to go to the movies*
aller aux discothèques *to go to discos*
aller aux parties (boum) *to go to parties*

9. Combien de personnes y-a-t-il dans (ta/votre) famille?
   How many people are there in your family?
   Il y a...personnes dans ma famille.
   There are ... people in my family.
   Qui sont-elles? *Who are they?*
   Il y a ma mère, mon frère et moi.
   They are my mother, my brother and I.
   Il y a mes parents, mes deux soeurs et moi.
   They are my parents, my two sisters and I.

10. A quelle école vas-tu?/ A quelle école allez-vous?
    What school do you attend?

    Je vais au lycée.
    I go to a high school.
    (May also be used to indicate American middle school)

Note: The preposition "to" in french is *"au"* (masculine) and *"à"* (feminine). Example:
Je vais au lycée (m.).
Je vais à l'école (f.).

11. Qu'est-ce que (tu étudies / vous étudiez) à l'école?
    What do you study in school?

    J'étudie ... ***I study ...***
    l'art *art*
    la biologie *biology*
    la science (générale) *general science*
    la musique *music*
    l'éducation physique *physical education*
    le français *French*
    la dactylo *typewriting*
    l'histoire *history*
    l'anglais *English*
    les mathématiques *mathematics*
    l'informatique *computers*
    la chimie *chemistry*
    la technologie *technology*
    la physique *physics*

12. Quel est (ton/votre) sujet favori?
    What is your favorite subject?
    Mon sujet favori est ....
    My favorite subject is ....

13. Parlons ici demain. *Let's speak here tomorrow.*

Aim II: *Each student will be able to ask a peer if s/he likes to do each of the following activities and be able to respond*

Conversation

Partners take turns (every other picture) asking each other *Est-ce que tu aimes...?* followed by the activity represented in the picture. Partners respond *j'aime...* if they like or *Non, je n'aime pas ...* if they don't like to do the activity. After completing one round, the other partner begins the second one. Remember to answer in complete sentences.

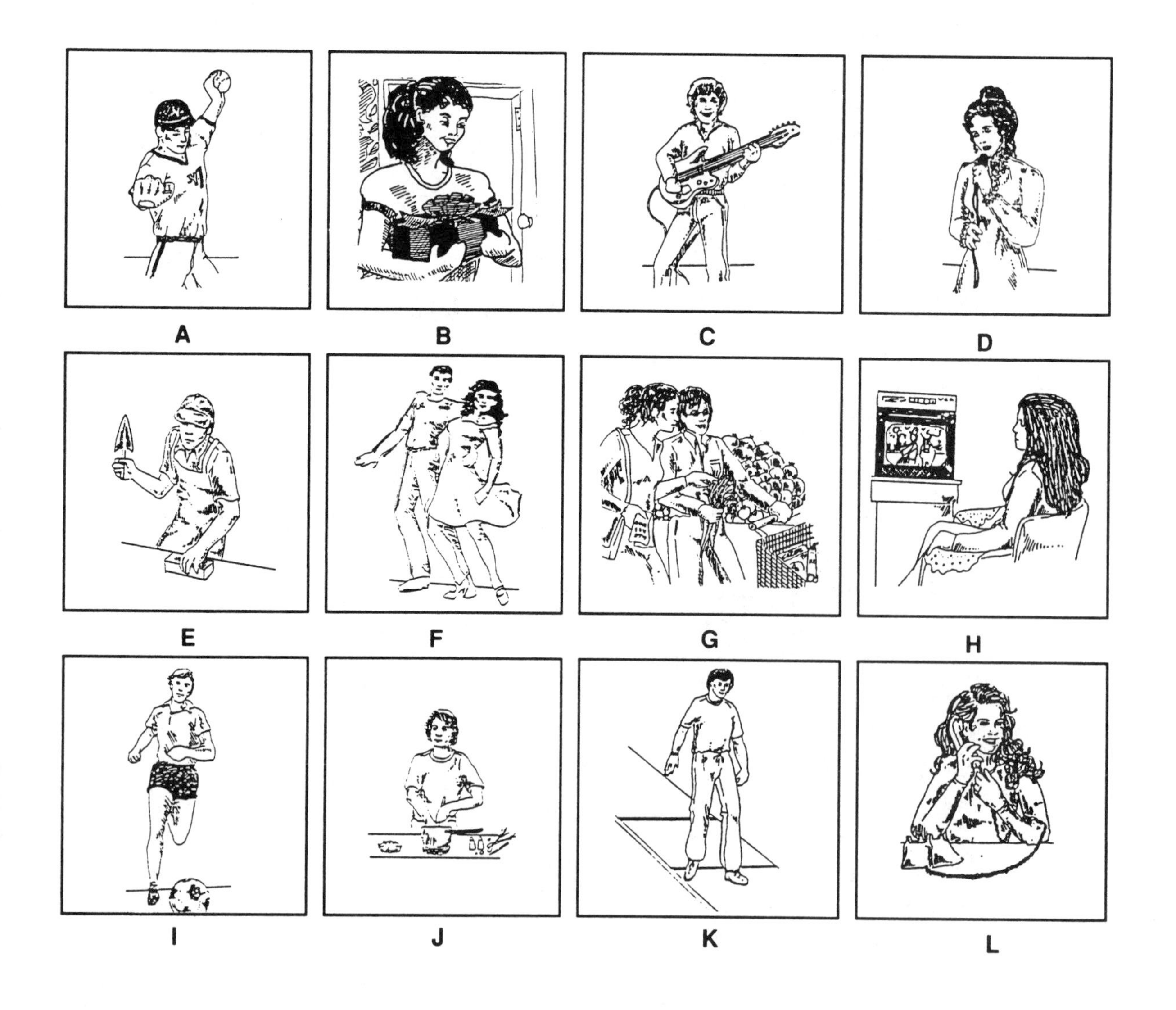

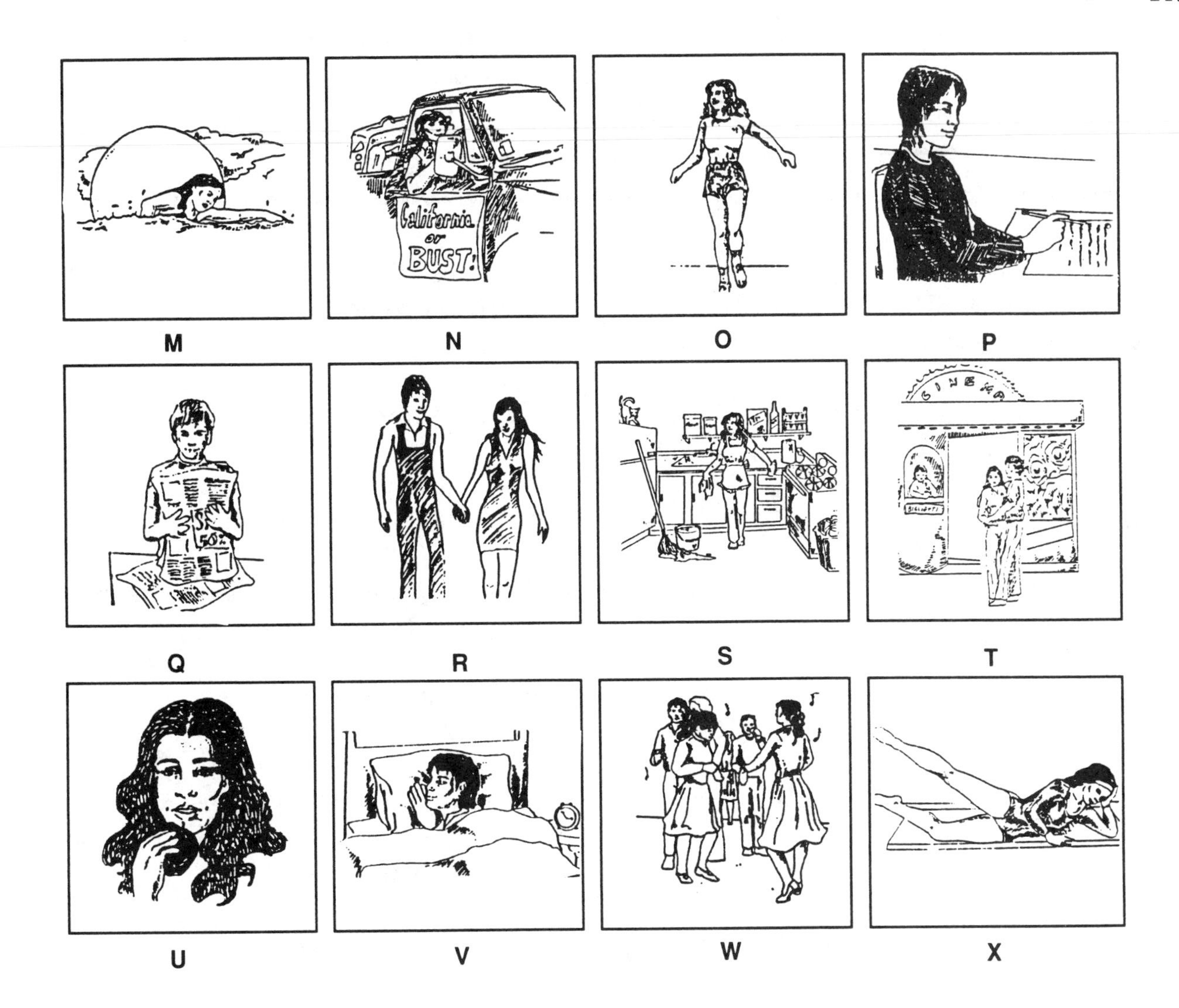

Exercice écrit

Write the five activities you most like to do and the five activities you don't like to do.

Aim III: *Each student will be able to ask a peer some basic questions about personal identification, family and school and be able to respond*

Conversation

Peer partners ask each other the following questions of personal identification, school and family. This **Conversation** can be repeated with a different partner.

1. Comment t'appelles-tu?
2. D'où es-tu?
3. Quel âge as-tu?
4. Quand est ton anniversaire?
5. En quelle année es-tu né(e)?
6. Où habites-tu?
7. Quel est ton numéro de téléphone?
8. Qu'est-ce que tu aimes faire pendant ton temps libre? (5 activités)
9. Combien de personnes y-a-t-il dans ta famille? Qui sont-elles?
10. A quelle école vas-tu?
11. Qu'est-ce que tu étudies à l'école?
12. Quel est ton sujet favori?

Exercice écrit

Write and answer the questions of the **Conversation,** numbers 1 - 12.

Résumé

One or two pairs of students can play the roles for the entire class followed by peer practice.

1. **Jean:**_____?

2. **Marie:** Je m'appelle Marie. Et toi?

3. **Jean:** __________.
__________?

4. **Marie:** Je suis des Etats-Unis. Et toi?

5. **Jean:** _____. Où habites-tu?

6. **Marie:** _____.

7. **Jean:** _____?

8. **Marie:** J'ai quatorze ans.

9. **Jean:** _____.

10. **Marie:** _____?

11. **Jean:** Mon anniversaire est le onze février. Et toi?

12. **Marie:** _____.

13. **Jean:** _____?

14. **Marie:** Je suis née en 19__.

15. **Jean:** _____?

16. **Marie:** J'aime jouer de la guitare, jouer au volleyball, aller au cinéma, sortir avec mes amies, et acheter des vêtements. Et toi?

17. **Jean:** _____.
_____________?

18. **Marie:** Mon numéro de téléphone est 792-5168.______?

19. **Jean:** Il y a cinq personnes dans ma famille: ma mère, ma tante, mes deux frères et moi. A quelle école vas-tu?

20. **Marie:** _____.

21. **Jean:** _____?

22. **Marie:** J'étudie l'anglais, les mathématiques, le français, la science, l'histoire et l'art.

23. **Jean:** Quel est ton sujet favori?

24. **Marie:** _____. Il est tard. Au revoir Jean.

25. **Jean:** Au revoir Marie.

J'aime acheter des vêtements.

Activité

Une lettre à un(e) ami(e) pour correspondre

Write a letter to a French-speaking pen pal. Tell as much about yourself as you can and then ask your pen pal at least five questions. Use the following format to indicate your city, the date, the salutation and the farewell.

New York, le ___ ___ 19__

Cher ami
(Chère amie)

____
____
____
____
____

A bientôt,
(Sign your name.)

Aim IV: *Each student will be able to ask an adult some basic questions of personal identification, about family and school and be able to respond*

Conversation

Peer partners play the role of two adults who do not know one another and ask each other the following questions.

1. Comment vous appelez-vous?
2. D'où êtes-vous? (pays)
3. Quel âge avez-vous?
4. Quand est votre anniversaire?
5. En quelle année êtes-vous né(e)?
6. Où habitez-vous?
7. Quel est votre numéro de téléphone?
8. Qu'est-ce que vous aimez faire pendant votre temps libre? (5 activités)

9. Combien de personnes y-a-t-il dans votre famille?

10. A quel cours du soir est-ce que vous allez?

11. Qu'est-ce que vous étudiez au cours du soir?

12. Quel est votre sujet favori?

Exercice écrit

Write and practice the questions of the **Conversation,** numbers 1 - 12.

Activité

Interview a French-speaking person in your community. Be prepared to state in class what you learned about the person.

1. Greet the person.
2. State your name.
3. Tell the person in what school you study French.
4. Tell the person that you would like to ask him/her some personal questions and that your homework assignment is to interview a French-speaking adult in your community.
5. Ask the person his/her name.
6. Ask the person where s/he is from.
7. Ask the person when his/her birthday is.
8. Ask the person where s/he lives.
9. Ask the person what s/he likes to do in his/her free time.
10. Ask the person how many people there are in his/her family and who they are.
11. Thank the person for the interview.

Vocabulaire

#1 Bonjour.
#4 J'aimerais vous poser quelques questions personnelles. Mon devoir est d'interviewer une personne qui parle français dans la communauté.
#11 ...pour l'interview.

Aim V: *Each student will be able to initiate and carry on a face-to-face conversation with both a peer and an adult*

Situations orales

Peer partners will play the roles in these situations exchanging at least 5 - 6 questions and answers. Partners can exchange roles when doing the situations a second time.

1. **Function:** Socializing

Roles: We are at a party. I am an exchange student who has recently arrived from France.

Purpose: We are socializing because you want to get to know me. You will begin the conversation.

2. **Function:** Providing and obtaining information

Roles: I have recently arrived with my family from France. You have stopped at my new home to inquire about babysitting possibilities.

Purpose: Since the ability to communicate in French is required, I will interview you to obtain personal information in French. I will begin the conversation.

Glimpses of France

UNIT SEVEN

Quelle heure est-il?

La maison et la vie chez soi

TOPIC

A. Telling time B. House and home

SITUATION

Interaction with individual peers and adults

FUNCTION

Providing and obtaining information about one's home (house or apartment)
Can express personal feelings about one's home and possessions

PROFICIENCY

Listening and speaking:
Can comprehend simple statements and questions and can respond appropriately with possible need for repetition
Can ask questions appropriate to the communicative situation
Writing:
Can write a letter to a French-speaking pen pal about one's home and the chores done by each family member

AIM I: Each student will be able to ask another person "What time is it?" and be able to answer the question

AIM II: Each student will be able to state the rooms of his/her house or apartment and the activities s/he does in each room

AIM III: Each student will be able to do a *"Résumé de grammaire"*: the use of singular and plural subject pronouns with regular -ER, -IR and -RE verbs in the present tense

AIM IV: Each student will be able to identify the principal furnishings and appliances in each room of the house

AIM V: Each student will be able to read with comprehension a dialogue between two teenagers who meet in France

AIM VI: Each student will be able to ask a peer or friend and adult basic questions about his/her house or apartment and be able to respond

Aim IA: *Each student will be able to tell time on the hour*

Exercice oral

Quelle heure est-il?

Il est dix heures.

Il est deux heures.

Il est sept heures.

Il est une heure.

Conversation

Peer practice in groups of two. One partner asks ""*Quelle heure est-il?* and the second responds by stating the appropriate time on each clock. Then partners reverse roles.

Exercice écrit

Write the time in French words of clocks 1 - 6.

Vocabulaire

Quelle heure est-il?
What time is it?
Il est dix heures. *It's ten o'clock.*
Il est une heure. *It's one o'clock.*

Aim IB: *Each student will be able to tell time between the hour and the half-hour*

Exercice oral

Quelle heure est-il?

Il est dix heures cinq.

Il est midi dix.

Il est neuf heures vingt.

Il est une heure vingt-cinq.

Conversation

Peer practice in groups of two.

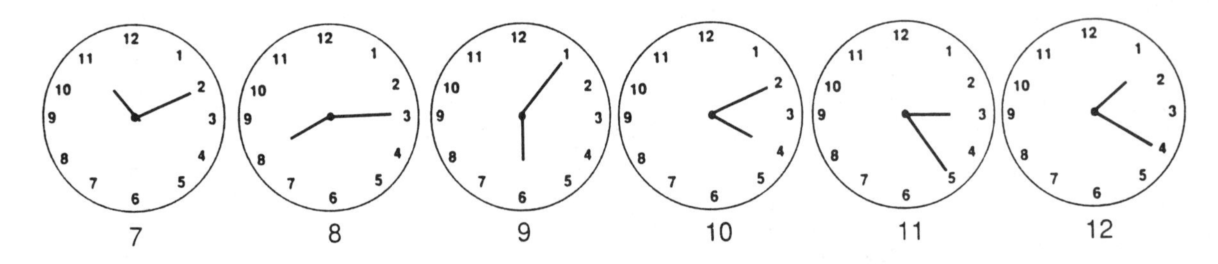

Exercice écrit

Write the time in French words of clocks 7 - 12.

Vocabulaire

Il est dix heures cinq.
It's five after ten.
It's ten o'five.
Il est une heure vingt-cinq.
It's twenty-five after one.
It's one twenty-five.

Aim IC: Each student will be able to tell the time a quarter after the hour in another common way

Exercice oral

Quelle heure est-il?

Il est dix heures et quart.

Il est cinq heures et quart.

Il est huit heures et quart.

Il est une heure et quart.

Conversation

Peer practice in groups of two.

Exercice écrit

Write the time in French words of clocks 13 - 18.

Vocabulaire

quart *quarter of an hour*

Il est dix heures et quart.
It's a quarter after ten.

Il est une heure et quart.
It's a quarter after one.
It's one-fifteen.

Aim ID: Each student will be able to tell time on the half-hour in another common way

Exercice oral

Quelle heure est-il?

Il est dix heures et demie.

Il est quatre heures et demie.

Il est sept heures et demie.

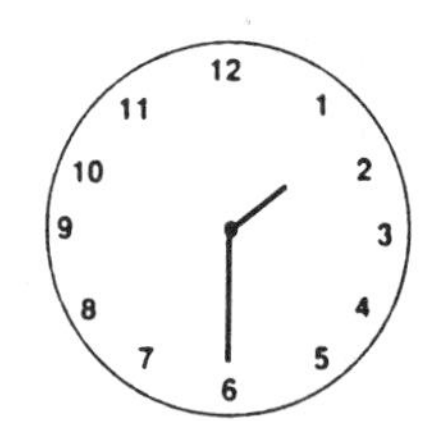

Il est une heure et demie.

Conversation

Peer practice in groups of two.

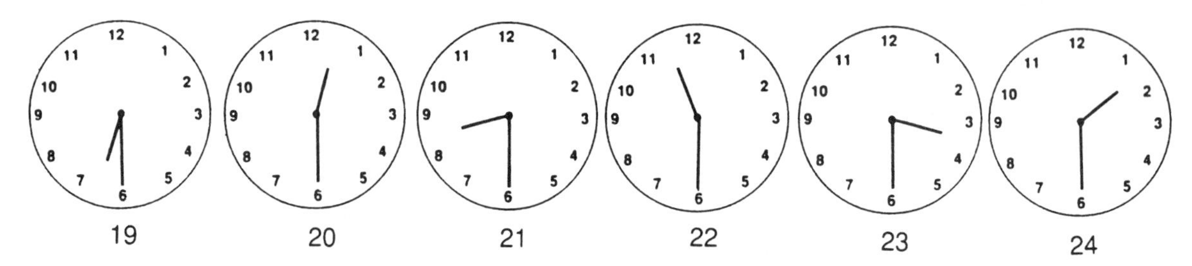

19 20 21 22 23 24

Exercice écrit

Write the time in French words of clocks 19 - 24.

Vocabulaire

demie *half an hour*

Il est dix heures et demie.
It's half past ten.

Il est une heure et demie.
It's half past one.
It's one-thirty.

Résumé partiel

Conversation:

Peer practice in groups of two. Each student asks his partner *Quelle heure est-il?* The partner then states the time indicated by the clocks in the first row (1 - 6). The second partner next asks *Quelle heure est-il?* and his partner states the time indicated in the second row (7 - 12). Then reverse roles to enable each partner to practice telling the time of the other clocks.

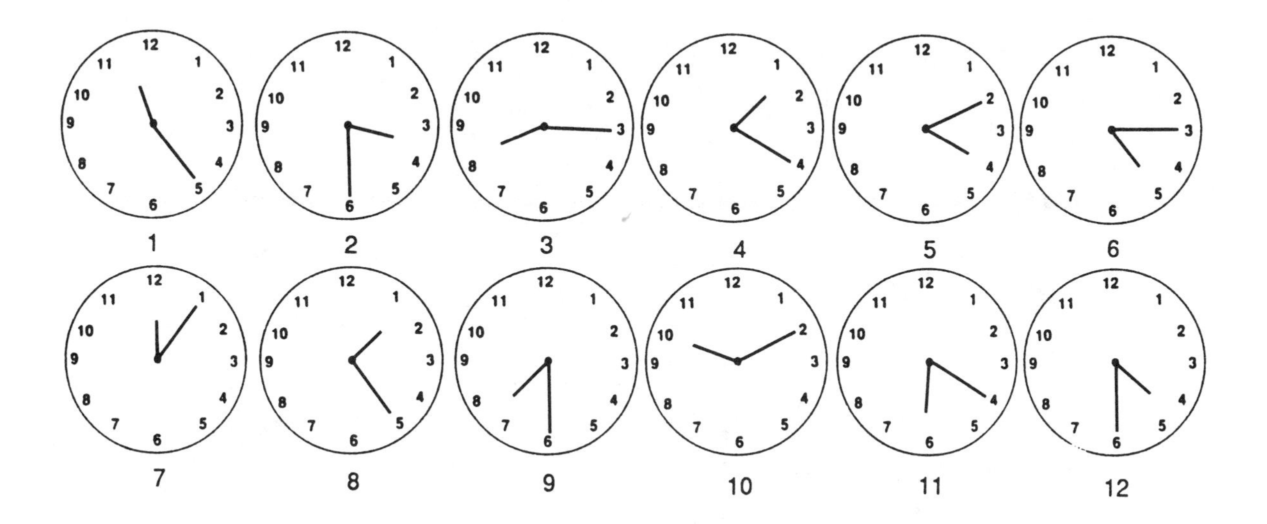

Exercice de compréhension

You will hear five different times. Choose the picture which corresponds to what you hear. Write only the letter.

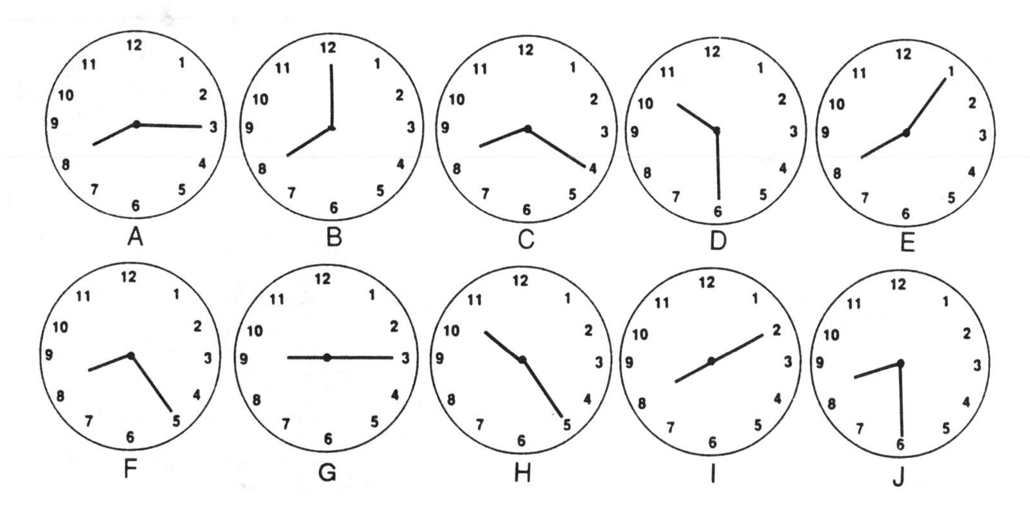

Aim IE: *Each student will be able to tell time between thirty-one minutes after the hour and the hour*

Exercice oral

Quelle heure est-il?

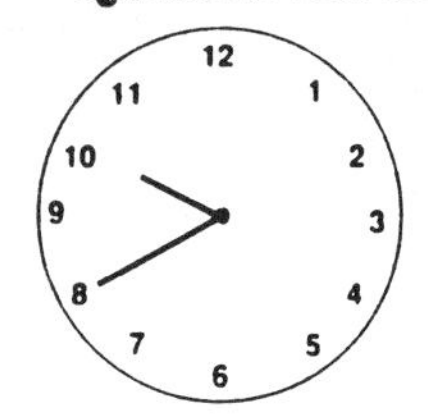

Il est dix heures moins vingt.

Il est huit heures moins cinq.

Il est quatre heures moins vingt-cinq.

Il est une heure moins dix.

Conversation

Peer practice in groups of two.

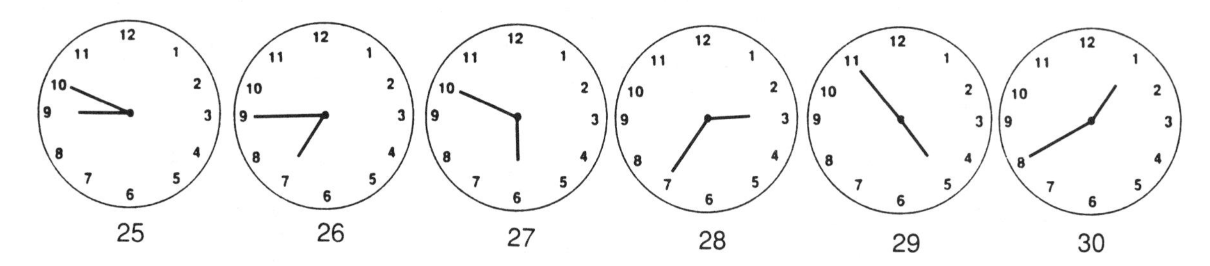

Exercice écrit

Write the time in French words of clocks 25 - 30.

Vocabulaire

Il est dix heures moins vingt.
It's twenty to ten.

Il est une heure moins dix.
It's ten to one.

Aim IF: *Each student will be able to tell the time a quarter to the hour in another way*

Exercice oral

Quelle heure est-il?

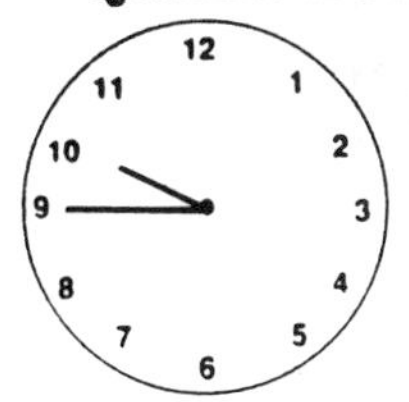

Il est dix heures moins le quart.

Il est quatre heures moins le quart.

Il est sept heures moins le quart.

Il est une heure moins le quart.

Exercice oral

Peer practice in groups of two.

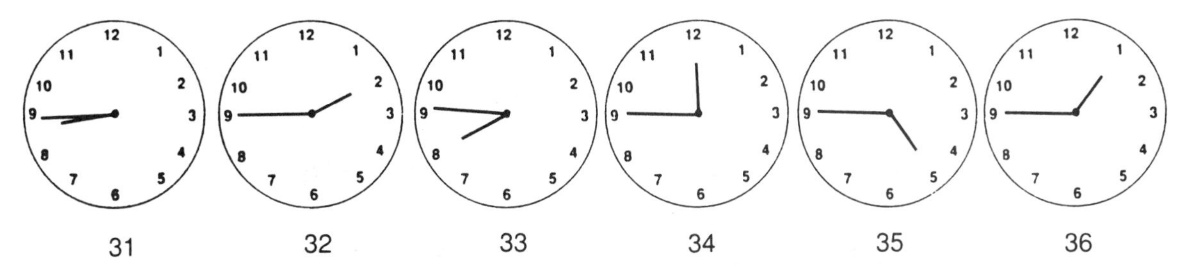

Exercice écrit

Write the time in French words of clocks 31 - 36.

Vocabulaire

Il est dix heures moins le quart.
It's a quarter to ten.

Il est une heure moins le quart.
It's a quarter to one.

Réfléchissons

1. How do we say "*It is one o'clock?*"

2. To state **any hour of the day,** what must precede the hour?
   "_____ *onze heures.*" 11:00 / "_____ *trois heures.*" 3:00

3. To state any time between **31 minutes after the hour and the hour**, what must be placed after the hour and before the minutes?
   *"Il est une heure____vingt." 12h40 **
   "Il est six heures____cinq." 5h55

4. To state **a quarter of an hour** before or after the hour, what expression can we use?
   "Il est une heure et____." 1:15 / *"Il est trois heures moins _____."* 2:45

5. To state **the half-hour past the hour,** what expression can we use?
   "Il est une heure et _____." 1:30 / *"Il est sept heures et_____."* 7:30

6. How do we say "**It is one fifteen?" and "It is four fifteen?"** How is the spelling of the word "**hour**" different in both cases? Why?

*When time is written in numbers the French use the format shown here.

Résumé: conversation

Peer practice in groups of two with a different partner. Alternate rows of clocks and then reverse roles to enable each partner to practice the other set of clocks.

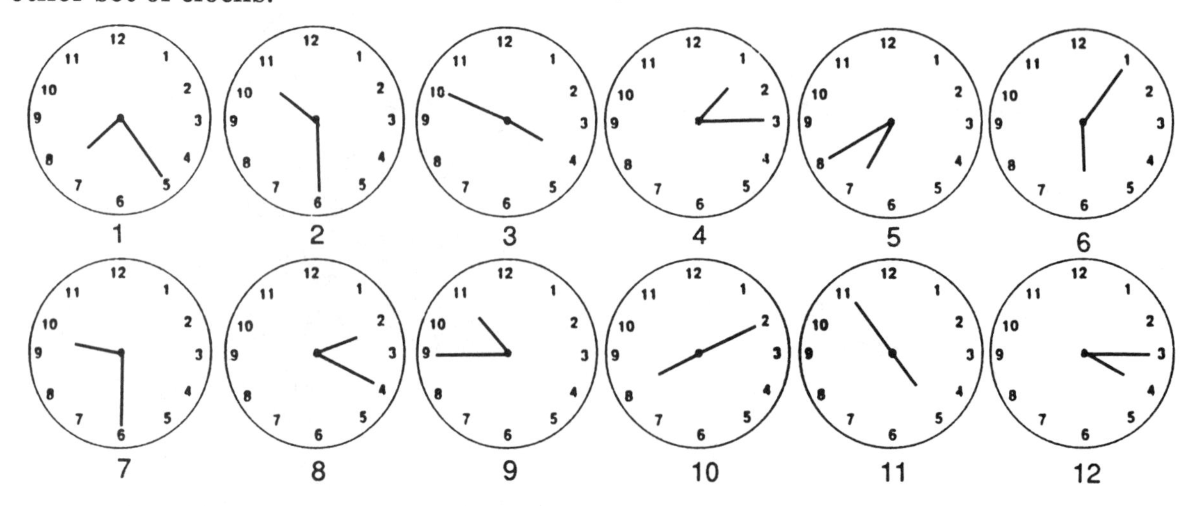

Résumé: compréhension

1. You will hear three times of the day; choose the picture which corresponds to what you hear. Write only the letter.

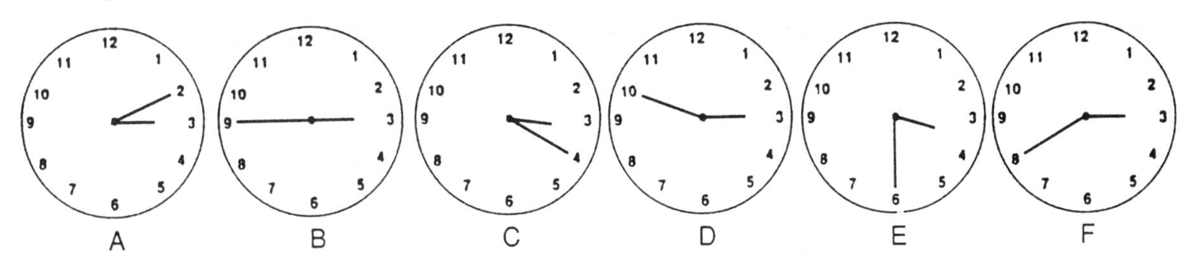

2. You will hear five different times. After the second repetition, write each time in numerals.

Example: *Il est onze heures moins le quart.* - Answer: 10h45
Il est une heure vingt. - Answer: 1h20

Résumé: exercice écrit

Write the following times in French words.

1. It's 8:26.
2. It's 4:45.
3. It's 1:30.
4. It's 11:55.
5. It's 2:10.
6. It's 9:35.
7. It's 1:14.
8. It's 6:40.
9. It's 3:19.
10. It's twenty to nine.
11. It's half past four.
12. It's a quarter to eleven.

Quelle heure est-il, s'il vous plaît?

Aim II: *Each student will be able to state the rooms of his/her house or apartment and the activities s/he does in each room*

Pratique orale 1

Les pièces de la maison

la cuisine

la salle à manger

la chambre

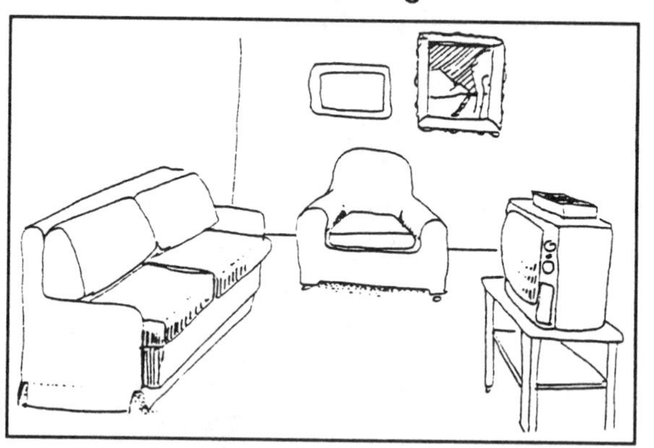

la salle de séjour

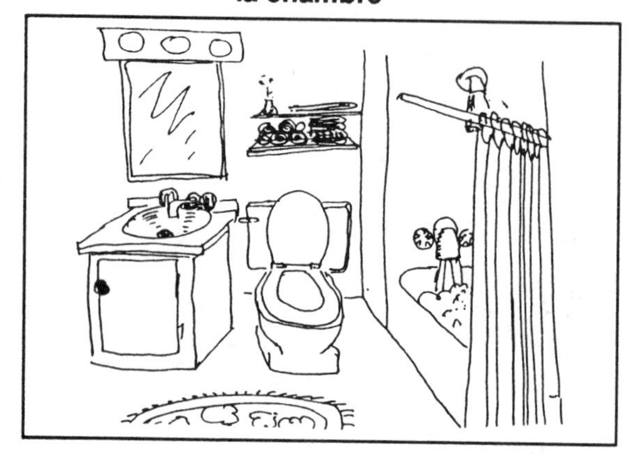

la salle de bain

l'autre chambre

Exercice oral 2

1. **Anne:** Où est-ce que tu regardes la télévision?
   Jean: Je regarde la télévision dans la salle de séjour.

2. **Philippe:** Où est-ce que tu manges?
   Hélène: Je mange dans la salle à manger.

3. **Rose:** Où est-ce que tu fais tes devoirs?
   Jacques: Je fais mes devoirs dans ma chambre.

4. **Antoine:** Où est-ce que vous faites la cuisine?
   Mme Vichy: Je fais la cuisine dans la cuisine.

5. **Marie:** Où est-ce que vous dormez?
   Mlle Rouet: Je dors dans ma chambre.

6. **Charles:** Où vous lavez-vous?
   M. Piret: Je me lave dans la salle de bain.

Réfléchissons

Recall how you answered the question *"Comment vous appelez-vous?"* Now look at the question and answer to number six in the **Exercice oral** above. Notice that the verb in number six is similar. How would you ask a peer "What's your name?" Now, how would Charles ask a peer question number six? How would you answer this question? Verbs that function in this way are called **reflexive verbs.**

Conversation

One partner asks the other questions 1 - 9. Then the second partner asks questions 10 - 18. Reverse roles and questions.

1. Où est-ce que tu étudies?
2. Où est-ce que tu dors?
3. Où est-ce que tu te laves?
4. Où est-ce que tu manges?
5. Où est-ce que tu écris des lettres?
6. Où est-ce que tu fais la cuisine?
7. Où est-ce que tu laves la vaisselle?
8. Où est-ce que tu écoutes la radio?
9. Où est-ce que tu fais tes devoirs?
10. Où est-ce que vous regardez la télévision?
11. Où est-ce que vous lavez les vêtements?
12. Où est-ce que vous vous reposez?
13. Où est-ce que vous faites des exercices?
14. Où est-ce que vous mettez la table?
15. Où est-ce que vous parlez au téléphone?
16. Où est-ce que vous lisez le journal?

Exercice écrit

Complete the following statements by writing the room or rooms in which you do the following activities.

1. Je regarde la télévision dans____.
2. Je lave la vaiselle dans ____.
3. J'écris des lettres dans____.
4. Je lave les vêtements dans____.
5. Je fais des exercices dans____.
6. Je mets la table dans____.
7. J'étudie dans____.
8. Je dors dans____.
9. Je fais la cuisine dans____.
10. Je fais mes devoirs dans____.
11. Je lis le journal dans____.
12. Je mange dans____.
13. J'écoute la radio dans____.
14. Je me lave dans ____.
15. Je parle au téléphone dans___.

Vocabulaire

Les pièces de la maison:

la salle de bain *the bathroom*
la cuisine *the kitchen*
la salle à manger *the dining room*
la chambre *the bedroom*
l'autre... *the other ....*
la salle de séjour *the living room*
le bureau *the study*

Où est-ce que...? *Where...?*

...tu **fais** la cuisine?/...vous **faites** la cuisine? *...do you cook?*

Je **fais** la cuisine... faire la cuisine *to cook*

... tu manges?/...vous mangez? *...do you eat?*

Je mange ... manger *to eat*

... tu **dors**?/...vous **dormez**? *do you sleep?*

Je **dors**... dormir *to sleep*

...tu écoutes la radio?/...vous écoutez la radio?

...do you listen to the radio

J'écoute écouter *to listen*

...tu parles au téléphone?/...vous parlez au téléphone?

... do you speak on the telephone? *?*

Je parle... parler *to speak*

... tu **fais** des exercices?/...vous **faites** des exercices? *do you exercise?*

Je **fais** faire *to do* des exercices *exercises*

... tu finis les devoirs? / ... vous finissez les devoirs?

... do you finish the homework?

Je finis... finir *to finish* les devoirs *homework*

...tu laves les vêtements?/...vous lavez les vêtements?

... do you wash clothes?

Je lave ... laver *to wash* les vêtements *clothes*

... tu **lis** le journal?/...vous **lisez** le journal?

... do you read the newspaper?

Je **lis**... lire *to read*

... tu regardes la télévision?/... vous regardez la télévision?

...do you watch television?

Je regarde... regarder *to watch, look at*

... tu **mets** la table?/...vous mettez la table? *... do you set the table?*

Je **mets**... mettre *to set the table*

... tu prends un bain?/...vous **prenez** un bain?

... do you take a bath?

Je prends un bain ... prendre un bain *to take a bath*

... tu te laves?/...vous vous lavez? *... do you wash up?*

Je me lave... se laver *to wash oneself*

Résumé

Tell a peer partner the activities (including chores) you do in each room of the house. State at least two or three for each room. Partners take turns.

Aim III: *Each student will be able to do a* "Résumé de grammaire": *the use of singular and plural subject pronouns with regular -ER, -IR and -RE verbs in the present tense*

Révision

parler au téléphone

je parl**e**	nous parl**ons**
tu parl**es**	vous parl**ez**
il parl**e**	ils parl**ent**
elle parl**e**	elles parl**ent**

laver la vaisselle

je lav**e**	nous lav**ons**
tu lav**es**	vous lav**ez**
il lav**e**	ils lav**ent**
elle lave	elles lav**ent**

Résumé de grammaire

finir les devoirs

je fin**is**	nous finiss**ons**
tu fin**is**	vous finiss**ez**
il fin**it**	ils finiss**ent**
elle fin**it**	elles finiss**ent**

vendre la maison

je vend**s**	nous vend**ons**
tu vend**s**	vous vend**ez**
il ven**d**	ils vend**ent**
elle ven**d**	elles vend**ent**

Réfléchissons

1. In what ways are the endings of regular --ER, -IR and -RE verbs in the present tense similar? In what way are they different?

Exercice écrit

A. Choose the correct form of the following -ER and -IR and -RE verbs.

1. Ma soeur _____ toujours ses devoirs.
   a. finissent b. finit c. finis d. finissons
2. Mon ami et moi_____ à beaucoup de questions dans la classe.
   a. répondez b. répond c. réponds d. répondons
3. Mes grands-parents_____à Tours en France.
   a. habitent b. habite c. habitez d. habites
4. M. Dupont_____-vous le journal tous les jours?
   a. vendons b. vends c. vend d. vendez
5. Louis, _____-tu beaucoup la télévision?
   a. regarde b. regardez c. regardes d. regardent

B. Write any possible subject pronoun

6. _____ vivons à San Francisco.
7. _____ comprends bien le français.
8. _____ regardent beaucoup la télévision.
9. _____ écris beaucoup de lettres.
10. _____ achète beaucoup de cadeaux.

C. Write the correct form of the infinitive in parentheses:

11. (travailler) Mes parents _____ beaucoup.
12. (répondre) Anne, tu_____toujours bien à tes questions.
13. (chanter) Mme Vichy, vous _____ très bien.
14. (finir) Nous _____ nos devoirs à dix heures.
15. (attendre) Charles _____ son amie après les classes.
16. (réfléchir) Je _____ avant de parler.
17. (vendre) Mon oncle et ma tante _____ leur maison.
18. (laver) Mon frère et moi _____ la vaisselle.
19. (choisir) Quel livre _____-tu?

Vocabulaire

choisir *to choose*
finir *to finish*
réfléchir *to reflect*
habiter *to live (in)*
avant de *before*
à dix heures *at 10 o'clock*
leur maison *their house*
attendre *to wait for*
vendre *to sell*
répondre aux questions *to answer questions*

Activité

Les activités et travaux domestiques de ma famille.
My family's activities and chores at home

A. Preparation

Write a list indicating the activities and chores done by each member of your family at home. Be prepared to share this list with your classmates.

B. Reporting out:

Students form groups of three or four. Each person in the group (one at a time) tells the other two or three activities and chores each family member does at home.

Examples:

Mon père regarde la télévision, sort les ordures et lit le journal.
Ma mère écoute la radio, fait la cuisine et lave les vêtements.
Ma soeur lave la vaisselle et parle beaucoup au téléphone. Elle et moi nous nettoyons la maison et écrivons beaucoup de lettres.
Mon frère fait des exercices. Lui et moi nous mettons la table.
Mon autre frère ne fait rien à la maison. Il dort beaucoup.

Vocabulaire

mon autre frère **ne** fait **rien.** *My other brother* ***doesn't*** *do* ***anything.***

nettoyer la maison *to clean the house*
je nettoie, tu nettoies, il/elle nettoie
nous nettoyons, vous nettoyez, ils/elles nettoient
mettre la table *to set the table*
je mets, tu mets, il/elle met
nous mettons, vous mettez, ils/elles mettent
sortir les ordures *to take out the garbage*
je **sors,** tu **sors,** il/elle **sort**
nous **sortons,** vous **sortez,** ils/elles **sortent**
dormir *to sleep*
je **dors,** tu **dors,** il/elle **dort**
nous **dormons,** vous **dormez,** ils/elles **dorment**
lire *to read*
je **lis**, tu **lis,** il/elle **lit**
nous **lisons,** vous **lisez,** ils/elles **lisent**
écrire *to write (irregular)*
j'**écris,** tu **écris,** il/elle **écrit**
nous **écrivons,** vous **écrivez,** ils/elles **écrivent**

Aim IV: *Each student will be able to identify the principal furnishings and appliances in each room of the house*

Exercice oral

les meubles de la maison

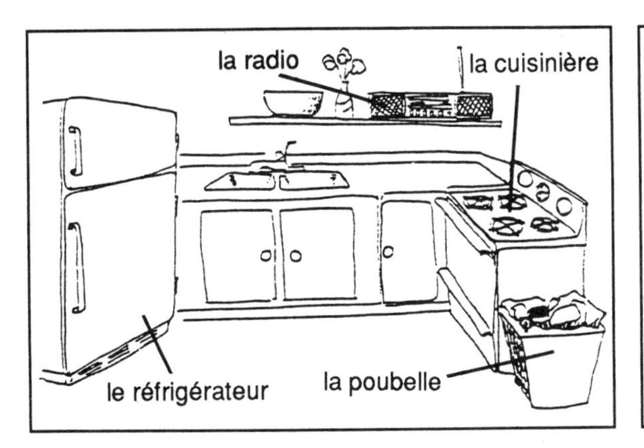

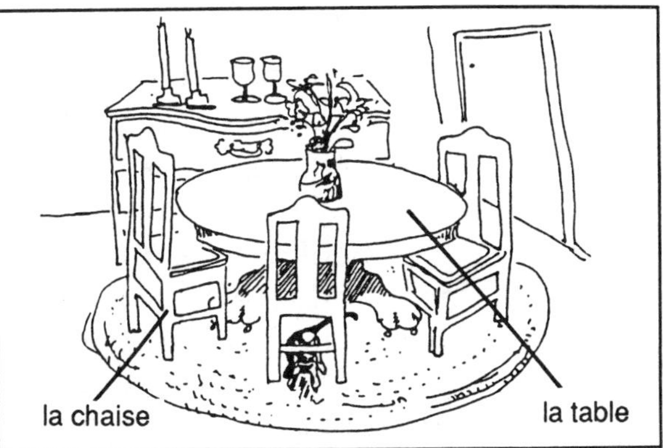

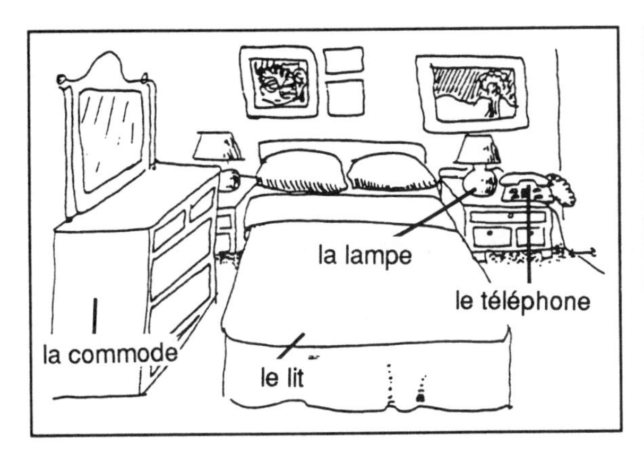

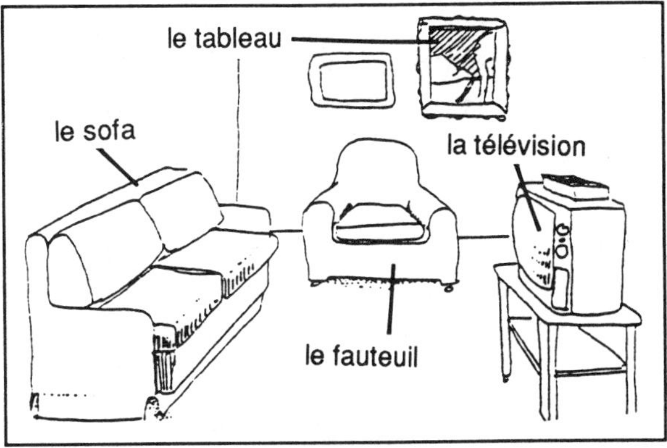

Conversation

Peer partners take turns asking the following questions to find out in what room each of the furnishings is located. ***Example:***

Dans quelle pièce est le lit?
Le lit est dans la chambre.

1. Dans quelle pièce est le lit?
2. Dans quelle pièce est le réfrigérateur?
3. Dans quelle pièce est la télévision?
4. Dans quelle pièce est la lampe?
5. Dans quelle pièce est la cuisinière?
6. Dans quelle pièce est la table?
7. Dans quelle pièce est le lavabo?
8. Dans quelle pièce est le téléphone?
9. Dans quelle pièce est le fauteuil?
10. Dans quelle pièce est la radio?
11. Dans quelle pièce est la commode?
12. Dans quelle pièce est la poubelle?
13. Dans quelle pièce est le bureau?
14. Dans quelles pièces sont les tableaux?
15. Dans quelles pièces sont les chaises?

Exercice écrit

Complete each sentence with the appropriate furnishings or appliance.

1. La mère de Françoise fait la cuisine dans______.
2. Les personnes dorment dans______.
3. Je me lave dans______.
4. Ma famille mange sur la ______de la salle à manger.
5. Je me douche dans la ______.
6. Nous gardons la nourriture dans______.
7. Nous regardons la télévision assis dans le______ou dans la______.
8. Ma grand-mère a beaucoup de______sur le mur.
9. Quand je fais mes devoirs, j'écris sur le______.
10. J'aime beaucoup la musique. J'écoute toujours mes disques sur le ______.
11. Ma soeur parle beaucoup au ______avec son ami.
12. Je prends un bain dans______.

Vocabulaire

les meubles de la maison ***the furniture of the house***

la baignoire	*the bathtub*	la lampe	*the lamp*
le fauteuil	*the armchair*	la table	*the table*
le lit	*the bed*	le réfrigérateur	*the refrigerator*
la commode	*the dresser*	le sofa	*the sofa*
le tableau	*the picture, the painting*	la télévision	*the television*
		le tourne-disque	*the record player, stereo*
la douche	*the shower*		
la cuisinière	*the stove*	le lavabo	*the sink (bathroom only)*
garder	*to keep*	le mur	*the wall*
ou	*or*	assis	*seated*

Révision de vocabulaire

la poubelle *the garbage can*
l'ordinateur *the computer*
le disque *the record*
le bureau *the desk*
la radio *the radio*
la chaise *the chair*
le téléphone *the telephone*

Aim V: ***Each student will be able to read with comprehension a dialogue between two teenagers who meet in France.***

Lecture première partie

Il est sept heures et demie du soir. Anne, la jeune fille américaine rencontre Jacques, le jeune homme français dans un café à Paris. Durant la conversation, ils parlent de leur vie de tous les jours.

1. **Anne:** Quelle est ton adresse?
2. **Jacques:** J'habite rue Cherbuliez au 14.
3. **Anne:** Est-ce que tu habites dans une maison ou un appartement?
4. **Jacques:** J'habite dans un appartement.

5. **Anne:** A quel étage habites-tu?
6. **Jacques:** J'habite au cinquième.
7. **Anne:** Combien d'étages y-a-t-il dans ton immeuble?
8. **Jacques:** Mon immeuble a huit étages.
9. **Anne:** Est-ce qu'il y a un ascenseur?
10. **Jacques:** Oui, il y en a deux.
11. **Anne:** Combien de pièces y-a-t-il dans ton appartement?
12. **Jacques:** Il y a six pièces dans mon appartement.
13. **Anne:** Quelles sont-elles?
14. **Jacques:** Il y a la salle de séjour, la cuisine, la salle à manger, la salle de bain et deux chambres.

15. **Anne:** Comment est ta chambre?
16. **Jacques:** Ma chambre est petite, mais je l'aime beaucoup parce qu'elle est très pratique. J'ai mon ordinateur, ma radio, ma télé et mon magnétoscope.
17. **Anne:** Comment est la cuisine?
18. **Jacques:** La cuisine est grande et très moderne. Ma mère y passe beaucoup de temps et elle a tout. Mon père ne fait rien dans la cuisine, mais quelquefois je lave la vaisselle si ma mère ne se sent pas bien.

Compréhension: vrai ou faux

If the statement is true, state *vrai.* If the statement is false, state *faux* and **correct the bold part.**

1. Il est **sept heures et quart** du soir.
2. Jacques habite dans **une maison.**
3. Il habite au **huitième** étage.
4. L'immeuble de Jacques a **deux** ascenseurs.
5. Il y a **sept** pièces dans l'appartement.
6. Sa chambre est **grande.**
7. Jacques aime sa chambre parce qu'elle **n'est pas pratique**.
8. Jacques a **une radio et un magnétoscope** dans sa chambre.
9. La cuisine de son appartement est très **vieille**.
10. La mère de Jacques passe **peu** de temps dans la cuisine.
11. Jacques lave la vaisselle **très souvent.**
12. **Son père** ne fait rien dans la cuisine.

Vocabulaire de la lecture

Américain/Américaine *American*
il/elle rencontre ... *he / she meets ...*
même ... *same ...*
durant la conversation *during the conversation*
la vie de tous les jours *every-day living*

Quelle est ton adresse? *What is your address?*
J'habite rue(avenue) ...au numéro...
I live on ... Street(Avenue), number ....
Est-ce que tu habites dans une maison ou un appartement?
Do you live in a house or in an apartment?
J'habite dans .... *I live in ....*

A quel étage habites-tu? *On what floor do you live?*
J'habite au...étage. *I live on the ... floor.*

premier *first* | cinquième *fifth* | neuvième *ninth*
deuxième *second* | sixième *sixth* | dixième *tenth*
troisième *third* | septième *seventh*
quatrième *fourth* | huitième *eighth*

Combien d'étages y a-t-il dans votre immeuble?
How many floors does your building have?
Dans mon immeuble il y a...étages. *My building has ... floors.*
Est-ce qu'il y a un ascenseur? *Is there an elevator?*
Il y a un ascenseur.. *It has...* Non, il n'y a pas... *No, It doesn't have...*
Est-ce qu'il y a une cour dans ta maison? *Does your house have a patio?*

le garage *garage* | le jardin *garden*
le sous-sol *basement* | les arbres *trees*
la terrasse *terrace* | les fleurs *flowers*

Combien de pièces y-a-t-il dans ta maison?
How many rooms are there in your house?
Il y a...pièces dans mon/ma... *There are ... rooms in my ...*
Quelles sont-elles? *What are they?*
Comment est ta chambre? *What is your bedroom like?*
ma chambre est: / **mon appartement** est:
grand (m)/grande (f) *large*
moyen (m)/moyenne (f) *medium*
petit (m)/petite (f) *small*
beau (m)/belle (f) *pretty*
laid (m)/laide (f) *ugly*
confortable, pratique *comfortable*
inconfortable *uncomfortable*
moderne *modern*
neuf (m)/neuve (f) *new*
vieux (m)/vieille (f) *old*
Un lit neuf (m). *A new bed.*
Une terrasse neuve (f). *A new terrasse.*

Note: In front of a vowel: un vieil appartement *an old apartment*
For a masculine noun: un vieux livre *an old book*
une vieille lampe *an old lamp*
un beau livre *a beautiful book*
un bel arbre *a beautiful tree*
une belle fille *a beautiful (pretty) girl.*

Comment est ta cuisine? *What is your kitchen like?*
La **cuisine** est
grande / moyenne / petite
belle / laide
moderne / neuve / vieille
confortable / inconfortable

Quelle est ta pièce favorite? *What is your favorite room?*
Ma pièce favorite est .... *My favorite room is ....*

le magnétoscope *VCR*
mais *but*
souvent *often*
quelquefois *sometimes*
passer beaucoup de temps *to spend a lot of time there*
elle/il a tout *she / he has everything*
si ma mère ne se sent pas bien *if my mother doesn't feel well*

sa maison/**son** appartement ***his/her*** *house / apartment*
sa chambre/**sa** salle de séjour ***his/her*** bedroom/living room

Mme Vinard-Vial aime faire la cuisine.

Lecture: deuxième partie

1. **Jacques:** Anne, quelle est ton adresse?
2. **Anne:** J'habite à la 94e rue au 847.
3. **Jacques:** Est-ce que tu habites dans une maison ou dans un appartement?
4. **Anne:** J'habite dans une maison.
5. **Jacques:** Combien d'étages y-a-t-il dans ta maison?
6. **Anne:** Il y a deux étages dans ma maison.
7. **Jacques:** Combien de pièces y-a-t-il dans ta maison?
8. **Anne:** Il y a neuf pièces.
9. **Jacques:** Quelles sont-elles?
10. **Anne:** Il y a la salle de séjour, la salle à manger, la cuisine, le bureau, trois chambres et deux salles de bain.
11. **Jacques:** Comment est la salle de séjour?
12. **Anne:** La salle de séjour est grande et très belle.
13. **Jacques:** Et comment est la cuisine?
14. **Anne:** La cuisine n'est ni grande ni petite, elle est moyenne.
15. **Jacques:** Et ton père, est-ce qu'il aide ta mère à la cuisine?
16. **Anne:** Certainement. Mon père lave la vaisselle après les repas. Ma mère travaille dans un bureau. Après le travail elle fait la cuisine. Ma soeur met la table, mon frère sort les ordures et j'essuie la vaisselle.
17. **Jacques:** Quelle est ta pièce favorite?
18. **Anne:** Ma pièce favorite est ma chambre. Elle est petite mais agréable. J'y étudie, je parle au téléphone avec mon amie, j'écoute la musique sur mon tourne-disque et je lis des romans.
19. **Jacques:** Est-ce qu'il y a une cour derrière la maison?
20. **Anne:** Non, il n'y a pas de cour, mais il y a un jardin avec des arbres et des fleurs. Mon père y travaille au printemps et en été. La maison a aussi un garage.

Compréhension de la lecture:

Answer the following questions with a complete sentence in French.

1. Quelle est l'adresse d'Anne?
2. Est-ce qu'elle habite dans une maison ou un appartement?
3. Combien de pièces est-ce qu'il y a dans sa maison?
4. Quelles sont les pièces de sa maison?
5. Comment est la cuisine?
6. Que fait le père d'Anne après le repas?
7. Où travaille la mère d'Anne?
8. Qui met la table?
9. Qui sort les ordures?
10. Qui essuie la vaisselle?
11. Quelle est la pièce favorite d'Anne?
12. Qu'est-ce qu'elle fait dans sa pièce favorite?
13. Est-ce qu'il y a une cour?
14. Qu'est-ce qu'il y a dans le jardin?
15. Quand est-ce que le père d'Anne travaille dans le jardin?

Vocabulaire de la lecture:

aider *to help*
j'**y** étudie *I study* ***there***
agréable *pleasant*
certainement *of course, certainly*
après le repas *after supper*
après le travail *after work*
essuyer *to dry*
j'essu**i**e, tu essu**i**es, il/elle essu**i**e
nous essuyons, vous essuyez, ils/elles essu**i**ent
derrière *behind*
aussi *also*

Les saisons de l'année

le printemps *spring*
l'été *summer*
l'automne *autumn, fall*
l'hiver *winter*

Aim VI: *Each student will be able to ask a peer or friend and adult basic questions about his/her house or apartment and be able to respond*

Conversation

Peer practice in groups of two.

1. Quelle est ton adresse?
2. Est-ce que tu habites dans une maison ou dans un appartement?
3. Combien d'étages est-ce qu'il y a dans ton immeuble (ou ta maison)?
4. A quel étage habites-tu?
5. Combien de pièces est-ce qu'il y a dans ta maison (ou ton appartement)?
6. Quelles sont-elles?
7. Comment est ta chambre?
8. Comment est la cuisine?
9. Comment est la salle de séjour?
10. Quelle est ta pièce favorite?
11. Est-ce qu'il y a un garage dans ton immeuble (ou ta maison?)
12. Est-ce qu'il y a une cour derrière ton immeuble (ou ta maison)?
13. Comment est-ce que tu aides dans ta maison?

Exercice écrit

1. Write and answer the questions of the **Conversation,** numbers 1 - 13.
2. Change each question, whenever necessary, of the **Conversation** to the appropriate form to ask an adult.

Activité

1. Draw a floor plan of your apartment or house. Label each room and draw or paste a picture of the major furnishings and appliances found in each room of your house. Write the name of each room and furnishing or appliance in French.

2a. Write a letter to a French pen pal in which you tell him/her the following about your home environment:

1. your address
2. if you live in an apartment or in a house
3. the number of rooms in your home and what they are
4. the number of floors in your house or apartment building
5. two things about each room (size and description)
6. two pieces of furniture (or appliances) in each room
7. in what room you spend a lot of time
8. what your favorite room is and why
9. what chores you do in the house
10. the chores other members of the family do in the house
11. if there is a patio, garden, basement or garage in your house, or a terrace in your apartment building

2b. Now ask him/her three questions about his/her house or apartment.

Use the following format to indicate your city, the date, the salutation and the farewell.

New York, le ___ ___ 19__

Cher ami_____,
(Chère amie)

____

____

____

____

____

____

____

A bientôt,
(Sign your name.)

Glimpses of France

UNIT EIGHT

La santé

Les passe-temps

TOPIC

A. Health and welfare B. Leisure

SITUATION

Informal everyday conversations with individual peers and adults

FUNCTION

Providing and obtaining information about one's health and leisure activities
Getting others to adopt a course of action by suggesting and advising
Expressing personal feelings

PROFICIENCY

Can comprehend simple statements and questions and can respond appropriately with possible need for repetition
Can ask questions appropriate to the communicative situation

AIM IA: Each student will be able to identify parts of the body and be able to state that a specific part hurts him/her

AIM IB: Each student will be able to state what's the matter with each of the following people and why each of them isn't going to school or work

AIM IC: Each student will be able to ask a peer and an adult questions related to health and be able to respond

AIM IIA: Each student will be able to ask a peer and an adult if s/he likes to play a particular sport and be able to respond

AIM IIB: Each student will be able to ask a peer and an adult "What sports do you play?" and be able to respond

AIM III: Each student will be able to read with comprehension a dialogue between two teenagers who meet in France

AIM IV: Each student will be able to ask a peer questions about his/her extracurricular activities after school, leisure activities during the weekend and the summer vacation, and be able to respond

Aim IA: *Each student will be able to identify parts of the body and be able to state that a specific part hurts him/her*

Exercice oral

Les parties du corps

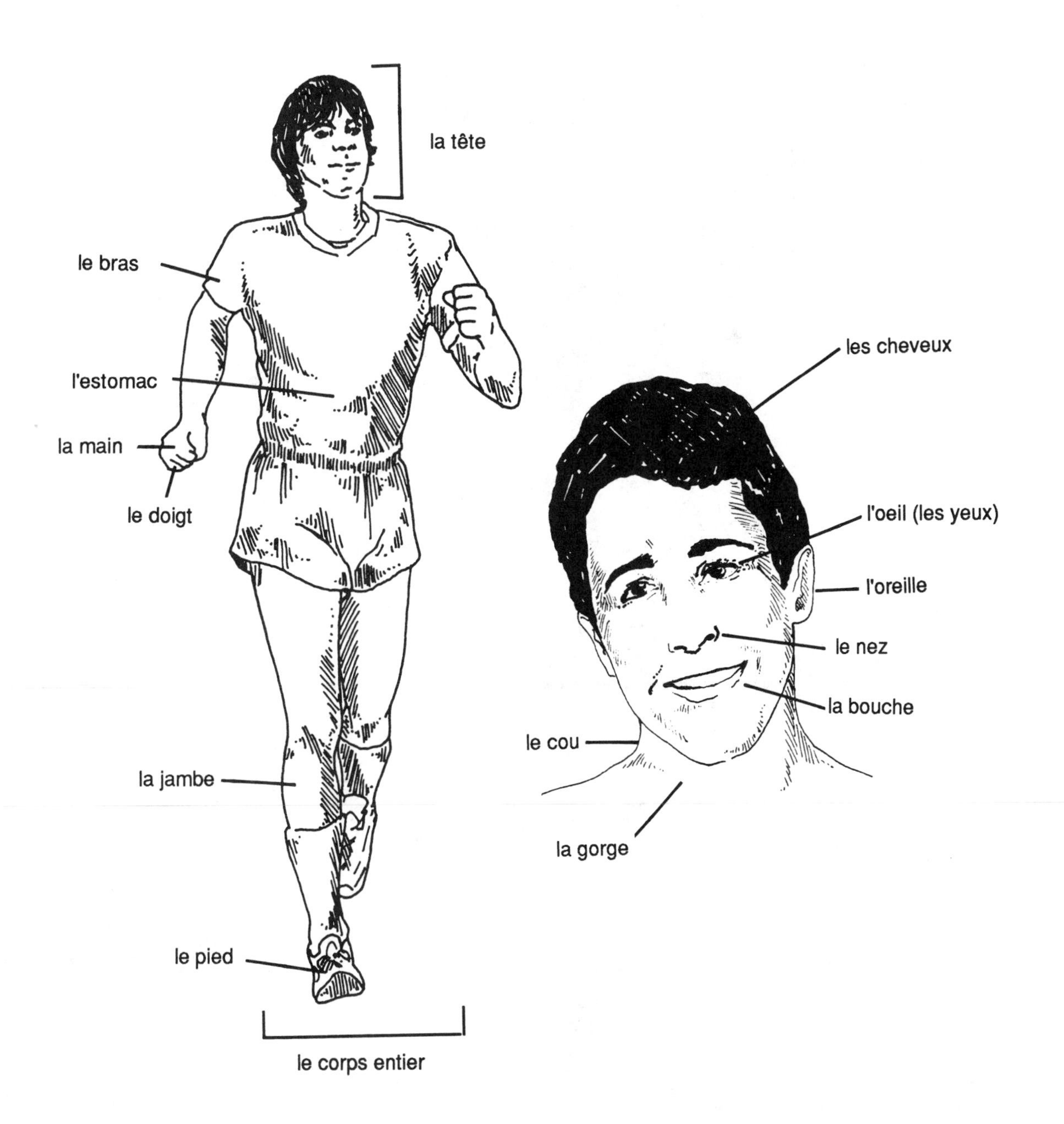

Conversation

Peer practice in groups of two.

A. One partner plays the role of the mother or father and asks his/her partner *Où as-tu mal?* The other partner, the son or daughter, points to the number on the diagram and indicates it is the part of his/her body that hurts.

Example:
Père ou mère: Où as-tu mal?
Le fils ou la fille: J'ai mal à la main.

B. Now partners change roles. This time the doctor asks the question, *Où avez-vous mal?* You, the patient, point to the part of your body which hurts and respond appropriately.

Example:
Le docteur: Où avez-vous mal?
Le malade: J'ai mal à la gorge.

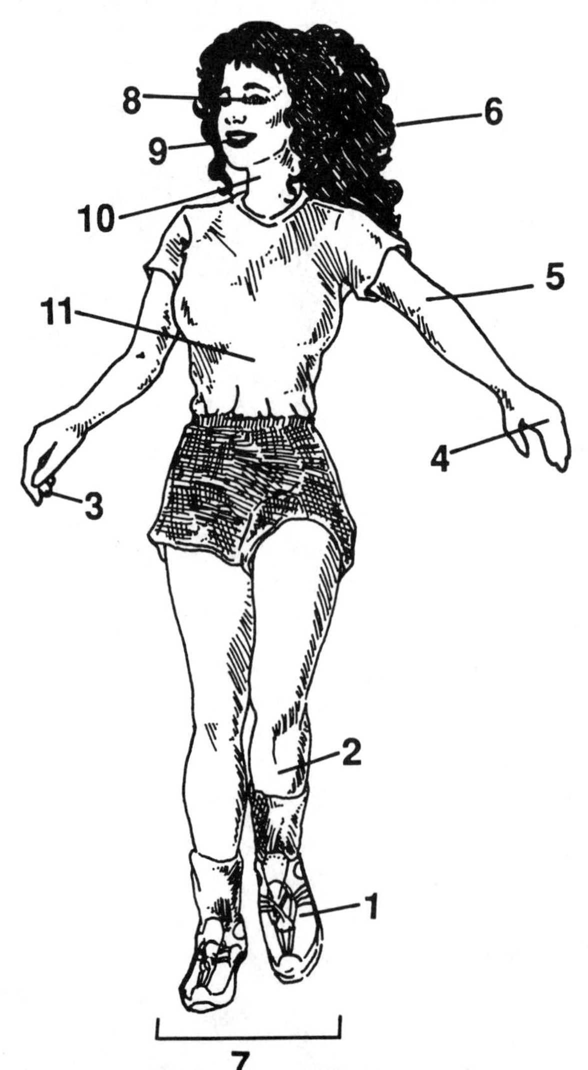

Exercice de compréhension

1. You will hear a few statements indicating that a specific part of the body hurts each of the following people. After the second repetition, choose the part of the body which corresponds to what you hear. Write only the letter.

Example: A. Charles a mal au bras.

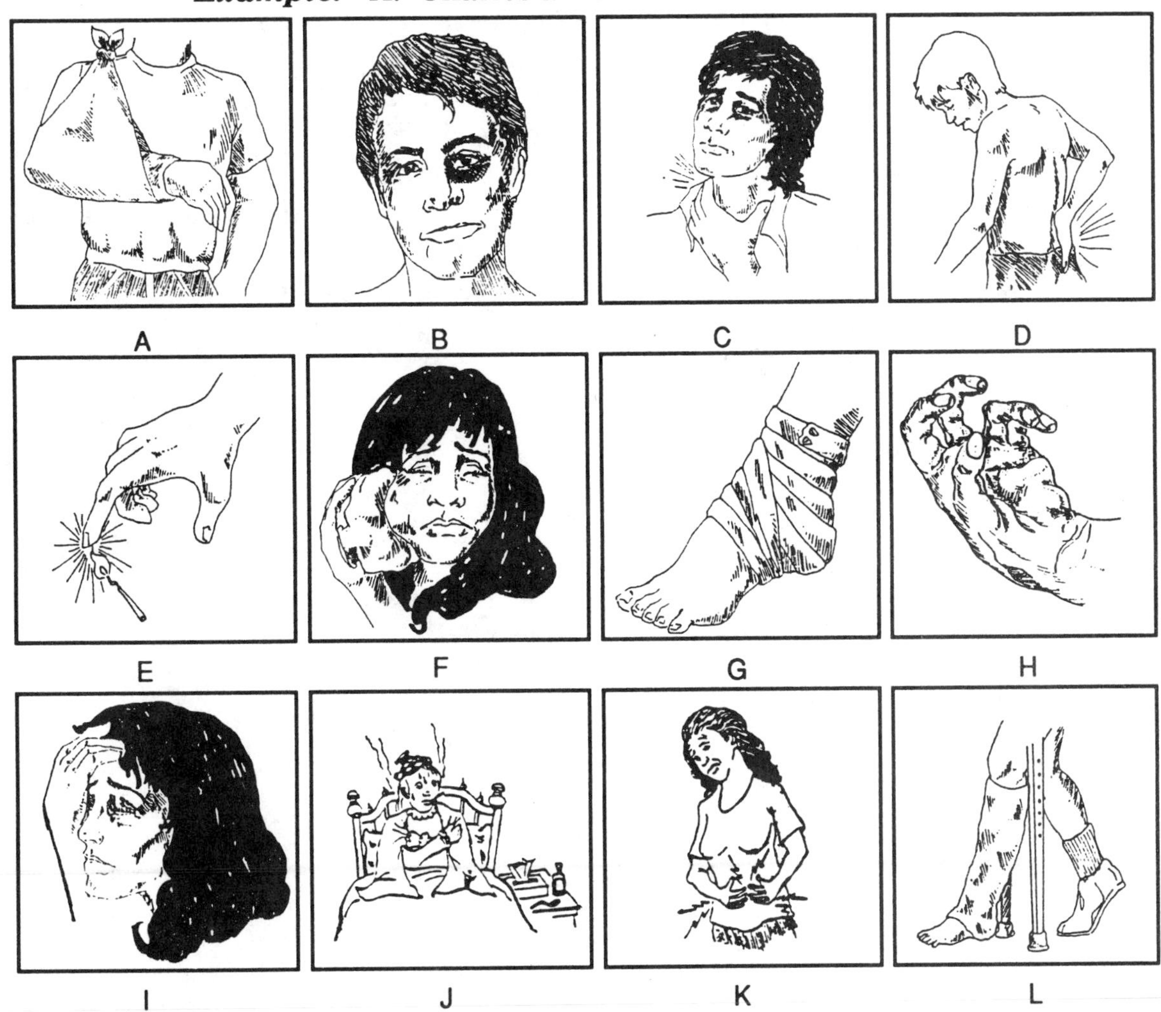

2. You may wish to play the game of "Simon Says" *("Jacques a dit")*

Jacques dit: Touchez la tête.
Jacques dit: Touchez le pied.

Play continues until one or more winners is declared.

Exercice écrit

Write five questions and answers of the **Conversation A,** and five of **B.** Use different parts of the body for each question.

Vocabulaire

Les parties du corps		***The parts of the body***	
la bouche	*the mouth*	la dent	*the tooth*
le bras	*the arm*	le nez	*the nose*
la tête	*the head*	l'oreille	*the ear*
le cou	*the neck*	la main	*the hand*
le doigt	*the finger*	l'oeil	*the eye* (les **yeux** *the **eyes***)
le dos	*the back*	la jambe	*the leg*
l'estomac	*the stomach*	les cheveux	*the hair*
la gorge	*the throat*	le pied	*the foot*

le corps entier *the entire body*

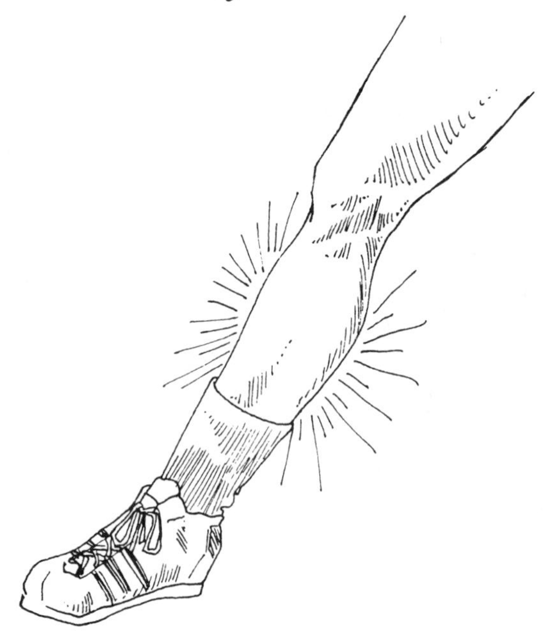

J'ai mal à la jambe.

Où as-tu mal? *What hurts you?*
Où avez-vous mal? *What hurts you?*
J'ai mal ... *... hurts me.*

le docteur *doctor*
la doctoresse *doctor*
le malade *patient*
la malade *patient*

Aim IB: *Each student will be able to state what's the matter with each of the following people and why each of them isn't going to school or work*

Exercice oral

Qu'est-ce qu'il a?/ Qu'est-ce qu'elle a?

Elle a de la fièvre.

Elle a un rhume.

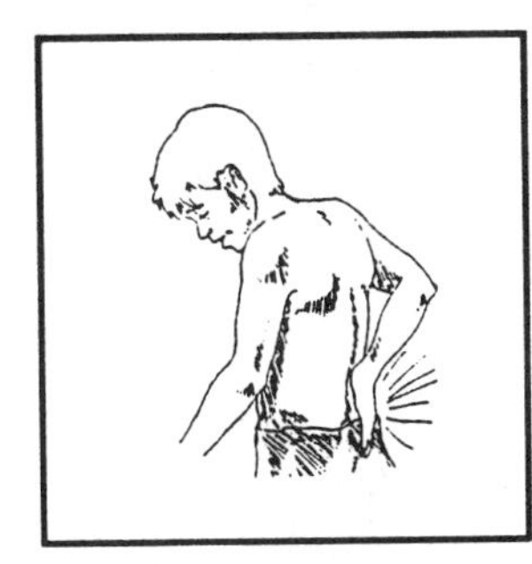

Il a mal au dos.

Elle a mal à la tête.

Elle a mal à l'estomac.

Il a mal à la gorge.

Conversation

1. One partner asks *Qu'est-ce qu'elle a?* or *Qu-est-ce qu'il a?* while pointing to each picture
A - H on the next page. The other partner responds appropriately. Then reverse roles.

2. Each student can change partners for this second **Exercice.** While pointing to each picture A - H one partner asks *Pourquoi est-ce qu'il (elle) ne va pas à l'école?* or *Pourquoi est-ce qu'il (elle) ne va pas travailler?* The other partner responds appropriately. Then reverse roles so that each partner can ask and answer all the questions.

Examples:

Jacques: Pourquoi est-ce qu'elle ne va pas à l'école?
Anne: Elle ne va pas à l'école parce qu'elle a mal à l'estomac.

Hélène: Pourquoi est-ce qu'il ne va pas travailler?
Paul: Il ne va pas travailler parce qu'il a un rhume.

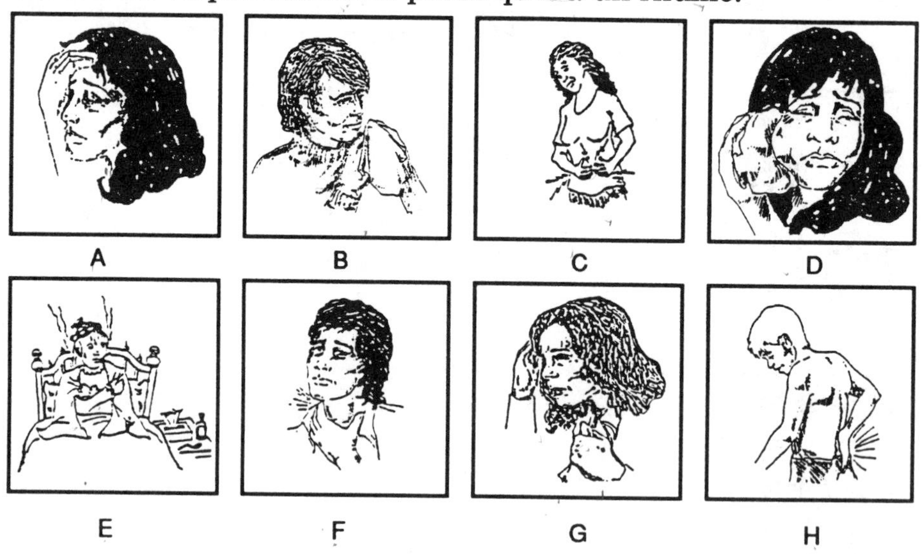

Exercice de compréhension

You will hear a few statements indicating that something is the matter with each of the following people. Refer to pictures A - H in the **Conversation** above. After the second repetition, choose the picture which corresponds to what you hear. Write only the letter.

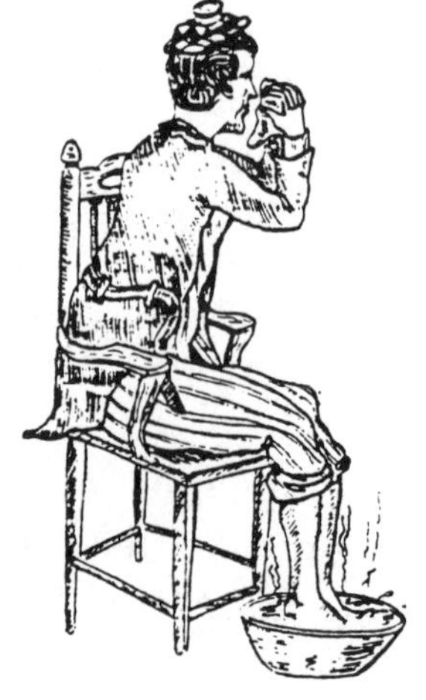

Pourquoi est-ce qu'il ne va pas travailler?

Exercice écrit

1. Write both the questions and the answers to the **Conversation,** number 2.
2. Complete each sentence by choosing an appropriate expression of health.

1. Madame Caillot prend de l'aspirine quand __.
2. Monsieur Carnot se repose au lit quand___.
3. Mademoiselle Cordier prend de L'alka- seltzer quand___.
4. Thérèse parle peu et ne chante pas quand___.
5. Charles va chez le docteur quand___.
6. Mon frère ne va pas à l'école aujourd'hui parce qu'il a ___.
7. Mon père ne va pas travailler aujourd'hui parce qu'il a ___.
8. Ma grand-mère est à l'hôpital parce qu'elle a___.
9. Ma soeur ne parle pas au téléphone aujourd'hui parce qu'elle a___.
10. Mon ami mange peu parce qu'il a___.

Vocabulaire

Qu'est-ce qu'il a? *What's the matter with him?*
Qu'est-ce qu'elle a? *What's the matter with her?*
Il/Elle a de la fièvre. *He / she has a fever.*
...a un rhume. *...has a cold.*
...a mal à la tête. *...has a headache.*
...a mal au dos. *...has a backache.*
...a mal à l'estomac. *...has a stomachache.*
...a mal à la gorge. *...has a sore throat.*
...a mal aux dents. *...has a toothache.*

Pourquoi est-ce qu'il/elle ne va pas à l'école?
Why isn't he / she going to school?
Il/Elle ne va pas à l'école parce qu'il/elle a...
He / she isn't going to school because...
Pourquoi est-ce qu'il/elle ne va pas travailler?
Why isn't he / she going to work?
Il/Elle ne va pas travailler parce qu'il/elle...
He / she isn't going to work because ...
se reposer au lit *to rest in bed*
être à l'hôpital *to be in the hospital*
aller chez le docteur *to go to the doctor*
Il/Elle va ... *He / she goes ...*
prendre de l'aspirine *to take aspirin*

Aim IC: *Each student will be able to ask a peer and an adult questions related to health and be able to respond*

Exercice oral

A. ***Jean rencontre Marie.***

1. **Jean:** Bonjour! Comment vas-tu?
2. **Marie:** Ça va très bien. Et toi?
3. **Jean:** Ça ne va pas très bien.
4. **Marie:** Qu'est-ce que tu as?
5. **Jean:** J'ai mal à la tête.

B. ***Anne appelle Paul au téléphone.***

1. **Paul:** Allô? Qui est-ce?
2. **Anne:** C'est moi, Anne. Quoi de neuf?
3. **Paul:** Ça ne va pas très bien.
4. **Anne:** Qu'est-ce que tu as?
5. **Paul:** Je suis malade. J'ai de la fièvre.
6. **Anne:** Je suis navrée. J'espère que ça ira mieux bientôt.
7. **Paul:** Merci. Et toi, comment vas-tu?
8. **Anne:** Ça va...

C. ***Madame Corail rencontre Monsieur Pinot.***

1. **Mme Corail:** Bonjour, M. Pinot. Comment allez-vous?
2. **M. Pinot:** Je suis un peu fatigué. Et vous?
3. **Mme Corail:** J'ai mal à la gorge et à l'estomac.
4. **M. Pinot:** Pourquoi n'allez-vous pas chez vous?
5. **Mme Corail:** Bonne idée. Je vais chez moi maintenant.

D. ***Charles rencontre sa maîtresse.***

1. **Charles:** Bonjour, Mlle Plon. Comment allez-vous?
2. **Mlle Plon:** Pas très bien.
3. **Charles:** Qu'est-ce que vous avez?
4. **Mlle Plon:** Je suis très fatiguée et j'ai un mauvais rhume.
5. **Charles:** Je suis navré. J'espère que vous irez mieux bientôt.
6. **Mlle Plon:** Merci. Et toi, comment vas-tu?
7. **Charles:** Je suis un peu fatigué, mais ça va.

Conversation

1. Partners take turns playing the roles of the **Exercice oral.**

2. One partner asks the other the following health related questions. Then the second partner asks the first the same questions but this time treats him/her as an adult.

1. Comment vas-tu?
2. Ça va bien?
3. Tu es fatigué(e)?
4. Tu es malade?
5. Tu as un rhume?
6. Tu as de la fièvre?
7. Tu as mal à la tête?
8. Tu as mal à l'estomac?
9. Tu as mal à la gorge?
10. Tu as mal au dos?

Exercice écrit

Write the questions and answers of **Conversation, 2,** numbers 1 - 10.

Résumé

One or two pairs of students can play the roles for the entire class followed by peer practice.

A

Paul appelle Laure au téléphone jeudi.

1. **Laure:** Allô? Qui est-ce?
2. **Paul:** C'est moi, Paul. Tu vas à la partie samedi?
3. **Laure:** Non, je ne___pas à la partie. Je ne vais pas bien.
4. **Paul:** _______ ?
5. **Laure:** J'ai un rhume et j'ai mal à _______ .
6. **Paul:** Je suis navré.
7. **Laure:** Merci.
8. **Paul:** A bientôt, Laure.
9. **Laure:** _____.

B

M. Duchêne rencontre Mme Vichy au travail lundi.

1. **M. Duchêne:** Bonjour, Mme Vichy. _____?
2. **Mme Vichy:** Pas très bien aujourd'hui.
3. **M. Duchêne:** _____?
4. **Mme Vichy**: J'ai mal à la___.
5. **M. Duchêne:** Pourquoi est-ce que vous n'allez pas chez le docteur?
6. **Mme Vichy:** Bonne idée. Je ____ _____ chez le docteur demain.
7. **M. Duchêne:** _____!, Mme Vichy.
8. **Mme Vichy:** Merci beaucoup, M. Duchêne.
9. **M. Duchêne:** Au revoir, Mme Vichy.

Activités

Write both roles in dialogue form, giving each person a name. Then take turns playing the roles.

1. You meet one of your teachers between classes in the morning. Greet him/her and ask him/her how s/he is. The teacher responds that s/he is very tired and has a sore throat. You then state that you're sorry and that you hope s/he feels better soon. The teacher thanks you.

2. You see a good friend after classes. Greet him/her and find out how s/he is. S/he tells you that s/he isn't going to the party because of a bad cold. You then state that you're sorry and that you hope that s/he feels better soon. S/he thanks you.

3. You meet one of your friends between classes. You tell your friend that you don't feel well and that your entire body hurts you. S/he asks you "Why don't you go to the doctor after school?" You respond that "It's a good idea." Your friend says goodbye and that s/he is going home now.

4. You're in the doctor's office. It's afternoon. Greet the doctor. Ask him/her how s/he is. S/he responds "very well" and then asks you "What's the matter?" You tell him/her that you have a cold and a stomachache and that your entire body hurts you. The doctor takes your temperature and tells you that you have a fever. You say "I'm not going to school tomorrow!"

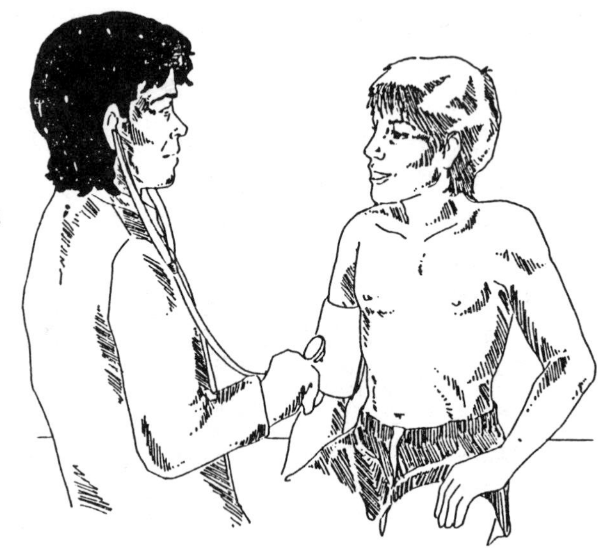

Vocabulaire

Qu'est-ce que tu as?/Qu'est-ce que vous avez? *What's the matter with you?*
J'ai ... *I have ...*
As-tu ...? *Do you have ...?*
Avez-vous ....? *Do you have ...?*
J'ai ... *I have ...*
Non, je n'ai pas ... *I don't have ...*
Tu es ...? *Are you ...?*
Vous êtes ...? Are you ...?
Je suis navré(e). *I'm sorry.*
J'espère que ça ira mieux bientôt! *Hope you feel better soon!*
J'espère que vous irez mieux bientôt! *Hope you feel better soon!*
appeler au téléphone *to call someone on the telephone*
Allô! *Hello! (used when speaking on the telephone)*
Qui est-ce? *Who's speaking?*
C'est moi,... *It's me,...*
Pourquoi est-ce que tu ne vas pas chez toi ...? *Why don't you go home?*
Pourquoi est-ce que vous n'allez pas chez vous ...? *Why don't you go home?*
Je vais... *I'm going ...*
Je ne vais pas... *I'm not going ...*
Bonne idée. *Good idea.*
maintenant *now*

Révision de vocabulaire

Quoi de neuf *What's new?*
Comment vas-tu? *How are you?*
Comment allez-vous? *How are you?*
Je vais bien. *I'm fine.*
Je suis fatigué(e). *I'm tired.*
Es-tu?...? *Are you...?*
Etes-vous...? *Are you...?*
Je suis.. *I'm...*
Je suis malade. *I'm sick*
Comme ci, comme ça. *So-so.*
Ça va. *I'm fine.*
Ça va très bien. *I'm very well.*
Pas très bien. *I'm not well.*
Je (ne) suis (pas)... *I'm (not)...*

être *to be*	
je **suis**	nous **sommes**
tu **es**	vous **êtes**
il **est**	ils **sont**
elle **est**	elles **sont**

avoir *to have*	
j'**ai**	nous **avons**
tu **as**	vous **avez**
il **a**	ils **ont**
elle **a**	elles **ont**

Aim IIA: *Each student will be able to ask a peer and adult if s/he likes to play a particular sport and be able to respond*

Exercice oral 1

Les sports

le baseball | le basketball | le football | le rugby

le tennis | le volleyball | le golf | le hockey

les boules | skier | nager | courir

Exercice oral 2

1. **Claudine:** Est-ce que tu aimes jouer au basketball?
   Pierre: Oui, j'aime jouer au basketball.

2. **Charles:** Est-ce que tu aimes faire du patin à glace?
   Cécile: Non, je n'aime pas faire de patin à glace.

3. **Jules:** Aimez-vous jouer au golf?
   Mme Monin: Oui, j'aime jouer au golf.

Conversation

One partner asks the **A** column questions and the other asks the **B** column. Then reverse roles.

A

1. Est-ce que tu aimes jouer au volleyball?
2. Est-ce que tu aimes jouer au tennis?
3, Est-ce que tu aimes jouer au basketball?
4. Est-ce que tu aimes jouer au football?
5. Est-ce que tu aimes faire du ski?
6. Est-ce que tu aimes courir?

B

7. Est-ce que vous aimez jouer au golf?
8. Est-ce que vous aimez jouer au hockey?
9. Est-ce que vous aimez jouer au football?
10. Est-ce que vous aimez nager?
11. Est-ce que vous aimez faire du patin à glace?

Exercice écrit

Write the questions and answers of the **Conversation,** numbers 1 - 11.

Aim IIB: *Each student will be able to ask a peer and adult "What sports do you play?" and be able to respond*

Exercice oral

1. **Rose:** A quels sports est-ce que tu joues?
   Marie: Je joue au tennis, au volleyball et je patine.

2. **Georges:** Quels sports fais-tu?
   Jean: Je joue au football et au hockey.

3. **Anne:** A quels sports est-ce que vous jouez?
   M. Bidot: Je joue au golf et je nage.

4. **Mlle Jocelin:** Quels sports faites-vous?
   M. Posna: Je joue au volleyball et je cours beaucoup.

Conversation

1. Ask two classmates near you *"A quels sports est-ce que tu joues?"*

2a. Ask your peer partner if he/she plays the following sports:
Est-ce que tu joues au ...?
a. volleyball *b. football* *c. hockey* *d. baseball*

2b. Now ask an adult if he/she plays the following sports:
Est-ce que vous jouez au ...?
a. golf *b. football* *c. basketball* *d. tennis*

Activité

On the first day of classes you meet an exchange student from France. He asks you what sports are played during each season in the United States. You respond. Name at least two sports played during each season.

Example A. *Quels sports fait-on au printemps?*
He also asks you what sports you watch on television.
Example B. *Quels sports est-ce que tu regardes à la télévision?*
You then ask him what sports do they play in France.
Example C. *Quels sports fait-on en France?*

Vocabulaire

Les sports ***sports***

le basketball *basketball*
le baseball *baseball*
le football *soccer / football*
skier/faire du ski *to ski*
le golf *golf*
le hockey *hockey*
le rugby *rugby*
les boules *boccie*
le tennis *tennis*
le volleyball *volleyball*
courir *to run*
nager *to swim*
patiner *to skate*
faire du patin à glace *to iceskate*
faire du vélo *to ride a bicycle*

Est-ce que tu aimes jouer ...? *Do you like to play ...?*
Est-ce que vous aimez jouer...? *Do you like to play ...?*
Oui, j'aime jouer ... *Yes, I like to play ...*
Non, je n'aime pas jouer... *No, I don't like to play...*

A quels sports est-ce que tu joues? *What sports do you play?*
A quels sports est-ce que vous jouez? *What sports do you play?*
Je joue... *I play...*

courir ***to run***

je **cours**	nous **courons**
tu **cours**	vous **courez**
il **court**	ils **courent**
elle **court**	elles **courent**

Note culturelle

1. Rugby is a very popular European sport that combines many of the elements of soccer and American football. Two teams of 15 members each try to advance the (football-shaped) ball over the opponent's goal by carrying or kicking. Players on the team in posession may not advance past the ball. An extremely rugged game, players generally do not wear protective pads as in American football. The game's formal origin and name come from the site of a boys' school founded in 1567 in Rugby, England, a borough in eastern Warwickshire.

2. *Les boules* or *pétanque* (known in Italy as *bocce)* is a national pastime of southern France, but played everywhere. Two teams of two or three players throw heavy steel balls in an attempt to come closest to a small wooden ball. Many elements of this game are similar to horshoes and shuffleboard.

Aim III: *Each student will be able to read with comprehension a dialogue between two teenagers who meet in France.*

Lecture: première partie

Anne, la jeune fille américaine, rencontre Jaqcues, le jeune français dans une discothèque à Paris où vont beaucoup de jeunes de son âge. Il est huit heures du soir et la musique commence.

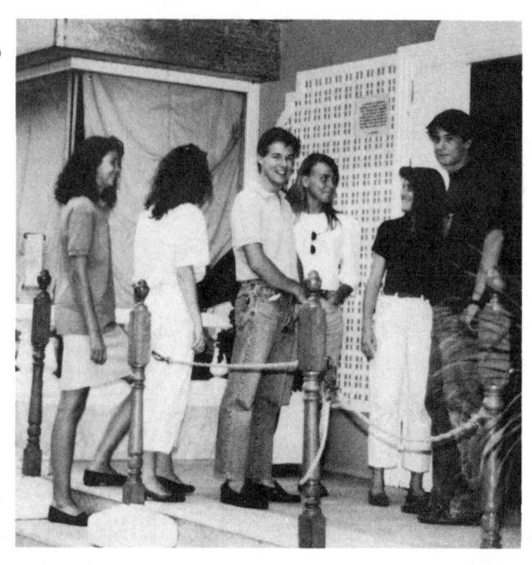

1. **Jacques:** Bonjour, Anne. Ça va?
2. **Anne:** Très bien. Et toi?
3. **Jacques:** Bien. Je suis content de te voir.
4. **Anne:** Moi aussi.
5. **Jacques:** Aimes-tu la musique?
6. **Anne:** Oui, beaucoup.
7. **Jacques:** Veux-tu danser?
8. **Anne:** Oui, je veux bien.
9. **Jacques:** Tu danses bien.
10. **Anne:** Merci. J'aime beaucoup danser. Aux Etats-Unis je vais souvent dans les discothèques.
11. **Jacques:** Avec qui y vas-tu?
12. **Anne:** Quelquefois avec mes amies et si j'ai rendez-vous avec un garçon, je vais avec lui.
13. **Jacques:** Ici en France les jeunes sortent pour aller au cinéma et aux discothèques en groupe ou avec une amie.
14. **Anne:** J'aime cette coutume.
15. **Jacques:** Qu'est-ce que tu fais à la fin de la semaine?
16. **Anne:** Et bien, samedi matin je joue au tennis, l'après-midi je fais des achats; le soir je sors avec mes amis ou avec un ami.

Compréhension de lecture:

If the statement is true state *vrai.* If the statement is false, state *faux* and **correct the bold part.**

1. C'est samedi, il est **dix heures** du soir.
2. Les deux jeunes se rencontrent dans **une bibliothèque**.
3. Jacques est **fatigué.**
4. Anne aime beaucoup **la musique.**
5. Elle danse très **mal**.
6. Anne **ne va pas souvent** dans les discothèques.
7. **Quelquefois** elle a rendez-vous avec un garçon.
8. Le samedi matin elle **joue au volleyball**.
9. Le samedi après-midi, elle **fait des achats**.
10. **Le dimanche** soir elle sort avec ses amies.

Vocabulaire de la lecture:

la discothèque *discotheque*
les jeunes *young people, teenagers*
le matin *in the morning*
l'après-midi *in the afternoon*
le soir *in the evening*
lundi matin
Monday morning
jeudi après-midi
Thursday afternoon
dimanche soir
Sunday evening

de son âge *of his/her age*
bien *well*
mal *badly*

Les jours de la semaine: lundi, mardi, mercredi, jeudi, vendredi, samedi, dimanche.

Je suis content de te voir! *How happy I am to see you!*
Moi aussi. *Me too.*

Veux-tu...? *Would you like to...?*
Oui, je veux... *Yes, I would like to....*
Non, je ne veux pas... *No, I wouldn't like to....*
Aimez-vous...? *Do you like to...?*
Oui, j'aime... *Yes, I like to...*
Non, je n'aime pas... *No, I don't like to...*

Avec qui vas-tu? *With whom do you go?*
Je vais avec... *I go with...*
Je vais seul(e). *I go alone.*
Si j'ai rendez-vous *If I have a date*
Est-ce que tu as rendez-vous avec...? *Do you have a date with...?*
Oui, j'ai rendez-vous avec... *Yes, I have a date with...*
Non, je n'ai pas rendez-vous. *No, I don't have a date.*
sortir: nous sortons... *to go out: we go out...*
Tu sors avec tes ami(e)s? *Do you go out with your friends?*
Oui, je sors avec mes ami(e)s. *Yes, I go out with my friends.*
Je sors avec un garçon. *I go out with a boy*
en groupe *in groups of friends*

la coutume *the custom :* cette coutume *that custom*
Qu'est-ce que tu fais à la fin de la semaine? *What do you do during the weekend?*

faire des achats *to go shopping*
Vas-tu faire des achats? *Do you go shopping?*
Je vais faire des achats *I go shopping.*
Je ne vais pas faire d'achats. *I don't go shopping.*

Lecture: deuxième partie

17. **Anne:** Le dimanche matin, je vais à l'église. L'après-midi je vais au parc avec mes amies et le soir j'étudie pour mes examens. Et toi? Qu'est-ce que tu fais à la fin de la semaine?
18. **Jacques:** Et bien, le samedi matin je joue au football; l'après-midi je sors avec mes amis et souvent nous allons au cinéma. Le dimanche je fais beaucoup de choses différentes.
19. **Anne:** Est-ce que tu participes à quelques activités après les classes?
20. **Jacques:** Non, je ne participe à aucune activité après les classes.
21. **Anne:** Pourquoi pas?
22. **Jacques:** Il y a peu d'activités à l'école. Après les classes, je sors avec mes amis faire une promenade. Et toi, Anne?
23. **Anne:** Je ne peux participer à aucune activité.
24. **Jacques:** Pourquoi est-ce que tu ne peux pas?
25. **Anne:** Parce que je n'ai pas le temps maintenant. Après les classes, je travaille dans un supermarché. L'année prochaine je veux devenir membre du club de théâtre dramatique.

Compréhension de la lecture:

Answer the following questions with a complete sentence in French.

11. Où va Anne le dimanche après-midi?
12. Quel sport Jacques fait-t-il le samedi matin?
13. Avec qui est-ce que Jacques va au cinéma?
14. Pourquoi est-ce qu'Anne ne peut pas participer à des activités après les classes?
15. Où travaille Anne après les classes?
16. Quand est-ce qu'Anne veut devenir membre du club de théatre dramatique?

Vocabulaire de la lecture:

Où vas-tu?/ Où allez-vous? *Where do you go...? / ...are you going?*

le cinéma *movie theater* — Je vais au cinéma.
l'école *school* — Je vais à l'école
l'église *church* — Je vais à l'église.
le parc *park* — Je vais au parc.
la plage *beach* — Je vais à la plage.

Je ne vais nulle part. *I don't go anywhere.*

faire du sport *to be involved in a sport*

Qu'est-ce que tu fais à la fin de la semaine?
What do you do during the weekend?
Je fais beaucoup de choses différentes. *I do many different things.*
Je sors avec mes amis... *I go out with my friends...*
bavarder *to chat*
faire une promenade *to take a walk*
Est-ce que tu participes à des activités après les classes?
Do you participate in any activity after classes?
Oui, je participe à... *I participate in/on the ...*
l'équipe de volleyball *volleyball team*
l'équipe de basketball *basketball team*
le club de théâtre dramatique *drama club*
le club de français *French club*
Non, je ne participe à aucune activité. *I don't participate in any activity.*
Il y a peu d'activités *There are few activities.*
Il y a beaucoup d'activités *There are many activities.*
Pourquoi est-ce que tu ne peux pas? *Why can't you?*
Parce que je n'ai pas le temps maintenant.
Because I don't have time now.
Je travaille dans un supermarché. *I work in a supermarket.*
Je veux être membre de... *I want to be a member of...*
devenir *to become*

pouvoir ***to be able, can***

je **peux**	nous **pouvons**
tu **peux**	vous **pouvez**
il **peut**	ils **peuvent**
elle **peut**	elles **peuvent**

vouloir ***to want***

je **veux**	nous **voulons**
tu **veux**	vous **voulez**
il **veut**	ils **veulent**
elle **veut**	elles **veulent**

Lecture: troisième partie

26. **Anne:** Où est-ce que tu vas pendant les grandes vacances?
27. **Jacques:** En été je vais à la plage avec ma famille pendant un mois. Et toi, où vas-tu?
28. **Anne:** Généralement, je ne vais nulle part. Je travaille dans un supermarché.
29. **Jacques:** Pourquoi est-ce que tu travailles tant?
30. **Anne:** Je travaille parce que j'ai besoin d'argent pour aller à l'université l'année prochaine.
31. **Jacques:** Samedi prochain, je vais au cinéma avec un groupe d'amis. Est-ce que tu veux venir avec nous?
32. **Anne:** Oui, d'accord. Quel film allons-nous voir?
33. **Jacques:** Je ne sais pas encore. A Paris il y a beaucoup de cinémas. Veux-tu que je t'appelle au téléphone la semaine prochaine?
34. **Anne:** D'accord. Voici mon numéro de téléphone.

Compréhension de la lecture:

Answer the following questions with a complete sentence in French.

17. Avec qui est-ce que Jacques va à la plage?
18. Où travaille Anne l'été?
19. Où est-ce qu'Anne va durant les vacances?
20. Pourquoi est-ce qu'elle travaille tant?
21. Est-ce qu'Anne veut aller au cinéma avec Jacques et ses amis?
22. Quand est-ce que Jacques va appeler Anne au téléphone?

Vocabulaire de la lecture:

Où est-ce que tu vas pendant les grandes vacances?
Where do you go during summer vacation?
Pourquoi est-ce que tu travailles **tant?** *Why do you work* **so much?**
J'ai besoin d'argent... *I need money...*
pour aller à l'université *to go to college*
Quand...? *When...?*
l'année prochaine *next year*
samedi prochain *next Saturday*
la semaine prochaine *next week*
Est-ce que tu veux venir avec nous? *Do you want to come with us?*
Je veux aller./Je ne veux pas aller. *I want to go. / I don't want to go.*
Quel film allons-nous voir? *What movie are we going to see?*
Je ne sais pas encore. *I still don't know.*
Veux-tu que je t'appelle? *Can I call you?*
D'accord. *Okay.*
Voici... *Here is...*

Note culturelle

1. The school day in France is divided into two sessions, one session in the morning from about 8:30 to 11:30 a.m. and an afternoon session from about 1:30 to 4:30 p.m. After classes French teenagers usually do homework from 4:30 to 6:00 p.m. While many high schools in the United States offer a wide variety of extracurricular activities, in France few schools do.

2. French teenagers do not usually entertain their friends at home. They meet their friends in the street, chat and walk in the neighborhood after school.

3. Jacques doesn't understand why Anne works so much. Why do many American teenagers work after school and during the summer? Few French teenagers work. Part time work does not exist.

Aim IV: *Each student will be able to ask a peer questions about his/her extracurricular activities after school, leisure activities during the weekend and the summer vacation, and be able to respond*

Conversation

Partners take turns asking one another the following questions about their leisure time activities.

1. a. Est-ce que tu participes à quelques activités à l'école après les classes?
   b. Quelles sont-elles?
   c. Si non, pourquoi?

2. Qu'est-ce que tu fais à la fin de la semaine?

3. Qu'est ce que tu fais après les classes?

4. a. Où est-ce que tu vas pendant les grandes vacances?
   b. Avec qui?

5. Quand est-ce que tu sors avec tes amis?

6. a. Est-ce que tu aimes aller au cinéma?
   b. Est-ce que tu veux aller au cinéma la semaine prochaine?
   c. Quel film est-ce que tu veux voir?

7. a. Est-ce que tu aimes danser?
   b. Est-ce que tu veux aller à la discothèque samedi prochain?
   c. Avec qui est-ce que tu veux y aller?

8. a. Est-ce qu'il y a beaucoup de cinémas près de ta maison?
   b. Est-ce que tu aimes mieux aller au cinéma ou aller à la discothèque?
   c. Pourquoi?

9. a. A quels sports est-ce que tu joues?
   b. Quel est ton sport favori?

Vocabulaire: près de *near* loin de *far* mieux *better*

Exercice écrit

Write the questions and answers of the **Conversation,** numbers 1 - 9.

Activité

A. Preparation:

Think about when you do your leisure activities and complete numbers 1 - 4f below. An activity can be placed in more than one category.

B. Reporting out:

Students form groups of three or four. Each person in the group (one at a time) states two or three activities he/she does at these times.

1. Après les classes à l'école je...
2. Après les classes je...
3. Pendant les grandes vacances je...
4. A la fin de la semaine:
    a. Le samedi matin je...
    b. Le samedi après-midi je...
    c. Le samedi soir je...
    d. Le dimanche matin je...
    e. Le dimanche après-midi je...
    f. Le dimanche soir je...

Pendant les grandes vacances je fais du vélo.

UNIT NINE

La nourriture et la boisson

Dans un restaurant

TOPIC

A. Food and drink B. In a restaurant

SITUATION

Interaction with individual peers and adults

FUNCTION

Introducing one friend to another
Expressing personal feelings and preferences about foods, drinks and meals
Suggesting a course of action, thanking, apologizing

PROFICIENCY

Can comprehend simple statements and questions and respond appropriately with possible need for repetition
Can read a menu to be able to order a meal

AIM I: Each student will be able to identify foods in several categories and be able to state if s/he likes or doesn't like each one: A. meat, fish and chicken, B. fruits and vegetables, C. other common foods and desserts, D. drinks

AIM II: Each student will be able to identify the three meals of a typical day in the United States, and be able to ask a peer and an adult what s/he eats and drinks for each of these meals

AIM III: Each student will be able to ask a peer and adult at what time s/he eats a particular meal

AIM IV: Each student will be able to ask a peer and an adult questions related to foods, drinks and meal-taking

AIM V: Each student will be able to identify the items of a table place setting and be able to indicate that one or more are missing from a particular one

AIM VI: Each student will be able to demonstrate his/her comprehension of two dialogues by answering questions

AIM VII: Given a menu of a French restaurant, each student will be able to order a meal, express satisfaction or dissatisfaction with the meal and ask for the bill

AIM VIII: Each student will be able to state numbers 100 - 2,000 and review numbers below 100 in order to be able to read the price of foods on a French menu

Aim IA: *Each student will be able to identify the following foods in the category of meat, fish and chicken and be able to state if s/he likes or doesn't like each one*

Exercice oral 1

La viande, le poisson et la volaille

Exercice oral 2

1. **Thomas:** Est-ce que tu aimes le poulet?
   Hélène: Oui, j'aime le poulet.

2. **Laure:** Est-ce que vous aimez le bifteck?
   Mme Sanlis: Non, je n'aime pas le bifteck.

Conversation 1

1. Est-ce que tu aimes le poisson?
2. Est-ce que tu aimes le poulet?
3. Est-ce que tu aimes le rosbif?
4. Est-ce que tu aimes le jambon?
5. Est-ce que tu aimes le bifteck?
6. Est-ce que vous aimez les hamburgers?
7. Est-ce que vous aimez les côtelettes de porc?
8. Est-ce que vous aimez la saucisse chaude?
9. Est-ce que vous aimez le veau?
10. Est-ce que vous aimez le mouton?

Exercice oral 3

1. **Anne:** Qu'est-ce que tu aimes mieux, la viande ou le poulet?
   Paul: J'aime mieux le poulet.
2. **Jean:** Qu'est-ce vous aimez mieux, le jambon ou les hamburgers?
   M. Courlet: J'aime mieux le jambon.

Conversation 2

1. Qu'est-ce que tu aimes mieux, le bifteck ou la saucisse chaude?
2. Qu'est-ce que tu aimes mieux, la côtelette de porc ou le rosbif?
3. Qu'est -ce que tu aimes mieux, le poulet ou le mouton?
4. Qu'est-ce que tu aimes mieux, le veau ou les hamburgers?
5. Qu'est-ce que vous aimez mieux, le jambon ou le poisson?
6. Qu'est-ce que vous aimez mieux, le poulet rôti ou le poulet en sauce?
7. Qu'est-ce que vous aimez mieux le bifteck bien cuit ou le bifteck saignant?
8. Qu'est-ce que vous aimez mieux, le veau rôti ou le veau en sauce?

Exercice écrit

Write and answer the questions of the **Conversation 1,** numbers 1 - 10 and the **Conversation 2,** numbers 5 - 8.

Vocabulaire

La viande ***meat***

le bifteck *steak*
le porc *pork*
la côtelette de porc
pork chop
le mouton *lamb*
le hamburger *hamburger*
le jambon *ham*
la saucisse *sausage*
le rosbif *roast beef*
le veau *veal*

le poisson *fish*

le poulet *chicken*

rôti *roasted*
bien cuit *well done*
frit *fried*
saignant *rare*
en sauce *in a sauce*
chaud(e) *hot*

Est-ce que tu aimes...?/ Est-ce que vous aimez...? *Do you like ...?*
J'aime... *I like...;* Je n'aime pas... *I don't like....*
Qu'est-ce que tu aimes mieux? / Qu'est-ce que vous aimez mieux?
What do you like better?
J'aime mieux... *I like ...better.*
Je n'aime ni...ni... *I don't like either... or...*

Résumé

Compréhension:

You will hear five foods of the group comprising meat, fish and chicken. After the second repetition, choose the picture, by letter, which corresponds to what you hear.

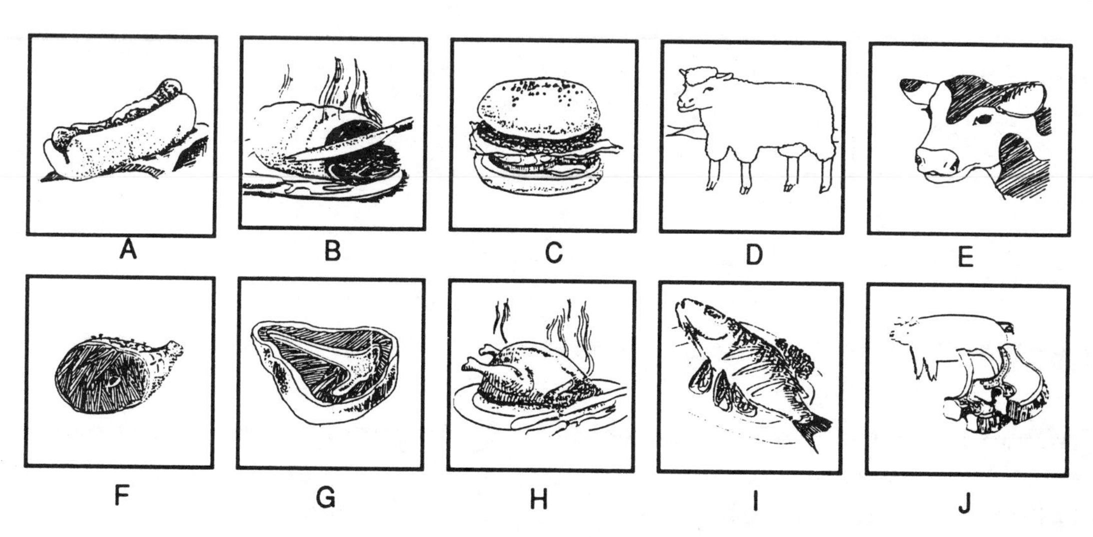

Conversation

Each partner asks the other if he/she likes to eat the foods represented by the pictures of the **compréhension.** Partners take turns asking the questions. ***Examples:***

1. **Jules:** Est-ce que tu aimes manger le jambon?
   Marie: Oui, j'aime manger le jambon.

2. **Julie:** Est-ce que tu aimes manger le poulet?
   Jean: Non, je n'aime pas manger le poulet.

Aim IB: *Each student will be able to identify the following foods in the category of fruits and vegetables and be able to state if he / she likes or doesn't like each one*

Exercice oral 1

Les fruits et les légumes

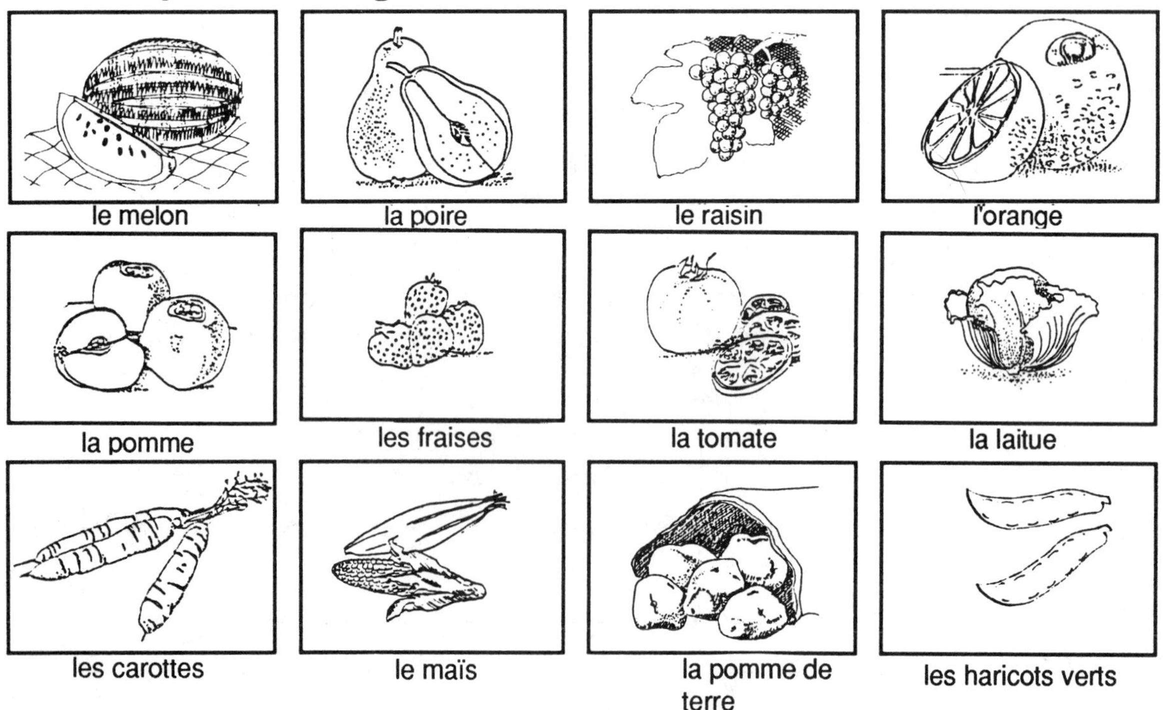

Exercice oral 2

1. **Antoine:** Qu'est-ce que tu préfères, la poire ou la pomme?
   Thérèse: Je préfère la pomme.

2. **Yvonne:** Qu'est-ce que vous préférez, la salade ou la tomate?
   M. Talbot: Je préfère la salade.

Conversation 1

1. Est-ce que tu aimes la pomme?
2. Est-ce que tu aimes les poires?
3. Est-ce que tu aimes les oranges?
4. Est-ce que tu aimes le melon?
5. Est-ce que tu aimes les fraises?
6. Est-ce que tu aimes le raisin?
7. Est-ce que vous aimez les pommes de terre?
8. Est-ce que vous aimez les tomates?
9. Est-ce que vous aimez les carottes?
10. Est-ce que vous aimez la salade?
11. Est-ce que vous aimez le maïs?
12. Est-ce que vous aimez les haricots verts?

Conversation 2

1. Qu'est-ce que tu préfères, le melon ou l'orange?
2. Qu'est-ce que tu préfères, le raisin ou les fraises?
3. Qu'est-ce que tu préfères, la poire ou la pomme?
4. Qu'est-ce que vous préférez, la salade ou les carottes?
5. Qu'est-ce que vous préférez, le maïs ou la tomate?
6. Qu'est-ce que vous préférez, la pomme de terre ou les haricots verts?

Exercice écrit

1. Write and answer the questions of the **Conversation 1,** numbers 1 - 12 and **Conversation 2** numbers 2, 4, and 6.

2. a. Quel est ton fruit favori?/ Quel est votre fruit favori?
   b. Quels sont tes fruits favoris?/ Quels sont vos fruits favoris?
   c. Quel est ton légume favori?/ Quel est votre légume favori?

Vocabulaire

Les fruits	***fruits***
la fraise	*strawberry*
le melon	*melon*
l'orange	*orange*
la poire	*pear*
la pomme	*apple*
le raisin	*grape*

Les légumes	***vegetables***
la carotte	*carrot*
les haricots verts	*green beans*
le maïs	*corn*
la pomme de terre	*potato*
la laitue	*lettuce*
la tomate	*tomato*

Qu'est-ce que tu **préfères**?/ Qu'est-ce que vous préférez?
what do you prefer?
Je **préfère**... *I prefer...*

Résumé

Compréhension:

You will hear five foods of the group comprising fruits and vegetables. After the second repetition, choose the picture, by letter, which corresponds to what you hear.

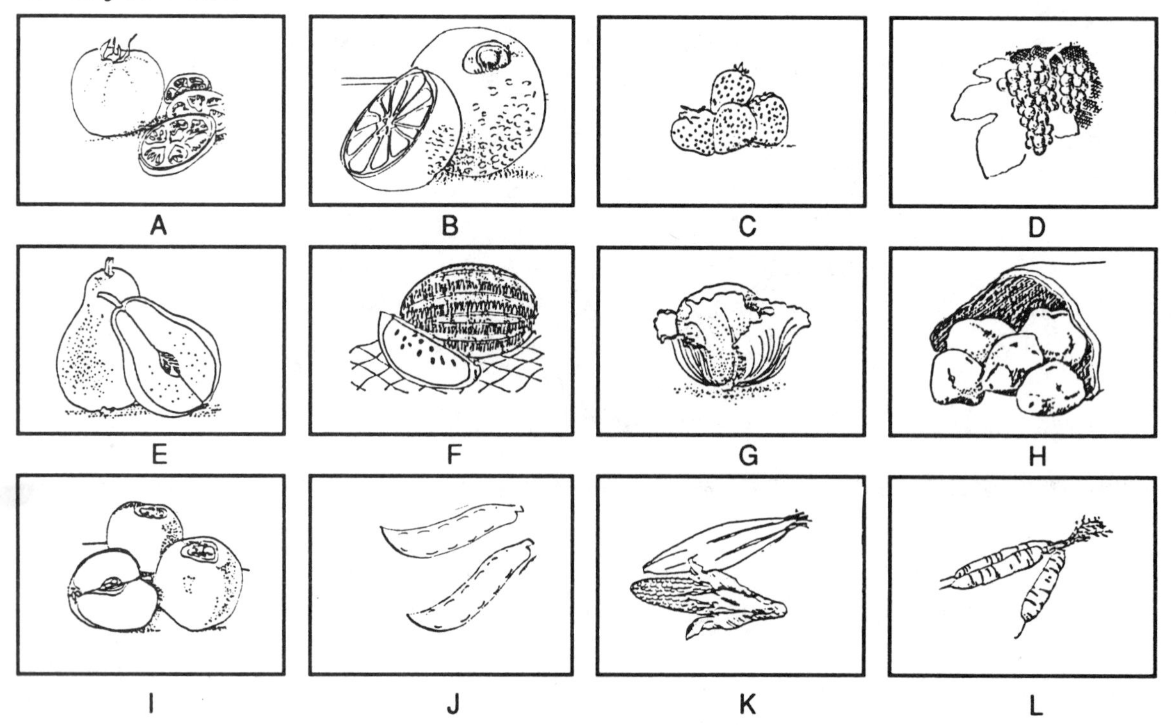

Aim IC: *Each student will be able to identify the following foods in the categories of other common foods and desserts*

Exercice oral 1

Autres nourritures courantes

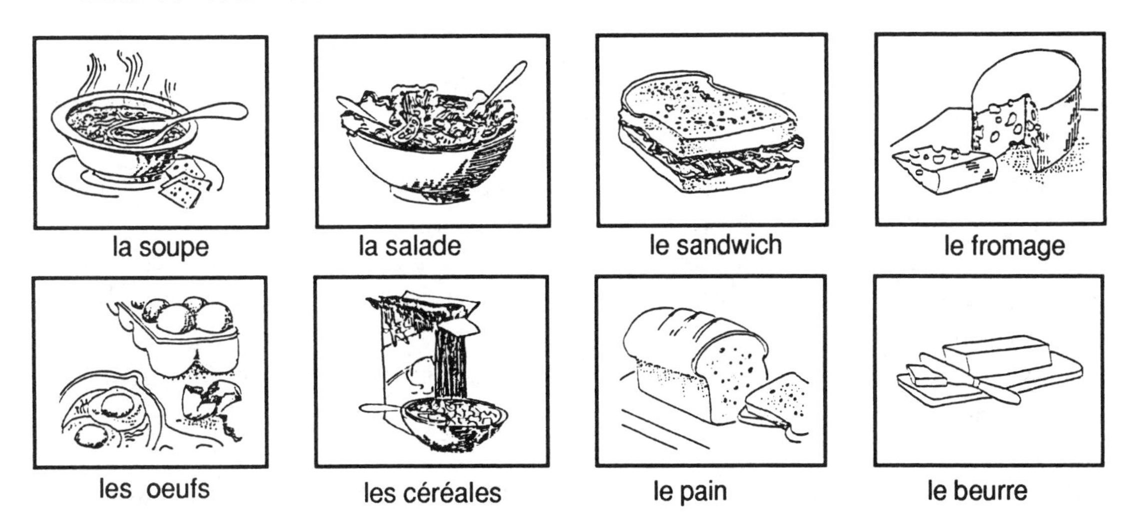

la soupe — la salade — le sandwich — le fromage

les oeufs — les céréales — le pain — le beurre

Exercice oral 2

Les desserts

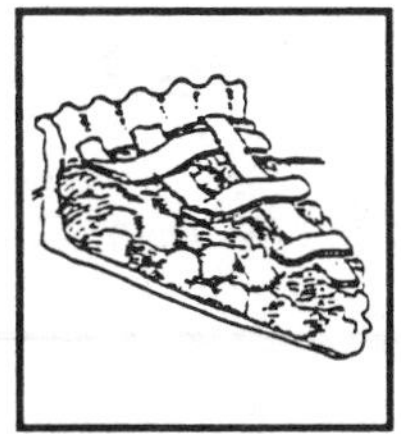

la tarte

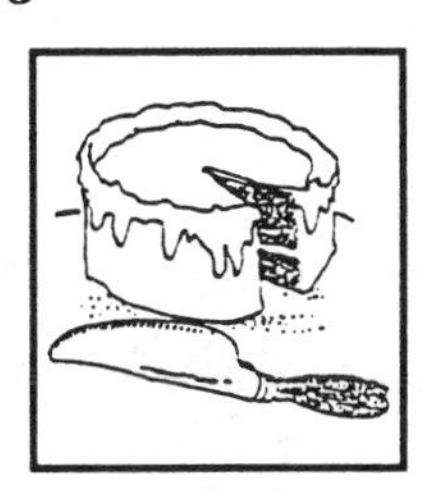

le gâteau

les fruits

la glace

le pudding

Conversation 1

1. Est-ce que tu aimes les céréales?
2. Est-ce que tu aimes la salade?
3. Est-ce que tu aimes la soupe aux légumes?
7. Est-ce que vous aimez le fromage?
8. Est-ce que vous aimez le pudding?
9. Est-ce que vous aimez le gâteau?

4. Est-ce que tu aimes le pain avec du beurre?

5. Est-ce que tu aimes la tarte?

6. Est-ce que tu aimes les oeufs?

10. Est-ce que vous aimez le sandwich au jambon?

11. Est-ce que vous aimez la glace?

12. Est-ce que vous aimez les fruits?

Conversation 2

1. Qu'est-ce que tu aimes mieux, la soupe de poulet ou la soupe de poisson?
2. Qu'est-ce que tu aimes mieux, la glace au chocolat ou à la vanille?
3. Qu'est-ce que tu aimes mieux, la glace à la fraise ou le pudding au chocolat?
4. Qu'est-ce que tu aimes mieux, le sandwich au fromage ou le sandwich au thon?
5. Qu'est-ce que vous aimez mieux, les céréales ou les oeufs sur le plat?
6. Qu'est-ce que vous aimez mieux, les fruits ou la tarte aux pommes?
7. Qu'est-ce que vous aimez mieux, les frites ou la salade?
8. Qu'est-ce que vous aimez mieux, le pain avec du beurre ou le pain avec de la confiture?

Exercice écrit

1. Write and answer questions of the **Conversation 2.**
2. a. Quelle est ta nourriture favorite?/ Quelle est votre nourriture favorite?
   b. Quelle est ta soupe favorite?/ Quelle est votre soupe favorite?
   c. Quel est ton dessert favori?/ Quel est votre dessert favori?

Vocabulaire

autres nourritures courantes *other common foods*

le beurre *butter*
les céréales *cereal*
la salade *salad*
le fromage *cheese*
la glace *ice cream*
les frites *french fries*
le pain *bread*
les oeufs *eggs*
la soupe *soup*
les desserts *desserts*
la tarte *pie*
les oeufs sur le plat *fried eggs*
le thon *tunafish*
le sandwich *sandwich*
la confiture *jam*
le gâteau *cake*
le pudding *pudding*

Résumé

Compréhension:

You will hear five foods of the group comprising other common foods and desserts. After the second repetition, choose the picture, by letter, which corresponds to what you hear.

Conversation:

Each partner asks the other if he/she likes to eat the foods represented by pictures M - X above. Partners take turns asking the questions.

Examples:

1. **Jean:** Est-ce que tu aimes les fruits?
   Rachelle: Oui, j'aime les fruits.

2. **Anne:** Est-ce que tu aimes le pain?
   Jacques: Non, je n'aime pas le pain.

Aim ID: *Each student will be able to identify the following drinks and be able to state if s/he likes or doesn't like each drink*

Exercice oral

Les boissons

l'eau

le lait

le jus d'orange

le thé

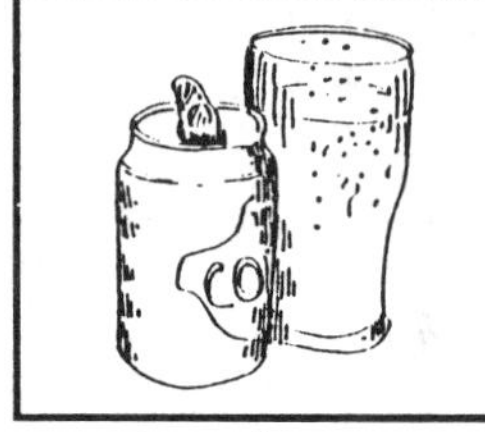
le soda

le chocolat chaud

le café

Conversation 1

1. Est-ce que tu aimes le café?
2. Est-ce que tu aimes le lait?
3. Est-ce que tu aimes le soda?
4. Est-ce que tu aimes l'eau?
5. Est-ce que vous aimez le chocolat chaud?
6. Est-ce que vous aimez le thé?
7. Est-ce que vous aimez le jus d'orange?

Conversation 2

1. Qu'est-ce que tu préfères, le lait ou l'eau?
2. Qu'est-ce que tu préfères, le soda ou le jus d'orange?
3. Qu'est-ce que tu préfères, le chocolat chaud ou le thé?
4. Qu'est-ce que vous préférez, le thé ou le café?
5. Qu'est-ce que vous préférez, le jus de tomate ou le jus de pomme?
6. Qu'est-ce que vous préférez, l'eau ou le soda?

Exercice écrit

1. Write and answer the questions of the **Conversation 1,** numbers 1 - 7 and the **Conversation 2,** numbers 1 - 6.

2. Quelle est ta boisson favorite?/ Quelle est votre boisson favorite?

Vocabulaire

Les boissons ***drinks***

l'eau *water*
le café *coffee*
le chocolat chaud
hot chocolate
le jus d'orange
orange juice
le lait *milk*
le soda *soda*
le thé *tea*

Résumé

Compréhension:

You will hear the names of four drinks. After the second repetition, choose the picture, by letter, which corresponds to what you hear.

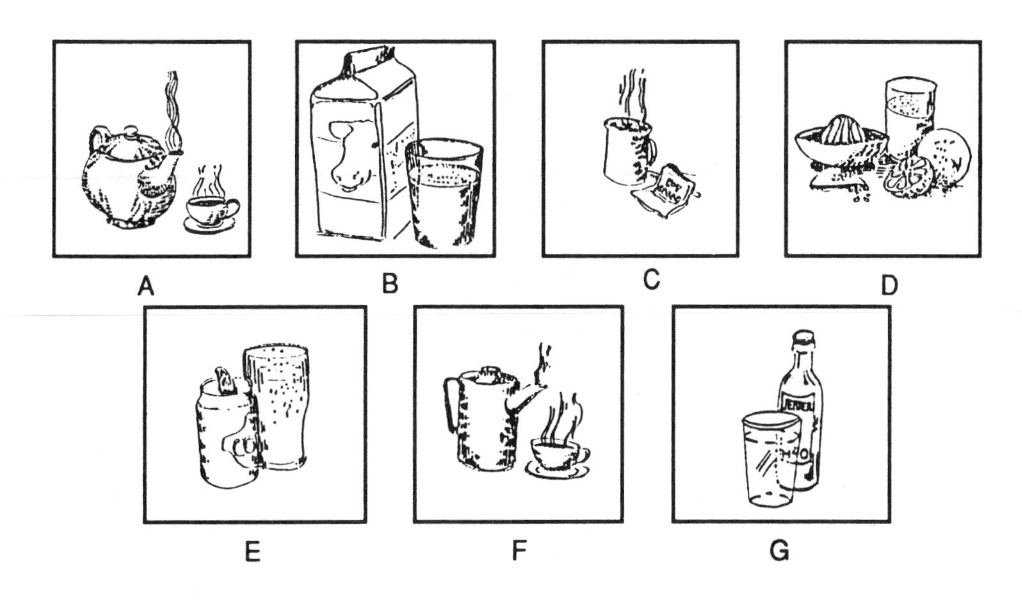

Conversation:

Each partner asks the other if he/she likes to drink the beverage represented by the pictures of the **Compréhension.** Partners take turns asking the questions. ***Examples:***

1. **Laure:** Est-ce que tu aimes le lait?
   Hélène: Oui, j'aime le lait.

2. **Jean:** Est-ce que tu aimes le thé?
   Anne: Non, je n'aime pas le thé.

Aim II: *Each student will be able to identify the three meals of a typical day in the United States*

Each student will be able to ask a peer and an adult what s/he eats and drinks for each meal of the day

Exercice oral 1

Les trois repas de la journée aux Etats-Unis

le petit déjeuner

le déjeuner

le dîner

Exercice oral 2

1. **Marie:** Qu'est-ce que tu manges pour le petit déjeuner?
   Thomas: Pour le petit déjeuner, je mange des céréales et du pain avec du beurre.
   Marie: Et qu'est-ce que tu bois?
   Thomas: Je bois du lait ou du chocolat chaud.

2. **Marie:** Qu'est-ce que tu manges pour le déjeuner?
   Thomas: Pour le déjeuner, je mange une pizza ou un hamburger.
   Marie: Et qu'est-ce que tu bois?
   Thomas: Je bois un soda.

3. **Marie:** Qu'est-ce que tu manges pour le dîner?
   Thomas: Pour le dîner, je mange un bifteck ou du poulet avec des frites et de la salade.
   Marie: Et qu'est-ce que tu bois?
   Thomas: Je bois de l'eau ou un soda.
   Marie: Et pour le dessert?
   Thomas: Un morceau de gâteau.

4. **Jean:** Qu'est-ce que vous mangez pour le petit déjeuner?
   Mlle Plon: Pour le petit déjeuner, je mange des oeufs sur le plat, du jambon et du pain.
   Jean: Et qu'est-ce que vous buvez?
   Mlle Plon: Je bois du jus d'orange et du café.

5. **Jean:** Qu'est-ce que vous mangez pour le déjeuner?
   Mlle Plon: Pour le déjeuner, je mange une saucisse chaude.
   Jean: Et qu'est-ce que vous buvez?
   Mlle Plon: Je bois du thé.

6. **Jean:** Qu'est-ce que vous mangez pour le dîner?
   Mlle Plon: Pour le dîner, je mange du poisson ou de la viande en sauce.
   Jean: Et qu'est-ce que vous buvez?
   Mlle Plon: Je bois du thé.
   Jean: Et pour le dessert?
   Mlle Plon: Un morceau de gâteau.

Conversation

Use different foods and drinks in your answers for numbers 1 - 3 and numbers 4 - 6.

1a. Qu'est-ce que tu manges pour le petit déjeuner?
 b. Et qu'est-ce que tu bois?

2a. Qu'est-ce que tu manges pour le déjeuner?
 b. Et qu'est-ce que tu bois?

3a. Qu'est-ce que tu manges pour le dîner?
 b. Et qu'est-ce que tu bois?

4a. Qu'est-ce que vous mangez pour le petit déjeuner?
 b. Et qu'est-ce que vous buvez?

5a. Qu'est-ce que vous mangez pour le déjeuner?
 b. Et qu'est-ce que vous buvez?

6a. Qu'est-ce que vous mangez pour le dîner?
 b. Et qu'est-ce que vous buvez?
 c. Et qu'est-ce que vous mangez pour le dessert?

Exercice écrit

Write and answer the questions of the **Conversation.**

Vocabulaire

Les trois repas de la journée ***The three meals of the day***

le petit déjeuner *breakfast*
le déjeuner *lunch*
le dîner *supper*

Qu'est-ce que tu manges pour ...?/Qu'est-ce que vous mangez pour ...?
What do you eat for ...?
Pour...je mange *For...I eat....*
Pour le petit déjeuner je ne mange rien.
For breakfast I don't eat anything.
Qu'est-ce que tu bois?/
Qu'est-ce que vous buvez?
What do you drink?
boire ***to drink*** *(irregular)*

Je **bois**	nous **buvons**
tu **bois**	vous **buvez**
il/elle **boit**	ils/elles **boivent**

Je bois... *I drink*
le dessert *for dessert*
un morceau *a piece of...*
la pizza *pizza*

Activité

Le menu idéal

1. **Preparation:**

You have invited a French-speaking friend to spend an entire day with you. Plan *three complete meals* consisting of your favorite foods and drinks to share with him/her. Draw or bring pictures from magazines of the foods and drinks you plan to serve. Organize your pictures by meal. Label the name of each meal but not the individual foods or drinks.

2. **Reporting out:**

Class members divide themselves into groups of four. Each member of the group first tells about what s/he and his/her guest eat for breakfast, lunch and supper, while pointing to the appropriate pictures. ***Example:***

a. Pour le petit déjeuner nous mangeons_______ et nous buvons________.
b. Pour le déjeuner nous mangeons_______ et nous buvons________.
c. Pour le dîner nous mangeons_______ et nous buvons________
et pour le dessert nous mangeons_________.

Aim III: *Each student will be able to ask a peer and an adult at what time s/he eats a particular meal*

Exercice oral

1. **Thérèse:** A quelle heure est-ce que tu prends ton petit déjeuner?
   Alfred: Je prends mon petit déjeuner à sept heures et demie.

2. **Georges:** A quelle heure est-ce que tu prends ton déjeuner?
   Jean: Je prends mon déjeuner à une heure et quart.

3. **Hélène:** A quelle heure est-ce que tu prends ton dîner?
   Raoul: Je prends mon dîner à six heures et demie.

4. **Julie:** A quelle heure est-ce que vous prenez votre petit déjeuner?
   Mme Colin: Je prends mon petit déjeuner à huit heures moins le quart.

5. **Antoine:** A quelle heure est-ce que vous prenez votre déjeuner?
   Mlle Fierte: Je prends mon déjeuner à midi et demi.

6. **M. Sanyo:** A quelle heure est-ce que vous prenez votre dîner?
   Mme Josselin: Je prends mon dîner à sept heures.

Conversation

1. A quelle heure est-ce que tu prends le petit déjeuner?
2. A quelle heure est-ce que tu prends le déjeuner?
3. A quelle heure est-ce que tu prends le dîner?
4. A quelle heure est-ce que vous prenez le petit déjeuner?
5. A quelle heure est-ce que vous prenez le déjeuner?
6. A quelle heure est-ce que vous prenez le dîner?

Exercice écrit

1. Write the questions and the answers of the **Conversation,** numbers 1-6.
2. Write the following hours in French:

a. at 9:30	e. at 4:45	i. at 12:30
b. at 2:10	f. at 8:14	j. at 3:13
c. at 10:15	g. at 1:25	k. at 11:20
d. at 3:55	h. at 6:40	l. at 1:35

Vocabulaire

A quelle heure est-ce que (tu prends/ vous prenez) le petit déjeuner?
At what time do you eat breakfast?
A quelle heure est-ce que (tu prends/ vous prenez) le déjeuner?
At what time do you eat lunch?
A quelle heure est-ce que (tu prends/ vous prenez) le dîner?
At what time do you eat supper?
Je prends...à une heure. *I eat...at one.*
Je prends...à... *I eat...at....*
prendre ***to take (a meal)***

je prends	nous **prenons**
tu prends	vous **prenez**
il/elle prend	ils/elles **prennent**

Aim IV: *Each student will be able to ask a peer and an adult questions related to foods, drinks and meal-taking*

Exercice oral

1a. **Raoul:** Est-ce que tu as faim?
Hélène: Oui, j'ai très faim.

1b. **Raoul:** Qu'est-ce que tu manges quand tu as faim?
Hélène: Quand j'ai faim, je mange un sandwich ou une pizza.

2a. **Rose:** Est-ce que vous avez soif?
M. Satin: Oui, j'ai très soif.

2b. **Rose:** Qu'est-ce que vous buvez quand vous avez soif?
M. Satin: Quand j'ai soif, je bois de l'eau ou un soda.

1c. **Raoul:** Avec qui est-ce que tu prends le déjeuner?
Hélène: Je prends le déjeuner avec mon amie Corine.

1d. **Raoul:** Où est-ce que tu prends le déjeuner?
Hélène: Je prends le déjeuner dans la cafétéria de l'école.

2c. **Rose:** Avec qui est-ce que vous prenez le petit déjeuner?
M. Satin: Je prends le petit déjeuner seul.

2d. **Rose:** Où est-ce que vous prenez le petit déjeuner?
M. Satin: Quelquefois, je prends le petit déjeuner à la cafétéria du travail et quelquefois à la maison.

Conversation

1. Est-ce que tu as faim?
2. Qu'est-ce que tu manges quand tu as faim?
3. Avec qui est-ce que tu prends le petit déjeuner?
4. Avec qui est-ce que tu prends le dîner?
5. Où est-ce que tu prends le déjeuner?
6. Est-ce que vous avez soif?
7. Qu'est-ce que vous buvez quand vous avez soif?
8. Avec qui est-ce que vous prenez le déjeuner?
9. Avec qui est-ce que vous prenez le dîner?
10. Où est-ce que vous prenez le petit déjeuner?

Exercice écrit

Write and answer the questions of the **Conversation,** numbers 1 - 10.

Aim VIA: ***Each student will be able to read the dialogue*** "L'heure de manger" ***and demonstrate comprehension by answering a series of true-false questions***

Lecture: première partie

C'est jeudi après-midi. Jacques rencontre son amie Anne à la bibliothèque de l'école à Paris. Il l'invite au restaurant où il va manger avec Michel.

1. **Jacques:** Bonjour, Anne. Comment vas-tu? Cela fait longtemps que je ne t'ai pas vue.
2. **Anne:** Ça va, j'ai un examen d'histoire aujourd'hui à trois heures. Je suis fatiguée d'étudier. A propos, quelle heure est-il?
3. **Jacques:** Je ne sais pas. Je n'ai pas ma montre.
4. **Un autre jeune:** Il est midi.
5. **Anne:** Merci.
6. **Jacques:** C'est l'heure de manger. Mon ami Michel et moi nous allons manger dans un restaurant près de l'école. Pourquoi est-ce que tu ne manges pas avec nous?
7. **Anne:** D'accord, j'aimerais bien. On dit que la nourriture est bonne.
8. **Jacques:** Elle est excellente. Quelquefois, je mange ici avec des amis.

Compréhension de lecture

If the statement is true, state *vrai;* if the statement is false, state *faux* and **correct the bold part.**

1. Jacques rencontre Anne à **la cafétéria** de l'école.
2. Cela fait **trois jours** que Jacques n'a pas vu Anne.
3. Anne a un examen de **mathématiques.**
4. Jacques ne sait pas l'heure parce qu'**il n'a pas sa montre aujourd'hui.**
5. Jacques et Michel vont manger dans un restaurant **loin de** l'école.

Vocabulaire de la lecture:

Il **l'**invite... *He invites* **her**

1. Cela fait **longtemps** que je ne t'ai pas vu/vue.
   I haven't seen you for a ***long time.***
2. Je suis fatigué(e) de.... *I'm tired of....*
   à propos *by the way2*

3. Je ne sais pas *I don't know.*
   savoir *to know:* Je **sais**... tu **sais**... il/elle **sait**...
   nous savons... vous savez... ils/elles savent...
   la montre *wrist watch*
6. C'est l'heure de... *It's time to...*
   près de *near*
   loin de *far from*
7. J'aimerais bien *I would like to.*
   On dit que... *They say* ***that***

Functions of Language:

We use language to carry out many functions in the process of communication. Answer the following questions in French to review some of these frequently used phrases which appear in the **première partie.**

How would you say:

1. to a friend, that you haven't seen him/her in a long time?
2. that you are tired of doing a particular activity?
   a. I'm tired of studying.
   b. I'm tired of working.
3. that you don't know something?
4. that it's time to do a certain activity?
   a. It's time to enter.
   b. It's time to eat.
   c. It's time to leave.
5. that you accept an invitation given to you?
   a. Okay.
   b. I would like to.

Lecture: deuxième partie

Jacques et Anne vont au restaurant à pied où ils rencontrent Michel qui attend à la porte.

9. **Jacques:** Bonjour, Michel. Je te présente mon amie Anne.
10. **Michel:** Bonjour, Anne.
11. **Anne:** Enchantée.
12. **Jacques:** Entrons au restaurant.
13. **Michel:** J'ai très faim.
14. **Anne:** Moi aussi.

(Les trois jeunes gens entrent au restaurant et s'asseyent à une table.)

15. **Anne:** Où sont les toilettes pour dames?
16. **Jacques:** C'est au fond, à droite.
17. **Anne:** Excusez-moi, s'il vous plaît.
18. **Michel:** Et les toilettes pour hommes? Où sont-elles?
19. **Jacques:** Aussi au fond, à gauche.
20. **Michel:** Excusez-moi, s'il vous plaît.

(Cinq minutes après, Anne et Michel reviennent à la table.)

Compréhension de lecture: vrai ou faux

If the statement is true, state *vrai:* if the statement is false, state *faux* and **correct the bold part.**

6. Jacques et Anne vont au restaurant **en métro.**
7. Michel attend **à la porte** du restaurant.
8. **Jacques** présente Anne à Michel.
9. Michel et Anne ont très **soif.**
10. Les toilettes pour dames sont au fond **à gauche.**

Vocabulaire de la lecture:

...**qui** attend à la porte... ***who** is waiting at the door*

9. Je te présente mon ami(e)
   I want to introduce you to my friend...
11. Enchanté(e). *Pleased to meet you. / It's a pleasure.*
12. Entrons... *Let's enter, go into*
    Ils s'asseyent à une table *They sit down at a table.*
14. Moi aussi. *Me too.*
15. les toilettes *the bathroom:*
    Où sont les toilettes? *Where is the bathroom?*
    pour dames *women's* pour hommes *men's*
16. C'est au fond ... *It's in the back ...*
    à droite *on the right*
17. Excusez-moi, s'il vous plaît. *Excuse me. (Used to excuse yourself when leaving the company of others)*
19. à gauche *on the left*
20. revenir *to return:* ils reviennent

Functions of Language:

In French how would you:

6. a. introduce one friend to another?
   b. indicate that you are pleased to meet the other person?
   c. respond if you were the other person ("I'm delighted.")?
7. suggest a course of action to one or more people?
   a. Let's go into the restaurant.
   b. Let's eat.
   c. Let's leave.
8. find out where someone or something is located?
   a. Where is the restaurant?
   b. Where is the bathroom?
   c. Where is Mary?
9. indicate that something is located on the left? on the right?
10. excuse yourself when in the company of others?

Compréhension de lecture:

1. Quand est-ce que Jacques et Anne se rencontrent?
2. A quelle heure est l'examen d'Anne?
3. Pourquoi est-ce qu'Anne ne sait pas l'heure qu'il est?

Jacques et Anne mangent au restaurant.

4. Quelle heure est-il? Est-ce que c'est l'heure de manger?
5. Où est le restaurant?
6. Comment est la nourriture?
7. Qui attend à la porte du restaurant?
8. Qui a très faim?
9. Où sont les toilettes pour dames?
10. Où sont les toilettes pour hommes?

Aim VIB: *Each student will be able to read the dialogue* "Dans un restaurant" *and demonstrate comprehension by answering a series of true / false questions*

Lecture: première partie

Il est midi et demi. Les trois jeunes gens, Jacques, Anne et Michel sont assis dans un restaurant à Paris. Jacques appelle le serveur.

1. **Jacques:** Garçon! Le menu, s'il vous plaît.
   (Le garçon apporte le menu et ils le regardent pendant cinq minutes.)
2. **Jacques:** Garçon! Il me manque une cuillère.
3. **Le serveur:** Je suis navré. La voici. Qu'est-ce que vous désirez manger pour commencer?
4. **Anne:** Une assiette de crudités, s'il vous plaît.
5. **Michel:** Une assiette de charcuterie, s'il vous plaît.
6. **Le serveur:** Et vous, monsieur?
7. **Jacques:** Apportez-moi le pâté maison, s'il vous plaît. C'est mon pâté favori.
8. **Le serveur:** Et ensuite?
9. **Anne:** Une côtelette de porc s'il vous plaît.
10. **Michel:** J'aimerais de la choucroute.
11. **Jacques:** Et pour moi, du poulet rôti avec des frites.
12. **Le serveur:** Qu'est-ce que vous désirez boire?
13. **Anne:** De l'eau minérale gazeuse s'il vous plaît.
14. **Michel:** Un Orangina.
15. **Le serveur:** Et vous monsieur, que désirez-vous boire?
16. **Jacques:** Apportez-moi de l'eau minérale non gazeuse, s'il vous plaît.

Compréhension de lecture:

If the statement is true, state *vrai;* if the statement is false, state *faux,* and **correct the bold part.**

1. Les trois jeunes gens regardent le menu pendant **une demi-heure.**
2. Il manque **un couteau** à Jacques.
3. Pour commencer Anne désire **une assiette de charcuterie.**
4. Le pâté favori de Jacques, c'est **le pâté maison.**
5. Ensuite, Michel désire **l'assiette de crudités.**
6. Anne veut boire de **l'eau minérale non gazeuse.**

Vocabulaire

avant *before;* après *after*
ensuite *then* pour commencer *to start* pour finir *to finish*
ils sont assis *they are seated*
il apporte la carte *he brings the menu*
apporter *to bring:* J'apporte, tu apportes, il/elle apporte
ils **le** regardent *they look at **it:*** **le** menu
pendant quelques minutes *for a few minutes*
3. Je suis navré. *I'm sorry.*
Le voilà. *Here it is.* (**le** couteau)
La voilà. *Here it is.* (**la** cuillère)
désirer *to wish, to desire*
Qu'est-ce que vous désirez manger?
What do you wish to eat?
pour commencer *to begin*
d'abord *first*
ensuite *then*

Note: The French generally eat their main meal at lunch time, usually from 12:30 to 2:30 p.m. It consists of:

1. *La soupe du jour* and/or *les hors-d'oeuvre* such as *une assiette de crudités* (tomatoes, cucumbers, various greens, etc. with oil, vinegar and mustard dressing.
2. *Une assiette de charcuterie* (various slices of sausages, salami, ham, etc...or pâté).
3. Then they have a dish of meat or fish with vegetables or potatoes, cheese and dessert.

The French eat every dish separately. They do not put everything together. Specific dishes are from various regions, such as *la choucroute* , which is saurkraut cooked in wine or beer with smoked pork, various sausages, potatoes and spices. This dish is from Alsace.

7. Apportez-moi ... *Bring me ...*
11. le riz *rice*
le poulet avec des frites *chicken with french fries*
pour moi *for me*
12. Qu'est-ce que vous désirez boire?
What do you wish to drink?
13. de l'eau minérale gazeuse *carbonated bottled water*
14. Un orangina. *A soda.*
16. de l'eau minérale non gazeuse *non-corbonated bottled water*

Lecture: deuxième partie

(Le serveur apporte le pain et les boissons)

17. **Michel:** Passez-moi le pain s'il vous plaît.
18. **Anne:** Le voici.
19. **Michel:** Merci.
20. **Jacques:** Bon appétit.
21. **Michel et Anne:** Merci.
(Le serveur apporte le deuxième plat.)
22. **Jacques:** Comment est la nourriture?
23. **Michel:** La nourriture est délicieuse.
Je l'aime beaucoup.
24. **Anne:** Je l'aime beaucoup aussi.
25. **Jacques:** Garçon! Qu'est-ce qu'il y a pour le dessert?
26. **Le serveur:** Il y a de la glace, des gâteaux ou des fruits.
27. **Anne:** Une glace au chocolat.
28. **Michel:** Un morceau de tarte aux fraises.
29. **Jacques:** Une glace au café..
30. **Le serveur:** Vous désirez du café?
31. **Anne, Michel et Jacques:** Non, merci.
32. **Jacques:** Apportez-moi l'addition, s'il
vous plaît.
33. **Le serveur:** Oui, monsieur.
34. **Anne:** Après ce repas excellent, je suis
prête à passer mon examen.
*(Les trois jeunes gens payent, laissent un
pourboire et sortent du restaurant).*

Compréhension de lecture:

If the statement is true, state *vrai;* if the statement is false, state *faux* and **correct the bold part.**

7. Le serveur apporte le pain et les boissons **après** les hors-d'oeuvre.
8. Jacques, Anne et Michel aiment **beaucoup** la nourriture.
9. Pour le dessert, Michel veut de **la glace.**
10. Jacques et Michel **boivent du café.**
11. **Anne** demande l'addition.
12. Ils laissent **un pourboire.**

Vocabulaire de la lecture:

17. Passer *to pass:* Passez-moi *Pass me...*
20. Bon appétit! *Bon appétit*
22. Comment est la nourriture? *How is the food?*
23. Je l'aime beaucoup. *I love it.* Elle est délicieuse. *It's delicious.*
25. Qu'est-ce qu'il y a pour le dessert? *What is there for dessert?*
29. café au lait *coffee with milk*
32. l'addition *the bill*

Je suis prêt(e) *I'm ready...*
payer *to pay*
laisser un pourboire *to leave a tip*
sortir de.. *to leave...*
demander *to ask for:* Je demande *I ask*

Functions of Language:

1. What would you say to get a waiter's attention?
2. What are four ways to order something in a restaurant?
3. What are three ways to express satisfaction with a meal?
4. What would you say to indicate that you're missing a part of your place setting?
5. How would you say "Hearty appetite!"

Note culturelle

The dialogue that takes place in a restaurant in Paris **(Lecture: deuxième partie)** reveals some differences between French and American culture with regard to eating customs. Can you answer the following questions?

1. At what time do the French eat their principal meal of the day? and the Americans?
2. How many main dishes are served at this principal French meal? How does this meal differ from the American lunch?
3. What is always brought to the table without request?
4. What are some typical French main dishes?
5. What are some typical French desserts?

Aim VII: *Given a menu of a French restaurant, each student will be able to order a meal, express satisfaction or dissatisfaction with the meal and ask for the bill*

Activité A

The class is divided into groups of four or five. One student plays the role of the waiter and the others are the diners for the main meal of the day. You are in a restaurant in Paris called *La Brasserie.*

a. Call the waiter (get his attention) and ask for a menu.
(The waiter brings the menu.)
b. Each diner states that one part of his place setting is missing.
(The waiter brings the missing item to each diner.)
c. The waiter asks what each diner wants to eat for the first and second course and each diner states his order from the menu given.
d. The waiter asks what each diner wishes to drink and each diner states his order.
(The waiter leaves to place his orders with the kitchen and returns with the bread and drinks.)
e. Each diner makes some "small talk" while waiting for the meal. One can comment about the weather, about how many people (few or many) there are in the restaurant or about its size (large or small) or beauty.
f. The waiter serves the first dish telling each diner in French "Here is...", naming the dish ordered by each person.
g. The waiter next serves the second dish stating "Here is...."
h. The waiter then asks each diner if s/he desires coffee and each diner expresses his preference.
i. Each diner then expresses satisfaction or dissatisfaction with the meal.
j. One diner gets the waiter's attention and asks for the bill.
k. The diners pay the bill, leave a tip in accordance with the kind of service given by the waiter and say goodbye.

Activité B

This same activity is repeated with students changing roles. The diners return to the same restaurant on another occasion. The second time they have a different waiter and, of course, want to try different dishes.

La Brasserie

Hors d'Oeuvres et Potages

Salade de Fruits 25fr ~ Escargots 35fr
Soupe à l'Oignon Gratinée 20fr ~ Pâté de Canard 40fr

On Recommande

Crevettes aux Herbes 84fr ~ Boudin Blanc 66fr
Quiche Lorraine 72fr ~ Poitrine de Poulet au Citron 71fr
Fettuccine aux Champignons 81fr ~ Fusilli aux Fruits de Mer 67fr
Crêpe de Poulet 65fr

Oeufs et Omelettes

Oeufs Bénédictine 48fr ~ Omelette Lorraine 52fr
Omelette Igor 50fr ~ Omelette au Saumon Fumé 47fr

Buffet Froid et Sandwiches

Steak Tartare 60fr ~ Poitrine de Poulet avec Epinards 77fr
Salade Niçoise 77fr ~ Salade verte 68fr

Desserts et Pâtisserie

Tarte aux Pommes 23fr ~ Fraises aux Chocolats Noir et Blanc 25fr
Mousse de Cassis 20fr ~ Gâteau au Chocolat 18fr

Boissons

Café 12fr ~ Thé 12fr
Espresso 15fr ~ Café au Lait 17fr
L'eau minérale 10fr

Aim VIII: *Each student will be able to state numbers 100 - 2000 and review numbers below 100 in order to be able to read the price of foods on a French menu*

Exercice oral

les numéros 100 - 2000

100	cent	600	six cents
200	deux cents	700	sept cents
300	trois cents	800	huit cents
400	quatre cents	900	neuf cents
500	cinq cents	1000	mille
		1200	mille deux cents, douze cents
		1800	mille huit cents , dix-huit cents
		2000	deux mille

1. Numbers *21,31,41,51,61,71* use the conjunction ***et*** (no hyphen)

quarante et un
soixante et un

The numbers *81,91 and 101* do not use the conjunction ***et.***

quatre-vingt-un
quatre-vingt-onze
cent un

2. Multiplied by another number, *vingt* and *cent* are plural, but when followed by another number, they are singular.

quatre-vingts	*quatre-vingt-huit*
deux cents	*deux cent douze*

3. Mille is never plural.

quatre mille
vingt mille cinquante

3. The format of numbers differs between France and the United States. The French use a period for our comma or space, and a comma replaces our decimal point.

French	***U.S.***
1.875	1,875
7,70	7.70

4. The *franc* is the French currency unit. Appearing as bills or coins in various denominations, it is divided into 100 *centimes* as well. The "exchange rate" (usually posted in major newspapers) should be consulted to determine the value of the *franc* against the dollar. Five to six francs to the dollar is a common equivalent.

Conversation 1

M. Henri is loading farm produce on his truck to take to the Saturday market in nearby Sisteron (a village in Provence). The amounts of all of the various items are listed below. Partners will take turns asking and answering questions according to the following model. Use complete sentences in French.

Example: 1200 tomatoes
Partner A: *Combien de tomates a M. Vial?*
Partner B: *M. Vial a mille deux cents tomates.*

1. 2000 strawberries
2. 1680 apples
3. 1975 potatoes
4. 1320 oranges
5. 550 melons
6. 350 pears
7. 735 carrots
8. 325 eggs

Mme Fontaine achète des fruits et des légumes le samedi.

Conversation 2

Peer partners take turns asking one another how much each of the following foods cost on the menu of *La Brasserie* ***Example:***

Philippe: Combien coûte la soupe à l'oignon gratinée?
Robert: La soupe à l'oignon gratinée coûte vingt francs.

Partner A

1. Combien coûte le Pâté de Canard?
2. Combien coûte la Salade de Fruits?
3. Combien coûtent les Escargots?
4. Combien coûte la Salade Niçoise?
5. Combien coûtent les Crevettes aux Herbes?
6. Combien coûte le Boudin Blanc?
7. Combien coûte la Crêpe de Poulet?
8. Combien coûte l'Omelette Lorraine?
9. Combien coûte le Fusilli aux Fruits de Mer?
10. Combien coûte l'Omelette Igor?

Partner B

1. Combien coûte l'Omelette au Saumon Fumé?
2. Combien coûte la Poitrine de Poulet au Citron?
3. Combien coûtent les Fettucine aux Champignons?
4. Combien coûtent les Oeufs Bénédictine?
5. Combien coûte la Mousse de Cassis?
6. Combien coûtent la Quiche Lorraine?
7. Combien coûte la Salade verte?
8. Combien coûte le Steak Tartare?
9. Combien coûte l'eau minérale?
10. Combien coûte le Gâteau au Chocolat?

Exercice écrit

Write each question and answer of the **Conversation, Partner A,** numbers 1 - 10.

Exercice de compréhension

Listen carefully as your teacher states a few numbers from 100 to 2000 in French. After the second repetition, write the number you hear in Arabic numbers. ***Example:***

sept cent trente-neuf 739
mille huit cent soixante-quatre 1,864

Vocabulaire

la salade de fruits *fruit salad*
les escargots *snails*
la salade verte *mixed green salad*
la soupe à l'oignon *onion soup*
les crevettes *shrimp*
le boudin blanc *white sausage*
la poitrine de poulet *chicken breast*
au citron *in lemon*
les champignons *mushrooms*
les oeufs *eggs*
Fusilli aux Fruits de Mer
corkscrew pasta with seafood
l'eau minérale *mineral water*
le saumon *salmon*
la Mousse de Cassis
black currant mousse

UNIT TEN

Les achats

TOPIC

Shopping

SITUATION

Interaction with individual peers and adults

FUNCTION

Socializing, obtaining and providing information
Expressing personal feelings about clothes
Suggesting a course of action

PROFICIENCY

Can comprehend simple statements and questions
and respond appropriately with possible need for repetition
Can buy an article of clothing in a store

AIM I: Each student will be able to identify some basic articles of men's and women's clothing

AIM II: Each student will be able to state what s/he wears on various occasions

AIM III: Each student will be able to ask what color an article of clothing is and be able to respond

AIM IV: Each student will be able to ask who possesses one or more articles of clothing and other objects and be able to respond

AIM V: Each student will be able to ask a peer and an adult questions related to shopping for clothes

AIM VIA: Each student will be able to read the dialogue *"Faire des achats"* and demonstrate comprehension by answering questions

AIM VIB: Each student will be able to read the dialogue *"Vous désirez?"* and demonstrate comprehension by answering questions

AIM VII: Each student will be able to buy an article of clothing in a store

Aim I: *Each student will be able to identify some basic articles of men's and women's clothing*

Exercice oral 1

les vêtements

Exercice oral 2

Deux conversations téléphoniques

1. *(Marcel téléphone à Jean.)*
   Jean: Allô!
   Marcel: C'est Jacques, ça va?
   Jean: Ça va bien, et toi?
   Marcel: Ça va très bien. Ce soir, je vais à une partie.
   Jean: Tant mieux! Est-ce que tu portes un costume pour la partie?
   Marcel: Oui, je porte toujours un costume et une cravate aux parties.

2. *(Hélène téléphone à Claire.)*
   Claire: Allô!
   Hélène: C'est Hélène, ça va?
   Claire: Ça ne va pas très bien.
   Hélène: Qu'est-ce que tu as?
   Claire: J'ai un rhume et de la fièvre. Je ne peux pas aller à la discothèque ce soir.
   Hélène: Je suis navrée!
   Claire: Qu'est-ce que tu vas porter?
   Hélène: Je vais porter une jupe, un joli chemisier et des chaussures neuves.
   Claire: Amuse-toi bien!
   Hélène: J'espère que ça ira mieux bientôt!

Réfléchissons

Functions of language:

1. What expression would be appropriate to respond to good news?
2. What expression would be appropriate to respond to bad news?
3. What would you say to a friend to wish him/her a good time?
4. What would you say to indicate you can't do a particular activity?
   a. I can't go.
   b. I can't work.
   c. I can't eat.

Conversation

You call your friend on the telephone in the morning before school. S/he responds appropriately (refer to **Exercice oral 2** and then you identify yourself. You then ask how s/he is and your friend responds. Next ask him/her if s/he is wearing the following articles of clothing today.

Questions pour hommes

1. Est-ce que tu portes une chemise?
2. Est-ce que tu portes un pantalon ou des jeans?
3. Est-ce que tu portes des chaussettes?
4. Est-ce que tu portes une ceinture?
5. Est-ce que tu portes un costume?
6. Est-ce que tu portes une cravate?
7. Est-ce que tu portes des tennis?
8. Est-ce que tu portes un chapeau?
9. Est-ce que tu portes un manteau ou une jaquette?

Questions pour femmes

1. Est-ce que tu portes un chemisier?
2. Est-ce que tu portes une jupe ou un pantalon?
3. Est-ce que tu portes une jaquette?
4. Est-ce que tu portes une ceinture?
5. Est-ce que tu portes une robe?
6. Est-ce que tu portes un chapeau?
7. Est-ce que tu portes des chaussures?
8. Est-ce que tu portes un pull-over?
9. Est-ce que tu portes un manteau?

Résumé

Ask three of your classmates the question, *Quels vêtements est-ce que tu portes aujourd'hui?* They should respond by stating at least five articles of clothing that they are wearing today.

Aim II: *Each student will be able to state what s/he wears or uses on various occasions*

Exercice oral 1

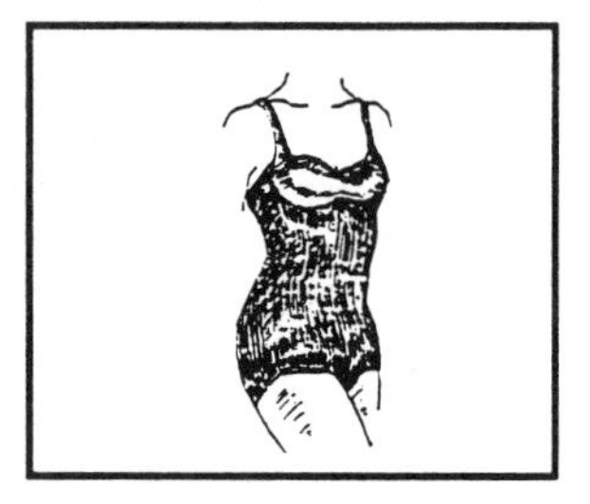
un maillot de bain

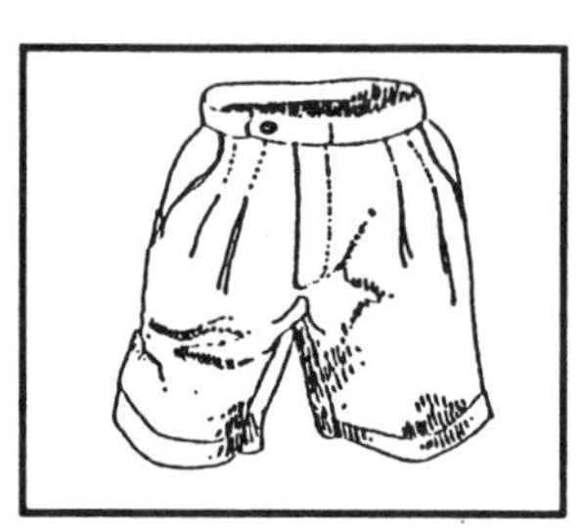
un short

un pull de coton

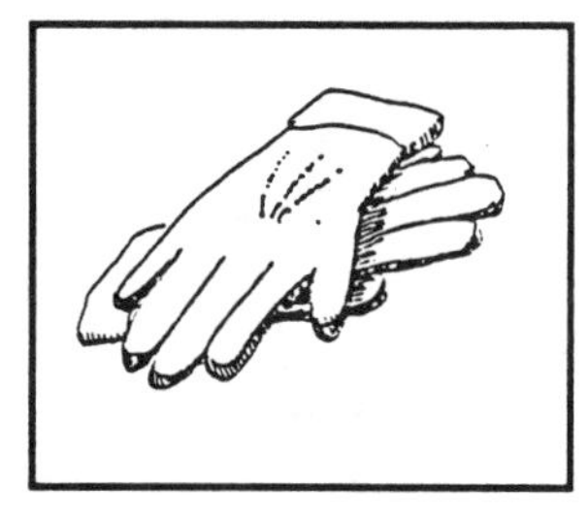
les gants

le parapluie

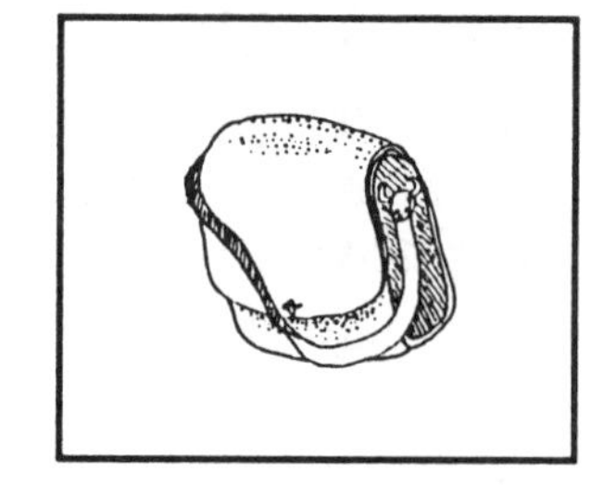
le sac

Exercice oral 2

1. **Laure:** Qu'est-ce que tu portes quand tu vas à un mariage?
   Thérèse: Quand je vais à un mariage, je porte une robe, des chaussures, un sac et un manteau.

2. **Robert:** Qu'est-ce que tu portes quand tu es à la maison?
   Antoine: Quand je suis à la maison je porte des jeans, un pull de coton, des chaussettes et des tennis.

Conversation

1. Qu'est-ce que tu portes quand tu vas à l'école?
2. Qu'est-ce que tu portes quand tu vas à une partie ou à une discothèque?
3. Qu'est-ce que tu portes quand tu vas à la plage?
4. Qu'est-ce que tu portes quand tu vas à la distribution des prix?
5. Qu'est-ce que tu portes quand tu vas à un match de baseball?
6. Qu'est-ce que tu portes quand tu vas à un mariage?
7. Qu'est-ce que tu portes quand tu es à la maison?

Exercice écrit

1. Write both the questions and the answers of the **Conversation,** numbers 1 - 7.

2. Complete each sentence with the appropriate articles of clothing or accessories for each of the following weather conditions.

a. Quand il fait très froid, Charles porte _____ et _____.
b. Quand il fait très chaud, Marie porte _____ et _____.
c. Quand il fait beau, je porte _____ et _____.
d. Quand il pleut, je porte _____et_____.
e. Quand il neige, je porte _____ et _____.

Exercice de compréhension

Listen carefully as your teacher states a few articles of clothing and accessories. After the second repetition, write the letter which corresponds to what you hear.

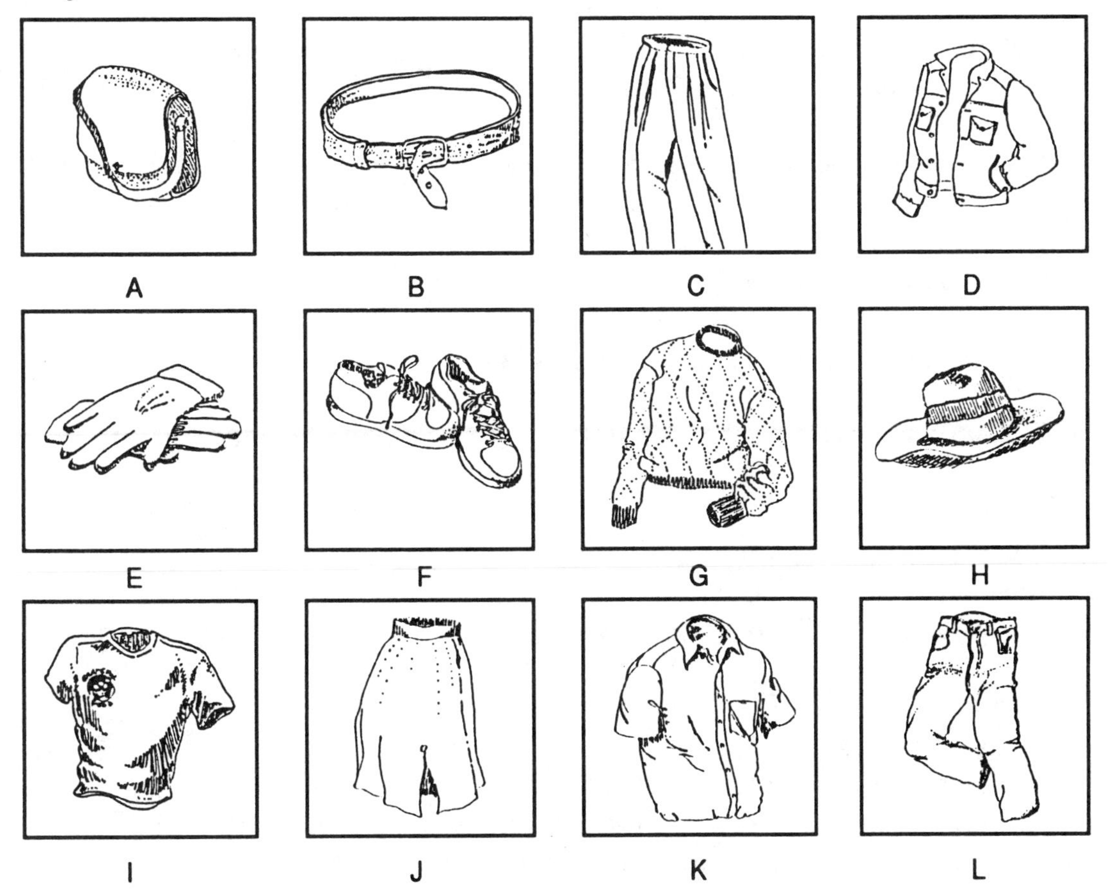

Vocabulaire

Les vêtements *clothing*

le manteau *overcoat*
le chemisier *blouse*
les chaussettes *socks*
la chemise *shirt*
le sac *pocketbook*
le blouson *jacket*
la ceinture *belt*
la cravate *tie*
la jupe *skirt*
les lunettes *eyeglasses*
les lunettes de soleil *sunglasses*
les gants *gloves*
les chaussures *shoes*
la jaquette *jacket*

le pantalon *pants*
le short *shorts*
les jeans *bluejeans*
le parapluie *umbrella*
les sandales *sandals*
le chapeau *hat*
le pull de coton *sweatshirt*
le pull-over *sweater*
les tennis *sneakers*
le costume *suit*
la robe *dress*
le maillot de bain *bathing suit*

Est-ce que tu portes ...? *Are you wearing ...? / Do you wear ...?*
Quels vêtements est-ce que tu portes aujourd'hui? *What clothes are you wearing today?*
Qu'est-ce que tu portes quand tu vas à...? *What do you wear when you go to ...?*

un mariage *a wedding*
la distribution des prix *the graduation*
la plage *the beach*
un match de baseball *a baseball game*

Une conversation au téléphone *a telephone conversation*

Allô! *Hello!*
C'est moi,... *It's me, ...*
ce soir *this evening*
Tant mieux! *or* Je suis content(e). *How happy I am! (In response to good news).*
Je suis navré(e)! *How sorry I am! (In response to bad news).*
Je ne peux pas ... *I can't ...*
Je ne peux pas aller... *I can't go...*
Amuse-toi bien! *Hope you have a good time!*
Remets-toi vite! *Hope you feel better soon!*

Aim III: *Each student will be able to ask what color an article of clothing is and be able to respond*

Exercice oral 1

Les couleurs **(Teacher's presentation)**
(Note: The colors are listed in the ***Vocabulaire.****)*

Exercice oral 2

1a. **Jean:** De quelle couleur est la robe?
Marie: La robe est blanche.

1b. **Jean:** De quelles couleurs sont les robes?
Marie: Les robes sont blanches.

2a. **Annette:** De quelle couleur est la jupe?
Hélène: La jupe est blanche.

2b. **Annette:** De quelles couleurs sont les jupes?
Hélène: Les jupes sont blanches.

3a. **Jean:** De quelle couleur est le costume?
M. Coté: Le costume est bleu.

3b. **Jean:** De quelles couleurs sont les costumes?
M. Coté: Les costumes sont bleus.

4a. **Philippe:** De quelle couleur est la chemise?
Mme Coté: La chemise est bleue.

4b. **Philippe:** De quelles couleurs sont les chemises?
Mme Coté: Les chemises sont bleues.

Réfléchissons

Colors are adjectives because they describe nouns.

Colors agree in gender and number with the noun they describe.

1. What will determine which form of the adjective is to be used?

Note: This concept is called Noun-Adjective Agreement.

Conversation

Peer partners ask one another the following questions and answer according to the cue given in parentheses.

1. De quelle couleur est le chapeau? (noir)
2. De quelle couleur est la cravate? (rouge)
3. De quelle couleur est le pull-over? (jaune)
4. De quelle couleur est le sac? (bleu)
5. De quelle couleur est la ceinture? (grise)
6. De quelles couleurs sont les tennis? (blancs)
7. De quelles couleurs sont les chemises? (rouges)
8. De quelles couleurs sont les gants? (marron)
9. De quelles couleurs sont les jupes? (bleues)
10. De quelles couleurs sont les manteaux? (gris)

Exercice oral 3

Qu'est-ce qu'il/elle porte? / Qu'est-ce qu'ils/elles portent?

1a. Marie porte un manteau rouge.
Marie et Annette portent des manteaux rouges.

1b. Charles porte un chapeau bleu.
Charles et Pierre portent des chapeaux bleus.

2a. Jean porte une chemise rouge.
Jean et Pierre portent des chemises rouges.

2b. Claudine porte une jupe bleue.
Claudine et Rachelle portent des jupes bleues.

Réfléchissons

In the examples given, where are the adjectives placed in relation to the nouns they describe?

Exercice écrit

1. Write the questions and answers of the **Conversation,** numbers 1 - 10.

2. Write the following sentences using the appropriate form of the adjective (the color) in parenthesis.

a. Anne porte un chapeau_____. (rouge)
b. Marie porte une robe_____. (jaune)
c. Claudine porte une jupe_____. (noir)
d. Pierre porte une chemise_____. (orange).
e. Mon amie porte une ceinture_____. (bleu)
f. Les filles portent des pantalons_____. (bleu)
g. Mes amis portent des chaussures_____. (gris)
h. Mes amies portent des jaquettes_____. (vert)
i. Ils portent des chaussettes_____. (blanc)
j. Elles portent des sandales_____. (rose)

Activités

1. State the colors of the clothes that three of your classmates are wearing. ***Examples:***

a. Rose porte une jupe jaune, un chemisier rouge, une ceinture noire, et des chaussures noires.
b. Robert porte un pantalon bleu, une chemise blanche, une jaquette grise, des chaussettes grises et des chaussures noires.

2. State the colors of clothes that people are wearing from pictures or advertisements that you have cut out from magazines (four or five pictures).

3. State the colors of five classroom objects.

Vocabulaire

Les couleurs ***colors***

jaune *yellow*
orange *orange*
bleu *blue*
blanc *white*
gris *gray*
marron *brown (this form does not change)*
noir *black*
rouge *red*
rose *pink*
vert *green*

De quelle couleur est ...? *What color is ...?*
De quelles couleurs sont ...? *What color are ...?*

Aim IV *Each student will be able to ask who possesses one or more articles of clothing and other objects and be able to respond*

Exercice oral

1a. **Michel:** A qui est ce chapeau?
Hélène: Ce chapeau est à Marie.

1b. **Jean:** A qui sont ces chapeaux?
M. Josselin: Ces chapeaux sont à M. Gac.

2a. **Philippe:** A qui est cette jaquette?
Thérèse: Cette jaquette est à ma soeur.

2b. **Jacques:** A qui sont ces jaquettes?
Robert: Ces jaquettes sont à Mme Béziers.

3a. **Marie:** A qui est cette robe?
Roberte: Cette robe est la mienne.

3b. **Rose:** A qui sont ces robes?
Mme Saliba: Ces robes sont les miennes.

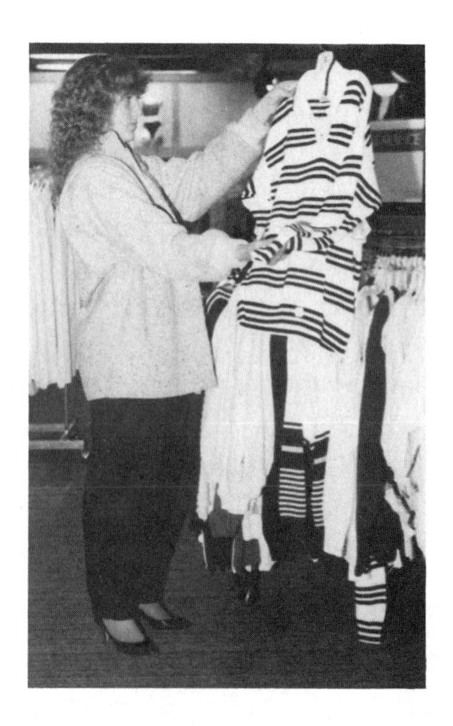

4a. **Thomas:** A qui est cette cravate?
Pierre: Cette cravate c'est la mienne.

4b. **Paul:** A qui sont ces cravates?
M. Jentil: Ces cravates sont les miennes.

Réfléchissons

1. What word indicates possession in French?

Note de grammaire

Demonstrative Adjectives

masculine

this(that) (before a consonant)	*ce*	*ce pantalon*
this(that) (before a vowel or mute "h")	*cet*	*cet ami*
	cet	*cet homme*
these (those)	*ces*	*ces chapeaux*

feminine

this(that)	*cette*	*cette robe*
these(those)	*ces*	*ces jupes*

Conversation

Respond according to the cue given.

1. A qui est ce parapluie? (Antoine)
2. A qui est cette jaquette? (Thérèse)
3. A qui est cette montre? (M. Pilon)
4. A qui est ce sac? (Mlle Saul)
5. A qui est ce livre? (le mien)
6. A qui est cette maison? (la mienne)
7. A qui sont ces chaussures? (les miennes)
8. A qui sont ces sandales? (les miennes)
9. A qui sont ces voitures? (mes parents)
10. A qui sont ces maisons? (le docteur)

Vocabulaire

A qui est ...? *Whose ... is ...?*
A qui sont ...? *Whose ... are ...?*
le mien/la mienne *mine*
les miens/les miennes *mine*
ce, cet *this, that (m.)* cette *this, that (f.)*
ces *these, those (m., f.)*

Exercice écrit

Write and answer the questions of the **Conversation,** numbers 1 - 10.

Aim V: *Each student will be able to ask a peer and an adult questions related to shopping for clothes*

Exercice oral

1a. **Jean:** Est-ce que tu aimes faire des achats?
Pierre: Non, je n'aime pas faire d'achats.
Jean: Pourquoi?
Pierre: Parce que je n'ai pas d'argent.

2a. **Jean:** Avec qui est-ce que tu fais des achats?
Pierre: Quelquefois je fais des achats avec mon amie et d'autres fois je fais des achats seul.

3a. **Jean:** Quand est-ce que tu fais des achats?
Pierre: Je fais des achats à la fin de la semaine ou les jours de fête.

4a. **Jean:** Comment est-ce que tu vas dans les magasins?
Pierre: Je vais dans les magasins à pied.

5a. **Jean:** Où est-ce que tu achètes tes vêtements?
Pierre: J'achète mes vêtements dans les magasins de mon quartier.

6a. **Jean:** Pourquoi est-ce que tu achètes tes vêtements dans ton quartier?
Pierre: J'achète mes vêtements dans mon quartier parce que les prix sont bas et il y a toujours beaucoup de soldes.

1b. **Annette:** Est-ce que vous aimez faire des achats?
Mme Dupont: Oui, j'aime faire des achats.
Annette: Qu'est-ce que vous aimez acheter?
Mme Dupont: J'aime acheter des vêtements pour sortir et pour travailler.

2b. **Annette:** Avec qui est-ce que vous faites des achats?
Mme Dupont: Je fais des achats seule ou avec mon mari.

3b. **Annette:** Quand est-ce que vous faites des achats?
Mme Dupont: Je fais des achats quand j'ai le temps et de l'argent.

4b. **Annette:** Comment allez-vous dans les magasins?
Mme Dupont: Je vais dans les magasins en autobus ou en métro. Quelquefois mon mari m'emmène en voiture.

5b. **Annette:** Où est-ce que vous achetez les vêtements?
Mme Dupont: J'achète les vêtements dans les grands magasins en ville.

6b. **Annette:** Pourquoi est-ce que vous allez en ville?
Mme Dupont: Je vais en ville parce qu'il y a un grand choix dans les magasins. J'aime aussi manger dans les restaurants en ville.

Conversation

1a. Est-ce que tu aimes faire des achats?
2a. Si tu n'aimes pas, pourquoi? Si tu aimes, qu'est-ce que tu aimes acheter?
3a. Avec qui est-ce que tu fais des achats?
4a. Quand est-ce que tu vas faire des achats?
5a. Comment est-ce que tu vas dans les magasins?
6a. Où est-ce que tu achètes les vêtements?
7a. Pourquoi est-ce que tu achètes tes vêtements là?

2a. Vous aimez faire des achats?
2b. Si vous n'aimez pas, pourquoi? Si vous aimez, qu'est-ce que vous aimez acheter?
3b. Avec qui est-ce que vous allez faire des achats?
4b. Quand est-ce que vous allez faire des achats?
5b. Comment est-ce que vous allez dans les magasins?
6b. Où est-ce que vous achetez les vêtements?
7b. Pourquoi est-ce que vous achetez les vêtements là?

Exercice de compréhension

Your teacher will ask you a few questions related to shopping. After the second repetition, answer each question with a complete sentence in French.

Vocabulaire:

Est-ce que tu aimes faire des achats?
Do you like to go shopping?
Pourquoi pas? *Why not?*
Parce que je n'ai pas d'argent. *Because I don't have money.*
Qu'est-ce que tu aimes acheter? / Qu'est-ce que vous aimez acheter?
What do you like to buy?
J'aime acheter des vêtements pour sortir et pour travailler.
...clothes to go out and to work
Avec qui est-ce que tu fais (vous faites)des achats...? *With whom...?*
Je fais des achats seul (seule). *I go shopping alone.*
Je fais des achats avec mon petit ami. *...with my steady boyfriend.*
Quand est-ce que tu fais (vous faites) des achats....? *When...?*
à la fin de la semaine *during the weekend*
un jour de fête *during a holiday*
quand j'ai le temps *when I have time*
quand j'ai de l'argent *when I have money*
quand il y a beaucoup de soldes *when there are many sales*
Comment est-ce que tu vas (vous allez) dans les magasins....?
How do you go to stores?
Je vais dans les magasins en bus *by bus*
en métro *by subway*
en voiture *by car*
Je vais dans les magasins à pied. *I walk to the stores.*
Quelquefois mon mari m'emmène en voiture.
Sometimes my husband takes me by car
Où est-ce que tu achètes (vous achetez)...? *Where do you buy...?*
dans les magasins du quartier *in the stores of my neighborhood*
dans les grands magasins là.
in the large department stores there
Pourquoi est-ce que tu vas (vous allez) en ville? *Why do you go downtown?*
...parce qu'il y a beaucoup de soldes. *...because there are many sales.*
...parce qu'il y a un grand choix. *...because there is a great selection.*
...parce que les prix sont moins chers. *...because the prices are less expensive.*

acheter ***to buy (irregular)***
j'achète, tu achètes, il/elle achète
nous achetons, vous achetez, ils/elles achètent

Activité

Your friend from France has come to visit you. He/she likes to go shopping for clothes and therefore asks you a few questions about your customs.

Tell him/her...

1. ...if you like to go shopping for clothes and what you like to buy.
   ...if you don't like to go shopping for clothes and why.
2. ...with whom you go shopping.
3. ...when you go shopping.
4. ...how you go to the stores.
5. ...where you buy your clothes (type of store).
6. ...two reasons you buy your clothes there.

Aim VIA: *Each student will be able to read the dialogue* "Faire des achats" *and demonstrate comprehension by answering a series of questions.*

Lecture: première partie

C'est vendredi après-midi. Anne, la jeune fille américaine demande à son amie française si elle veut aller faire des achats. Hélène dit oui. Les deux jeunes décident d'aller aux "Galeries Lafayette" un grand magasin parisien.

1. **Anne:** A propos, quelle heure est-il?
2. **Hélène:** Il est quatre heures et demie.
3. **Anne:** Je n'ai pas de classes cet après-midi. Et toi?
4. **Hélène:** Moi non plus.

5. **Anne:** Quelle chance! Pourquoi est-ce que nous n'allons pas faire des achats. J'ai besoin d'acheter une robe pour le mariage d'Isabelle.
6. **Hélène:** Qui est Isabelle? Je ne la connais pas.
7. **Anne:** C'est la fille aînée de la famille française avec qui j'habite. Elle va se marier dans deux mois.
8. **Hélène:** J'ai une bonne idée! Allons aux "Galeries Lafayette." Il y a un bon choix de robes et il y a aussi beaucoup de soldes maintenant . Je peux t'aider. J'aime beaucoup faire les achats. Est-ce que tu veux aller à pied ou prendre l'autobus?
9. **Anne:** Si ce n'est pas loin, allons à pied. J'ai besoin de maigrir et l'exercice est bon pour moi.

Compréhension de lecture:

If the statement is true, state *vrai*. If the statement is false, state *faux* and **correct the bold part.**

1. Anne et Hélène n'ont pas de classes **ce matin.**
2. Anne veut aller faire des achats parce qu'elle a besoin d'**un chemisier.**
3. **Hélène** va se marier dans deux mois.
4. Hélène dit qu'il y a **beaucoup de soldes** maintenant aux "Galeries Lafayette."
5. Anne et Hélène décident de **prendre l'autobus.**

Vocabulaire de lecture:

si **elle veut** aller *if **she wants** to go...*

Il (elle) **dit** oui. ***...says** yes.*

1. à propos *by the way*
3. ce matin *this morning* / cet après-midi *this afternoon*
   le matin *in the morning* / l'après-midi *in the afternoon*
4. Moi non plus. *Neither do I.*
5. Quelle chance! *What luck!*
   avoir besoin de *to need* / J'ai besoin de... *I need.....*
   ...pour le mariage de... *...for ...'s wedding*
6. Je ne **la** connais pas. *I don't know **her.***
   Je ne **le** connais pas. *I don't know **him.***
7. la **fille aînée** *the **oldest daughter***
   la plus jeune *the **youngest***
   ...va se marier *...is going to get married*
8. Allons... *Let us go...*
   Je **peux** t'aider. ***I can** help you.* J'aime beaucoup... *I love to...*
   prendre l'autobus *to take the bus*
9. **allons** à pied ***let's** walk.* maigrir *to lose weight*

Functions of Language:

1. Somebody tells you that he/she doesn't want to do a particular activity. How would you say "Neither do I."?
2. Somebody tells you some good news about himself/herself. How would you say "What luck!" or "How lucky!"?
3. Someone asks you if you know his friend. Respond "I don't know him." Someone asks you if you know her friend. Respond "I don't know her."
4. How would you say to somebody that you have a good idea?
5. How would you tell somebody that you love to... (do an activity)?
    a. I love to eat.
    b. I love to go shopping.
6. How would you tell somebody that...
    a. ...you need to buy clothes?
    b. ...you need to rest?
    c. ...you need to work?
    d. ...you need to lose weight?

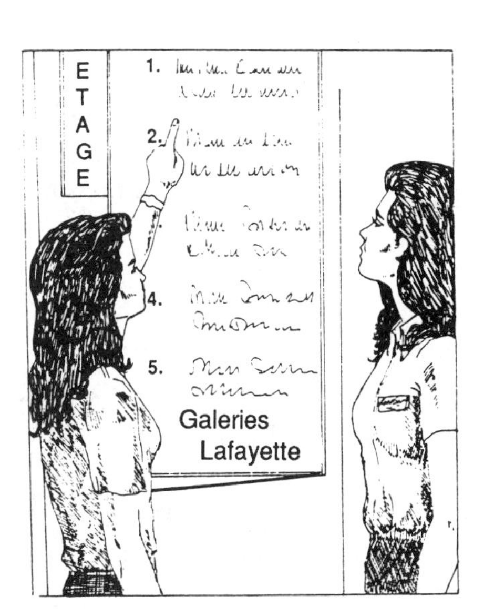

Lecture: deuxième partie

Les deux jeunes filles vont aux "Galeries Lafayette" à pied.

10. **Hélène:** S'il vous plaît, à quel étage est le rayon de vêtements pour jeunes filles?
11. **Vendeuse:** Au cinquième étage.
12. **Hélène:** Pouvez-vous me dire où est l'ascenseur?
13. **Vendeuse:** Allez tout droit.
14. **Anne:** Il y a beaucoup de monde dans ce magasin aujourd'hui.
15. **Hélène:** Tu as raison. Regarde! Voici les robes. Allons voir si tu vas trouver une belle robe pas chère.
16. **Anne:** Mon Dieu!, Hélène!

17. **Hélène:** Qu'est-ce que tu as?
18. **Anne:** Je ne peux rien acheter aujourd'hui. Je n'ai pas assez d'argent .
19. **Hélène:** Ne t'en fais pas! J'ai la carte de crédit de ma famille.
20. **Anne:** Merci beaucoup, Hélène. J'apprécie beaucoup ton aide.

Compréhension de lecture:

If the statement is true state *Vrai.* If the statement is false, state *Faux* and **correct the bold part.**

6. Le rayon de vêtements pour jeunes filles est au **premier étage.**
8. L'ascenseur est à **droite.**
9. Anne dit qu'elle ne peut rien acheter aujourd'hui parce qu'elle **n'a pas assez d'argent.**
10. Hélène répond qu'il n'y a pas de problèmes parce qu'elle a **la carte de crédit de son père.**

Vocabulaire de lecture:

10. A quel étage est...? *On what floor is...? (refer to Unit VII, Aim V)*
    le rayon de vêtements pour jeunes filles *...young people's clothing department*
11. la vendeuse *salesperson*
12. Pouvez-vous me dire...? *Can you tell me...?*
    l'ascenseur *the elevator*
13. Allez tout droit. *Go straight ahead.*
    C'est au fond. *It's in the back.*
15. Tu as raison. / Vous avez raison.
    You are right.
    Regarde! *Look!*
    Allons voir / Voyons voir ... *Let's see...*
    trouver *to find*
    pas chère *not expensive*
16. Mon Dieu! *My gosh!, Good heavens!*
17. Qu'est-ce que tu as? *What's the matter?*
18. Je ne peux pas.. *I can't...*
    rien *anything, nothing*
    assez d'argent *enough money*
19. Ne t'en fais pas! *Don't worry!*
    la carte de crédit *the credit card*
20. J'apprécie ton/votre aide.
    I appreciate your help.

Functions of Language:

7. How would you tell somebody that he/she is right? (agreement)
8. How would you tell a friend not to worry?
9. How would you ask a friend "What's the matter?"
10. How would you tell a friend that you appreciate something he/she did?
11. What would you say to a friend to have him/her look at something you are pointing out?
12. What expression would you use to indicate surprise or shock?
13. What would you ask a salesperson to find out some information?
14. How would you ask where something is located?
15. How would you tell a person to "Go straight ahead."?

Aim VIB: *Each student will be able to read the dialogue and demonstrate his / her comprehension by answering a series of questions*

Lecture

Anne et Hélène ont besoin de l'assistance d'une vendeuse.

1. **La vendeuse:** Vous désirez?
2. **Anne:** Je veux acheter une robe.
3. **La vendeuse:** Quel genre de robe cherchez-vous?
4. **Anne:** C'est pour un mariage.
5. **La vendeuse:** Quelle taille portez-vous? Nous avons un grand choix.
6. **Anne:** Je porte du 36.
7. **La vendeuse:** Et de quelle couleur?
8. **Anne:** Bleue, s'il vous plaît.

(La vendeuse apporte la robe.)

9. **Anne:** Qu'est-ce que tu penses?
10. **Hélène:** Elle est très jolie.
11. **Anne:** Je l'aime beaucoup.
12. **Anne:** Combien est-ce qu'elle coûte?
13. **Vendeuse:** Elle coûte 450 francs.
14. **Hélène:** Elle n'est pas chère.
15. **Anne:** Un moment. J'ai ma machine à calculer. 450 francs divisé par 6, cela fait 75 dollars. Ça va. Je l'achète.
16. **Vendeuse:** Est-ce que vous désirez autre chose?
17. **Anne:** Rien d'autre, merci.
18. **Vendeuse:** Est-ce que vous allez payer en espèces ou avec une carte de crédit?
19. **Anne:** Avec une carte de crédit.
20. **Anne:** Hélène, merci de m'avoir aidée. Est-ce que tu veux acheter quelque chose?
21. **Hélène:** Non, je n'ai besoin de rien. Allons prendre quelque chose.
22. **Anne:** Bonne idée. J'ai un peu faim.

Note:

Sizes:	**Women's dresses and suits**					**Men's suits and coats**				
Europe:	36	38	40	42	44	46	48	50	52	54
USA:	8	10	12	14	16	36	38	40	42	44

Compréhension de lecture:

1. Qu'est-ce qu'Hélène et Anne cherchent?
2. Quel genre de robe Anne veut-elle acheter?
3. Quelle taille porte-t-elle?
4. De quelle couleur Anne veut la robe?
5. Comment est la robe?
6. Est-ce qu'Anne aime la robe?
7. Combien coûte la robe?
8. Est-ce qu'Anne décide d'acheter la robe?
9. Comment est-ce qu'elle va payer?
10, Est-ce qu'elle veut autre chose?
11. Est-ce qu'Hélène veut acheter quelque chose?
12. Que font Hélène et Anne après être sorties du magasin?

Vocabulaire

l'aide *help*
chercher *to look for*
le vendeur *salesman*
la vendeuse *saleswoman*
décider de ... *to decide to ...*

1. Vous désirez?
   How can I help you?
   j'aimerais acheter...
   I would like to buy...
   je veux acheter... *I want to buy...*
3. Quel genre...? *What kind of...?*
4. C'est pour... *It is for ...*
5. Quelle taille portez-vous?
   What size do you wear?
   Je porte la taille ... *I wear size ...*
   elle apporte ... *she brings ...*
9. Qu'est-ce que tu penses?
   What do you think?
   Elle/Il essaye **...** *... **tries on ...***
12. Combien est-ce qu'il/elle coûte?
    How much does it cost?
    Il coûte/ elle coûte... *It costs ...*
14. Ça n'est pas cher. *It is not expensive.*
15. Un moment. *One moment.*
    la machine à calculer *calculator*
    divisé par ... *divided by ...*
    Ça va/ C'est bien. *It's fine. / It's okay.*
    Je **l'**achète. *I'll buy **it**.*; **une** robe, **un** chemisier
16. Vous désirez **autre chose**? *Do you wish **something else**?*
    Rien d'autre. ***Nothing** else.*
18. Est-ce que vous allez **payer**...? *Are you going **to pay** ...?*
    espèces *in cash*
    avec une carte de crédit *with a credit card*
20. Merci de votre aide. *Thanks for helping me.*
    Est-ce que tu veux acheter quelque chose?
    Do you want to buy something?
21. Allons prendre quelque chose. *Let's have a snack.*

Aim VII: Each student will be able to buy an article of clothing in a store

Activité 1

The class is divided into groups of two. One student plays the role of the salesperson and the other is the customer. You are in a department store in Paris called *Galeries Lafayette.*

1. The salesperson asks the customer how s/he can help.
2. The customer says that he wants to buy a shirt or a suit.
   The customer says that she wants to buy a dress or a coat.
3. The salesperson asks what kind of ..... s/he is looking for. The customer responds.
4. The salesperson asks what size is needed. The customer responds.
5. The salesperson asks what color is desired. The customer responds.
   (The salesperson brings the article of clothing requested.)
6. The customer responds that it is pretty and that s/he likes it very much.
7. The customer asks how much it costs.
8. The salesperson responds that it costs "..... *francs.*"
9. The customer states that the price is not expensive and that s/he will buy it.
10. The salesperson asks if anything else is needed.
11. The customer responds "Nothing else, thank you."
12. The salesperson asks if she is going to pay by cash or with credit card. The customer responds.

Note:
Sizes: Men's shirts

Europe:	36	37	38	39	41	42	43
USA:	14	14	15	15	16	16	17

Bank exchange rate: $1.00 = 6.00 francs

Activité 2

This same activity is repeated with students changing roles. This customer wants to buy a different article of clothing than the first customer.

UNIT ELEVEN

La France et sa géographie
Une promenade dans Paris
Voyager dans Paris et en Métro
La pendule de 24 heures
Voyager par la SNCF

TOPIC

A. France and its geography
B. A stroll through Paris C. Travel in Paris and on the *Métro*
D. The 24-hour clock D. Travel by railroad

SITUATION

Interaction with individual peers and adults

FUNCTION

Providing and obtaining information about travel, expressing personal feelings
Suggesting a course of action, socializing (thanking and leave-taking)

PROFICIENCY

Can comprehend simple statements and questions and
can respond appropriately with possible need for repetition
Can ask questions appropriate to the communicative situation
Can understand some aspects of French culture
Can ride the *Métro* and can purchase a railroad ticket

AIM I: By identifying cognates and answering questions, each student will be able to demonstrate his/her comprehension of a reading about France and its geography

AIM II: Each student will be able to identify some of the places visited by a resident of Paris or a visitor to the capital

AIM IIIA: Each student will be able to read a dialogue about transportation in Paris and demonstrate comprehension by answering true-false questions

AIM IIIB: Each student will be able to read a dialogue about traveling in the *Métro* and demonstrate comprehension by answering true-false questions

AIM IIIC: Each student will be able to use the map of Paris's *Métro* to visit the places of interest of his/her choice

AIM IV: Each student will be able to read the 24-hour clock in order to understand and use a railroad time schedule

AIM V: Each student will be able to ask directions to travel by bus and be able to buy a railroad ticket

Aim I: *By identifying cognates and answering questions, each student will be able to demonstrate his / her comprehension of a reading about France and its geography*

Lecture

1 La France est un pays d'Europe en forme d'hexagone. Elle
2 est entourée au nord par la Manche et la mer du Nord, à
3 l'ouest par l'océan Atlantique, au sud par la mer Méditerannée.
4 Les trois autres côtés sont des frontières continentales.
5 La France est bordée par six pays. Au nord-est: la
6 Belgique et le Luxembourg; à l'est: l'Allemagne, la Suisse et
7 l'Italie; au sud: l'Espagne. La France est un pays très varié, au
8 sud-ouest, les Pyrénées séparent la France de l'Espagne. Les
9 Alpes à l'est séparent la France de l'Italie et de la Suisse.
10 Le Jura est la frontière principale entre la France et la Suisse.
11 Les Vosges en Alsace séparent la France de l'Allemagne. Au
12 centre, le Massif Central est la chaîne de montagnes la plus
13 ancienne.
14 Il y a cinq fleuves importants en France. 1) *La Seine* qui
15 traverse Paris. 2) *La Loire,* le plus long fleuve de France qui
16 traverse la vallée de la Loire avec ses magnifiques châteaux.
17 3) *La Garonne,* le fleuve le plus court qui passe à Bordeaux. Il
18 produit beaucoup d'énergie hydro-électrique. 4) *Le Rhône,*
19 fleuve rapide et puissant traverse de lac de Genève et passe à
20 Lyon. Il se jette dans la mer Méditerranée près de Marseille.
21 5) *Le Rhin,* est la frontière naturelle entre la France et
22 l'Allemagne, c'est aussi le fleuve le plus long d'Europe.
23 La France est située en zone tempérée, parce qu'elle est
24 presque à égale distance du pôle Nord et de l'équateur. Paris se
25 trouve à la même latitude que Montréal (Canada). Cette
26 latitude, le relief moyen, l'influence du Gulf Stream, et la

27 proximité des quatre mers contribuent au climat modéré de la
28 France. La population est approximativement 60.000.000
29 d'habitants. Paris est la capitale. Il y a d'autres villes très
30 importantes: Lyon, Marseille, Bordeaux, Brest et Strasbourg.
31 La langue officielle est le français. On parle aussi d'autres
32 langues: le breton, le basque et le provençal.
33 Dans la mer Méditerranée, il y a une île qui fait partie de
34 la France, la Corse. La Corse est un Département français, on
35 l'appelle aussi l'île de beauté. C'est l'île où est né Napoléon
36 Bonaparte en 1764. La capitale est Ajaccio.

Vocabulaire de la lecture:

1 un hexagone *hexagon*
2 entouré(e) *surrounded*
nord *north* par *by*
la Manche *English channel*
la mer du Nord *North sea*
3 l'ouest *west*
l'océan Atlantique *Atlantic ocean*
sud *south*
la mer Méditerranée *Mediterranean sea*
4 le côté *side*
5 est bordé(e) *is bordered* l'Allemagne *Germany*
8 les Pyrénées *Pyrenees mountains*
séparer *separate*
10 entre *between*
12 la chaîne de montagnes *chain or range of mountains*
14 le fleuve *river*
15 traverser *to cross, to go through*
16 magnifiques châteaux *magnificent castles*
17 court *short:* le plus court *the shortest*
18 produire *to produce*

19 lac de Genève *Geneva lake*
puissant *powerful*
20 se jeter *to throw oneself (to empty)*
24 presque *almost* égale *equal*
pôle Nord *north pole*
équateur *equator*
25 la même latitude *the same latitude*
relief *relief (mountain ranges)*
moyen *average*
33 une île *an island*
34 La Corse *Corsica*

Compréhension de lecture:

I. What are cognates?

Cognates are words that look alike and have similar meanings in two languages. We can expect to find many cognates in French and English because of their common heritage, Latin. Recognizing cognates can help us to read. When we read we have to look up some words in the dictionary, while other words can be figured out because of their resemblance to English or by contextual clues.

Many of the cognates in this reading have not been listed in the dictionary section ***(Vocabulaire de lecture).*** Make a list of all the cognates you ahve found after reading the selection for the second time. List the line on which each is found and both English and French cognates. ***Examples:***

	French	**English**
Line 1	forme	form
Line 8	séparent	separate

II. Choose the letter for the correct answer:

1. La France est ...
   a. un continent b. une ville c. un pays d. une île.

2. La France est en ...
   a. Afrique b. Amérique du Nord c. Asie d. Europe

3. Au sud de la France il y a ...
   a. le Portugal b. l'Espagne c. l'Italie d. l'Angleterre

4. A l'ouest de la France il y a ...
   a. la mer du Nord c. l'océan Atlantique
   b. la mer Méditerranée d. la Manche

5. Les Vosges séparent la France de ...
   a. la Suisse b. l'Italie c. l'Allemagne d. l'Espagne

6. La Seine traverse ...
   b. Bordeaux b. Paris c. Brest d. Lyon

7. La Garonne est le fleuve le plus ...
   a. court b. long c. rapide d. puissant

8. Les Alpes qui séparent la France de l'Italie et la Suisse sont ...
   a. des montagnes b. un fleuve c. un océan d. la mer

9. Le Rhône se jette dans ...
   a. la Manche b. la mer du Nord c. le Rhin d. la mer Méditerranée

10. Paris est à la latitude de ...
    a. Strasbourg b. Lyon c. Montréal d. Brest

11. Paris est la capitale de ...
    a. le Luxembourg b. la Suisse c. l'Allemagne d. la France

12. L'énergie hydro-électrique est produite par ...
    a. la Seine b. la Loire c. la Garonne d. le Rhône.

13. La langue officielle de France est ...
    a. l'espagnol b. l'italien c. l'allemand d. le français

France is a member of the European Economic Community

Résumé de lecture:

1. Qu'est-ce qu'est la France?
2. Dans quel continent est la France?
3. Quel pays est au sud de la France?
4. Où est la Suisse?
5. Quels sont les six pays qui bordent la France?
6. Comment s'appellent les montagnes en France? Donnez les noms.
7. Donnez le nom des 5 fleuves français.
8. Donnez le nom des mers et de l'océan.
9. Quelle est la capitale de la France?
10. Quelle est la langue officielle de la France?
11. Combien d'autres langues parle-t-on en France?
12. Comment s'appelle l'île dans la mer Méditerranée?

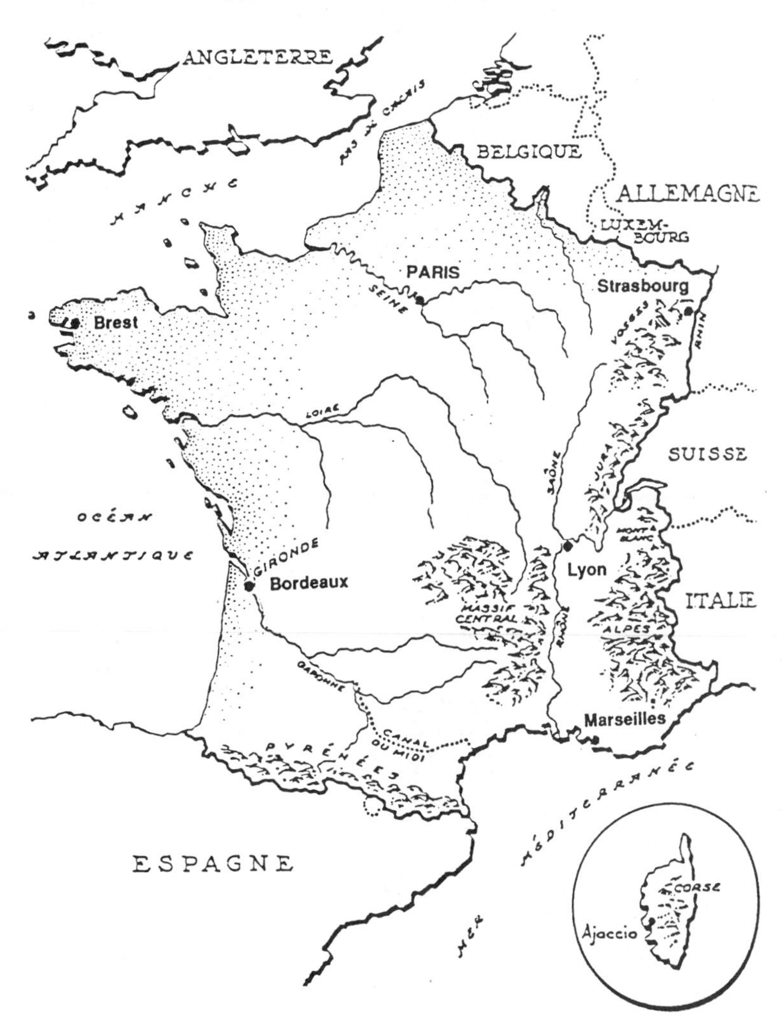

Aim II: *Each student will be able to identify some of the places visited by a resident of Paris or a visitor to the capital*

Arc de Triomphe

Tour Eiffel

Gare du Nord

Opéra

Sacré Coeur

Notre Dame

Hôtel de Ville

Sorbonne

Louvre

Hôtel des Invalides

St Germain des Prés

Panthéon

Conversation

Many American high schools and colleges throughout the United States have academic programs in many cities of France for a summer, a term or for the entire academic year. Anne is one of the American high school students who is participating in a program in Paris. During her stay in Paris she visits many places of interest. In the following peer practice partners take turns asking one another the name of the place Anne visits (represented by the symbol given) on a particular day and date as recorded in her diary. Begin with question number one.

1. Où est Anne le vendredi 6 septembre? (Le vendredi six septembre, Anne est à la gare du Nord.)

2. Où est Anne le mardi 15 octobre?

3. Où est Anne le mercredi 20 novembre?

4. Où est Anne le lundi 13 janvier?

5. Où est Anne le dimanche 9 février?

6. Où est Anne le jeudi 27 mars?

7. Où est Anne le vendredi 11 avril?

8. Où est Anne le dimanche 18 mars?

9. Où est Anne le samedi 14 juin?

10. Où est Anne le jeudi 31 juillet?

A stroll through Paris.

This is an opportunity for your French teacher to take you on a walk through Paris. The places that you will visit along your route are described in pictures and captions on the following pages.

Le Louvre - Situated in the old *Palais Royal,* this art museum is one of the most important in France and one of the biggest and richest in the world. Perhaps its most famous treasure is *La Jaconde,* known throughout the world as the famous "Mona Lisa", painted by Leonardo da Vinci. Also on view are the statues *Venus de Milo* and *la Victoire de Samothrace.*

Le Musée de Cluny - This building is a 15th century mansion built over the site of the Roman baths of the city. Belonging originally to the monks of the Cluny Abbey, this museum houses a magnificent tapestry collection (including the series *La Dame à la Licorne)* as well as many medieval art treasures.

L'Ile de la Cité - The history of Paris begins upon this small island in the Seine. It was here that the tribe of *Parisii* settled in approximately 250 B.C. Many of its oldest buildings disappeared in the rebuilding of the island during the 19th century but the feel and tone of Parisian history are still maintained by the presence of *la Cathédrale de Notre Dame,* the beautiful *Sainte Chapelle*, and the former city prison, *La Conciergerie.*

La Cathédrale de Notre-Dame de Paris - This magnificent cathedral begun in 1163 on the *île de la cité* is a tribute to French architecture. Built on a site that has seen worship for over 2000 years, the Cathedral took almost 100 years to complete. Its beautiful stonework and stained glass have survived in spite of the depredations of history; the Revolution took its toll when the site was declared a "Temple of Reason" and much statuary was destroyed. At one point the interior was altered to permit processions to move more freely, and some stained glass was removed to allow more light.

Victor Hugo drew attention to the state of disrepair in the 19th century and a major reconstruction and renovation was undertaken. A source of pride and inspiration to Parisian citizenry, the Cathedral is one of the central attractions of Paris.

L'Hôtel des Invalides - This building is a fine example of late 17th century architecture. Built to house wounded veterans, it serves primarily as a multi-faceted museum housing military artifacts. It has a beautiful cobbled courtyard still used for occasional ceremonies, and the setting is enhanced by the impressive dome that caps the *Eglise du Dôme* (Church of the Dome).

Within its walls lie the remains of Napoleon Bonaparte, encased in a series of coffins of pink marble. The *Code Napoléon* (still the basis of much of French law) is inscribed on the walls surrounding the tomb.

Le Panthéon - This mausoleum is situated in the Latin Quarter. Originally a church built to honor St. Geneviève (Patron of Paris), it houses the tombs of many French notables. Voltaire, Victor Hugo, Jean Jacques Rousseau and Emile Zola are buried here. The building bears the inscription, *"Aux grands hommes la Patrie reconnaissante".*

L'Opéra - This beautiful building was built in 1875 in the heart of the city. It is famous for the marble grand staircase and the luxurious foyer designed by Charles Garnier. Across from the Opera is the reknowned *Café de la Paix,* an international meeting place where one can hear every language in the world being spoken.

St-Germain-des-Prés - This is the oldest of Paris's churches and the burial place of most of the Merovingian kings. It is a historic anchor to the *Quartier Latin*, or "Left Bank", that section of Paris that evokes images of Bohemian coffee houses, artistic endeavors and intellectual ferment. Along the *"quais",* the large streets that line the banks of the Seine, the *"bouquinistes"* have settled, selling their second-hand books, pictures and cards. Often one is lucky enough to find an old and rare edition of a print or book.

La Sorbonne - This is the oldest University in Paris and represents the pinnacle of French higher education. It was begun by Robert de Sorbon as a theological college in 1253 for only 16 students, but grew rapidly. Today, its many buildings represent the restoration work undertaken by Cardinal de Richelieu.

La Tour Eiffel - The Eiffel tower was built by Alexandre Gustave Eiffel for the World fair of 1889. Considered an engineering marvel, its 7,000 tons of iron were in danger of removal after its 20-year concession expired. Saved by its utility as a radio tower, the Eiffel tower stands today as one of the major attractions of Paris. Visitors can climb stairs as far as the third deck, or use elevators which can reach the 1000 foot summit. Two restaurants are housed in the tower, and the structure affords magnificent views of the city.

Le Sacré-Coeur - This church, built in 1873, is a combination of Romanesque and Byzantine architecture. Standing white and imposing above the city from the hills of **Montmartre,** it is an impressive sight. **Montmartre** is one of the areas of Paris that has retained its hold on tourists despite the fact that the old thriving artistic community has departed. The church and the nearby famous square *place du Tertre* are reached by a set of imposing steps that rise to offer magnificent views of Paris by night.

L'Hôtel de Ville - This is a grand building of Renaissance design (rebuilt in 1874 after it was destroyed by the Communards) that today houses the government of the City of Paris. In earlier incarnations this building and site was often the focal point of upheaval in French history. It was here that Robespierre, fanatical leader of the "Reign of Terror" during the French Revolution, was cornered by a furious mob and sent to the guillotine.

La Conciergerie - This is one of the famous buildings situated on the *île de la cité*. A former prison, many of the victims of the French Revolution waited here to be taken to the guillotine in the **Place de la Concorde.** It was here that Marie Antoinette spent her last hours. Visitors can see some of the blades used on the *échafaud.*

La Place Charles de Gaulle - This famous intersection of 12 avenues surrounding the **Arc de Triomphe** used to be called **Place de l'étoile.** The arch itself was built by Napoleon Bonaparte to commemorate his victories. When the Empress Marie Louise was to make her triumphal entry into Paris beneath the Arch, only a few feet had been completed. Napoleon had a full size painted canavas ready for the occasion . The arch has magnificent relief sculptures, the most famous of which was done by the artist François Rude, depicting *la Marseillaise,* the departure of volunteers who fought for France in 1792. The top of the arch is one of the best places to view the city. The picture on page 282 looks down the famous *Avenue des Champs Elysées.*

Exercice écrit

Follow the examples given to answer questions 1 - 10 that follow.

Q: Quand vous êtes à Paris, où allez-vous pour voir le tableau de la Joconde?
A: Je vais au Louvre pour voir le tableau de la Joconde.

Q: Quand tu es à Paris, où vas-tu pour voir des animaux?
A: Je vais au Zoo de Vincennes pour voir des animaux.

Note: Remember that when the preposition *"à"* is followed by *"le"* we combine these two words to make *"au"*. (Example: ***à le*** *Louvre* = ***au*** *Louvre.)*
The *"à"* followed by *"la"* does not combine. (Example: ***à la*** *Tour Eiffel.)*
The "à" followed by *"les"* becomes *"aux"*. (Example: ***à les*** *Tuileries* becomes ***aux*** *Tuileries.)*

1. Quand vous êtes à Paris, où allez-vous pour faire des achats?
2. Quand vous êtes à Paris, où allez-vous pour écouter de la musique?
3. Quand vous êtes à Paris, où allez-vous à la messe?
4. Quand vous êtes à Paris, où allez-vous pour acheter des timbres?
5. Quand vous êtes à Paris, où allez-vous si vous êtes malade?
6. Quand vous êtes à Paris, où allez-vous pour chercher des vieux livres?
7. Quand vous êtes à Paris, où allez-vous pour voir un match de football?
8 Quand vous êtes à Paris, où allez-vous si vous voulez vous promener?
9. Quand vous êtes à Paris, où allez-vous si vous voulez voir le tombeau du soldat inconnu?
10. Quand vous êtes à Paris, où allez-vous si vous voulez changer de l'argent?

Vocabulaire

l'aéroport *airport*
la banque *bank*
le bois/le parc *park*
la cathédrale *cathedral*
le cinéma *movie*
l'église *church*
l'hôpital *hospital*
la messe *mass*
le musée *museum*
la poste *poste office*
le stade *stadium*
le zoo *zoo*

Quand vous êtes à Paris, où allez vous pour voir ...?
When you are in Paris, where do you go to see ...?
Quand tu es à Paris, où vas-tu pour voir ...?
When you are in Paris, where do you go to see ...?

Quand tu es à Paris, où vas-tu pour ...?

When you are in Paris, where do you go to see ...? (informal)

Quand je suis à Paris, je vais ...

When I am in Paris, I go ...

pour voir le tableau *to see a painting*
pour voir des animaux *to see animals*
pour faire des achats *to go shopping*
pour écouter de la musique *to listen to music*
pour aller à la messe *to go to church*
pour acheter des timbres *to buy stamps*
si vous êtes malade *if you are sick*
pour chercher des vieux livres *to buy old books*
pour voir un match de football *to see a football game*
pour vous promener *to take a walk*
pour changer de l'argent *to change money*

Révision

Les jours de la semaine

lundi, mardi, mercredi, jeudi, vendredi, samedi, dimanche

Les mois de l'année

janvier, février, mars, avril, mai, juin, juillet, août, septembre, octobre, novembre, décembre

Aim IIIA: *Each student will be able to read a dialogue about transportation in Paris and demonstrate comprehension by answering true-false questions*

Lecture

Charles, le frère de Françoise arrive à Paris pour passer deux semaines. Il demande à la réceptioniste de son hôtel comment aller à Paris.

1. **Charles:** Excusez-moi, comment peut-on aller à Paris?
2. **La réceptioniste:** Si vous n'êtes pas pressé et l'endroit est près, on peut y aller à pied.
3. **Charles:** Et si on est pressé?
4. **La réceptioniste:** Si on est pressé, le mieux est de prendre un taxi.
5. **Charles:** Est-ce qu'on peut louer une voiture?
6. **La réceptioniste:** Bien sûr, mais c'est très cher et il y a beaucoup de circulation dans Paris.
7. **Charles:** Et pour aller travailler ou visiter un endroit intéressant?
8. **La réceptioniste:** Pour aller travailler, il vaut mieux prendre l'autobus ou le métro.
9. **Charles:** Qu'est-ce que c'est le métro?
10. **La réceptioniste:** Le métro est le moyen de transport public le plus rapide de la capitale. Les américains l'appellent *"subway"*. Voulez-vous parler anglais?
11. **Charles:** Non monsieur, Je suis ici pour rendre visite à ma soeur et pour pratiquer le français. Je travaille dans une banque française à New York et je dois beaucoup parler français.
12. **La réceptioniste:** Voici un plan de métro. Pour avoir plus d'informations vous pouvez aller au bureau de tourisme qui est près de l'arrêt de la station de métro Opéra.
13. **Charles:** Merci beaucoup Madame.
14. **La réceptioniste:** Je vous en prie. Bonne journée.

Compréhension de lecture:

If the statement is true, state *Vrai*. If the statement is false, state *Faux* and **correct the bold portion.**

1. Si vous n'êtes pas pressé et l'endroit est près, on peut **prendre un taxi.**
2. Si on est pressé, on peut **aller à pied.**
3. Pour aller travailler on peut **prendre l'autobus.**
4. Le moyen de transport le moins **cher** de la ville est une voiture louée.
5. Le moyen de transport publique et plus rapide est **le métro.**
6. Charles est à Paris pour **rendre visite à sa soeur et pratiquer le français.**
7. Charles doit parler **français** dans la banque où il travaille.
8. La réceptioniste dit que c'est **difficile** de voyager par le métro.
9. Charles peut obtenir plus de renseignements au **Bureau de Tourisme.**
10. Le Bureau de Tourisme est **loin de** l'arrêt de métro "Concorde".

Vocabulaire de lecture:

l'autobus *bus* — prendre l'autobus *to take the bus*
la voiture *car* — prendre la voiture *to take the car*
louer une voiture *to rent a car*
une voiture louée *a rented car*
le métro *subway* — prendre le métro *to take the subway*
le taxi *taxi* — prendre un taxi *to take a taxi*

arriver *to arrive*
pour... *in order to ...*
pour passer *to spend time*
demander *to ask*
la réceptioniste *receptionist*
Comment peut-on circuler ...? ***How can one** get around ...?*
on ... *one ... (a person)*

Ligne 1: Excusez-moi. *Excuse me.*
Ligne 2: Si on **n'est pas pressé**... *If one **is not in a hurry**...*
si l'endroit est près... if the place is near ...
loin... *far*

Ligne 3: Si on **est pressé...** *If a person is **in a hurry...***
Ligne 4: le mieux c'est *the best thing is...*
Ligne 5: Est-ce qu'on peut louer une voiture? *Can we rent a car?*
Ligne 6: Bien sûr. *Of course.*
Ligne 7: pour aller travailler *to go to work*
pour aller visiter *to visit (a place)*
pour rendre visite *to visit (people)*
Ligne 8: il vaut mieux... *it's best to ...*
Ligne 10: le moyen de transport *means of transportation*
Ligne 11: pratiquer *to practice*
une banque *a bank*
je dois *I have to, I must*
Ligne 12: voici... *here is...*
un plan de métro *a map of the subway*
pour obtenir **plus** de renseignements *to obtain **more*** information
vous pouvez aller... *you can go...*
l'arrêt *the stop*
l'arrêt de métro *the subway stop*
l'arrêt d'autobus *the bus stop*
Ligne 14: Je vous en prie/de rien. *You're welcome.*
Question 8: il/elle dit *he / she says*

Note culturelle

Almost every city and town in france has a tourist office. Large cities like Paris have more than one branch. At the tourist office you can obtain a map of the city, a list of recommended hotels and restaurants and information about the entertainments available, including theater, movies and the opera. Local bus and train information is available as well.

The municipal town hall of Paris *(Hôtel de Ville de Paris)* provides tourist information to the millions who visit Paris each year. The most popular months are June through October.

Hôtel de Ville de Paris

Aim IIIB: *Each student will be able to read a dialogue about traveling in the Métro and demonstrate comprehension by answering true-false questions*

Lecture

Avec le plan de métro en main, Charles décide de visiter le bureau de tourisme afin d'obtenir plus de renseignements sur Paris et les alentours. Puisque sa soeur a des classes pendant la journée, Charles doit aller seul visiter plusieurs endroits intéressants. Il sort dans la rue et demande à un passant.

1. **Charles:** Excusez-moi, Monsieur, où est la station de métro s'il vous plaît?
2. **Le passant:** Venez avec moi. Je vais moi-même prendre le métro maintenant. Voici l'entrée. Cherchez toujours la pancarte avec le mot "métro".
3. **Charles:** Comment est-ce que je peux aller à la station "Concorde"?
4. **Le passant:** Vous avez un plan de métro?
5. **Charles:** Oui, le voici.
6. **Le passant:** Ah voilà! Regardez! Nous sommes ici à la Station "Leningrad" sur la ligne Porte de la Villette - Porte d'Ivry. Il faut aller direction Porte d'Ivry et changer à la station "Opéra". Quand vous descendez à "Opéra" cherchez la correspondance pour "Balard". Sur cette ligne en direction de "Balard", c'est le deuxième arrêt après "Opéra". Descendez à la station "Concorde" Cherchez le mot "Sortie Place de la Concorde" et vous y êtes. Dans le métro, pour ne pas se perdre, il faut toujours chercher la première et la dernière station de la ligne pour savoir quelle direction prendre. Vous comprenez?
7. **Charles:** Je comprends. Il faut chercher la fin de la ligne pour trouver le moyen le plus simple pour aller quelque part.
8. **Le passant:** C'est ça. A propos, où allez-vous?
9. **Charles:** Je vais au bureau de tourisme.
10. **Le passant:** C'est dans la rue de Rivoli à Côté de la Place de la Concorde. Je vous recommende de visiter le jardin des Tuileries sur la droite et vous trouverez le bureau de tourisme sur la gauche dans la rue de Rivoli sous les Arcades.
11. **Charles:** Merci beaucoup, vous êtes très aimable.

12. **Le passant:** Je vous en prie! Amusez-vous bien à Paris.
13. **Charles:** Au revoir! Merci beaucoup de votre amabilité.

Compréhension de lecture:

If the statement is true, state *Vrai.* If the statement is false state *Faux* and **correct the bold part.**

1. Charles doit aller seul visiter plusieurs endroits intéressants parce que sa soeur **est malade.**
2. Il demande à **une passante** où est la station de métro.
3. Le passant va prendre le métro **aussi** lui-même.
4. Charles tient **un plan de métro** dans la main.
5. Maintenant Charles est à la station **"Leningrad".**
6. Il doit changer à la station **"Opéra".**
7. Charles doit sortir à la station **"Balard".**
8. Le bureau de tourisme est **Place de la Concorde.**
9. Le passant recommande à Charles de visiter **le Jardin des Tuileries.**
10. Charles dit au passant, **"Merci beaucoup de votre amabilité."**

Vocabulaire de la lecture:

le plan de métro *subway map*
décider *to decide*
le bureau de tourisme *office of tourism*
obtenir *to obtain*
les renseignements *information*
les alentours *areas close to the city center*
puisque *because*
devoir *ought to*
il doit *he must, he has to*
seul(e) *alone*
un endroit *a place*
sortir dans la rue *go into the street*
le passant *a passer-by, someone*

Ligne 1: où est *where is*
je vais moi-même ... maintenant *I am going myself now*
voici l'entrée *here is the entrance*
cherchez *look for, watch out for*
le signe *the sign*

Ligne 6. Ah voilà! *Here it is!*
regardez *lt look*
la ligne *line*
changer *to change*
descendre *to get off*
direction *direction*
un arrêt *a stop*
la correspondance *transfer, connection*
le deuxième *second*
la sortie *exit*
vous y êtes *you are there*
se perdre to get lost
Vous comprenez? *Did you understand?*
Ligne 7: comprendre *to understand*
le moyen le plus simple *the easiest way*
la fin de la ligne *the end of the line*
Ligne 8: C'est ça. *That's it.*
à propos *by the way*
Ligne 10: Je vous recommende *I recommend*
Ligne 11: Vous êtes très aimable. *You are very kind.*
Ligne 12. Je vous en prie. *Don't mention it. / You are welcome.*

Note culturelle: Le Métro

The Paris *Métro* is one of the most comfortable underground urban transportation systems, and quite easy to use. There are 13 lines that whisk one throughout the city from 5:30 A.M. to 1:15 A.M. daily. A single ticket costs 5.20f, while a *carnet,* or 10-trip packet offers more value at 32.80f.

Many of the major attractions in Paris are found along Line 1. Tickets are also good for making connections with the *R.E.R.,* an inter-suburban high-speed rail system.

Aim IIIC: Each student will be able to use the map of the Paris *Métro* to visit the places of interest of his/her choice

Let's review how to travel the Paris Métro in preparation for your future trip to see the sights of Paris.

a. To find the subway look for a sign that says " _____."
b. Buy your ticket at the ticket window by saying *"Un ticket s'il vous plaît"* if you want one ticket, or *"Un carnet"* if you want a ten-trip ticket.
c. Insert your ticket in the opening in front of the machine. The machine will take your ticket, stamp it and slide it through to the other end where you will pick it up. Do not forget to take your ticket!
d. Let's say you are at the *Louvre* station (Line 1) and wish to go to the *Invalides* station to take a train to the palace at *Versailles*. Looking for the shortest and easiest route, you decide to go in the direction of _____ (look for the last stop on line 1). You then get off at the station called "_____" in order to change to line number ___, heading in the direction of "_____" (the last stop). After exiting the metro at the *Invalides* station, you then purchase a ticket on the *R.E.R.* (the French national railroad) for *Versailles*.

The ***Chateau de Versailles*** was built between 1662 and 1690 as a home and power base for Louis XIV, the Sun King. A visit to this beautiful estate southwest of Paris to view the art and architecture and to sense the history of this opulent period, will take a full day.

Exercice oral

Now it is your turn to use the map of the *Métro* to get around Paris. The map on the following page includes only the basic boulevards and avenues of the heart of Paris, and only three of the thirteen rail lines. The stop for the end of each line is preceded by the word "to" (line 8, south: <u>To</u> Porte d'Orleans, etc.) The places of interest are marked in black. Refer to the list below for the Métro station nearest your destination. Ask your peer partner who will play the role of *un passant* or *une passante* how you can go to the Métro station you desire. S/he will then give you instructions in French as you follow along on the map. Think for a moment to discover the easiest route. Be sure to thank the stranger who is kind enough to heop you. Take turns playing the roles of the tourist and the stranger. The stranger who is giving you instructions can follow the general model given in the dialogue of ***Aim IIIB,*** line 6.

les endroits intéressants	**station**
L'Arc de Triomphe	Charles de Gaulle/Etoile
Avenue des Champs Elysées	Champs Elysées
le jardin des Tuileries	Tuileries
Le Louvre	Louvre
L'Hôtel de Ville	Hôtel de Ville
L'Hôtel des Invalides	Invalides
La Sorbonne, Saint-Germain-des-Prés	St.-Germain-des-Prés
La Cathédrale de Notre-Dame, L'Ile de la Cité	Cité
Le Musée de Cluny, Le Panthéon	St.-Germain-des-Prés
L'Opéra	Opéra
La Tour Eiffel	Invalides
Le Sacré-Coeur	Rochechouart
La Conciergerie	Cité

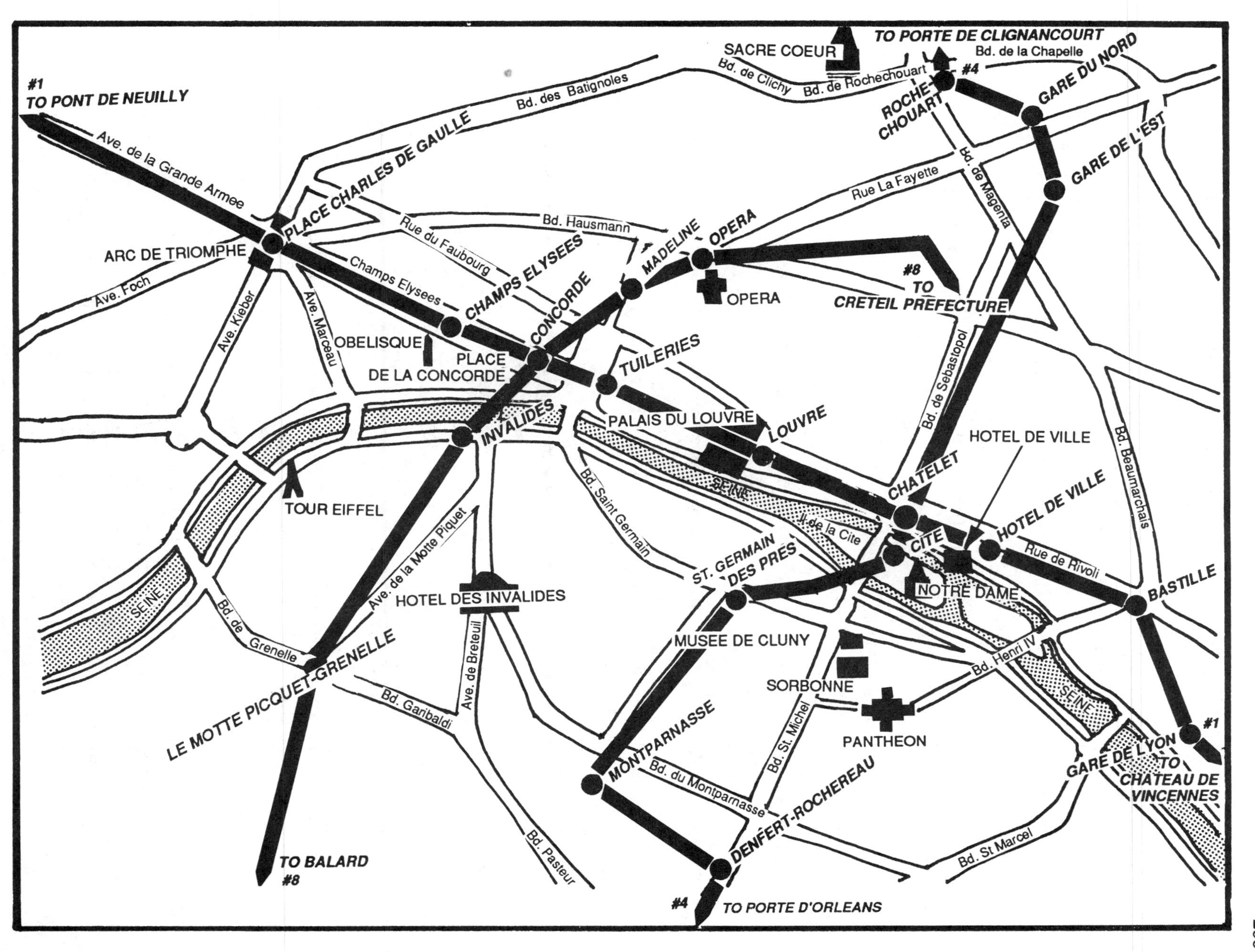
#1
TO PONT DE NEUILLY
Ave. de la Grande Armee
Bd. des Batignoles
PLACE CHARLES DE GAULLE
ARC DE TRIOMPHE
Ave. Foch
Ave. Kleber
Ave. Marceau
Champs Elysees
Rue du Faubourg
Bd. Hausmann
CHAMPS ELYSEES
OBELISQUE
PLACE
DE LA CONCORDE
CONCORDE
MADELINE
OPERA
OPERA
TUILERIES
PALAIS DU LOUVRE
LOUVRE
INVALIDES
SEINE
TOUR EIFFEL
SACRE COEUR
TO PORTE DE CLIGNANCOURT
Bd. de la Chapelle
Bd. de Clichy
Bd. de Rochechouart
#4
ROCHE
CHOUART
GARE DU NORD
GARE DE L'EST
Rue La Fayette
Bd. de Magenta
#8
TO
CRETEIL PREFECTURE
Bd. de Sebastopol
HOTEL DE VILLE
Bd. Beaumarchais
CHATELET
HOTEL DE VILLE
Rue de Rivoli
I. de la Cite
CITE
NOTRE DAME
BASTILLE
Bd. Saint Germain
ST. GERMAIN
DES PRES
Ave. de la Motte Piquet
HOTEL DES INVALIDES
SEINE
Bd. de Grenelle
LE MOTTE PICQUET-GRENELLE
MUSEE DE CLUNY
SORBONNE
Bd. Henri IV
SEINE
PANTHEON
Bd. Garibaldi
Ave. de Breteuil
Bd. St. Michel
MONTPARNASSE
Bd. du Montparnasse
DENFERT-ROCHEREAU
GARE DE LYON
#1
TO
CHATEAU DE
VINCENNES
Bd. St Marcel
Bd. Pasteur
TO BALARD
#8
#4
TO PORTE D'ORLEANS

1. Vous êtes à la station Charles de Gaulle - Etoile (ligne 1) et vous voulez visiter le Musée du Louvre.

2. Vous êtes à la station Denfert-Rochereau (ligne 4) et vous voulez visiter le jardin des Tuileries.

3. Vous êtes à la station Hôtel de Ville (ligne 1) et vous voulez visiter la Sorbonne.

4. Vous êtes à la station Opéra (ligne 8) et vous voulez visiter la Tour Eiffel.

5. Vous êtes à la station Balard (ligne 8) et vous voulez visiter L'Arc de Triomphe.

6. Vous êtes à la station Concorde (ligne 1) et vous voulez visiter le Sacré-Coeur.

Exercice écrit

Write three dialogues of the **Conversation** in which you follow the pattern of ***Aim IIIB,*** lines 3 and 6.

Activité

The class is divided into groups of two. One student plays the tourist and the other the resident of Paris. The tourist wishes to visit a French friend who lives near the Madeleine station (line 8). S/he is staying at a hotel near the intersection of the Boulevard du Montparnasse and Boulevard St. Michel.

1. The tourist says "Excuse me." to a stranger on the street and asks where *métro* station is.
2. The stranger answers that s/he should come with him because he is going to the *métro* now.
3. The tourist asks how s/he can get to the Madeleine station.
4. The stranger asks if s/he has a plan of the *métro.*
5. The tourist answers "Here it is."
6. The stranger explains in detail how s/he can get to his/her destination.
7. The stranger asks why s/he is going there.
8. The tourist responds that s/he is going there to visit a friend.
9. The tourist thanks the stranger and says that he is very kind.
10. The stranger replies "You're welcome." and says that he wishes the tourist a good time in Paris.

Aim IV: *Each student will be able to read the 24 - hour clock in order to understand a railroad time schedule*

Note culturelle

Most countries of the world employ the 24 - hour clock, and not the 12 - hour clock used in the United States. Departure and arrival times for buses, trains and airplanes are based on the 24 - hour clock.

In this system midnight is the starting point and is designated as 00:00. Thirty minutes after midnight is stated as 00:30. One hour after midnight is 01:00. Four hours and fifteen minutes after midnight is 04:15. Nine hours and forty-five minutes after midnight is 09:45. Eleven hours and twenty minutes after midnight is 11:20. As you can see, from 12 midnight (12:00 a.m.) to 12:59 (12:59 p.m.) this system is similar to that used in the United States. However, from 12:59 p.m. through 12 midnight the clock continues through the next eleven hours of the 24 - hour clock from 13:00 to 23:59. Study the following examples:

1:00 p.m. is noted as 13:00
1:10 p.m. is noted as 13:10
2:30 p.m. is noted as 14:30
5:50 p.m. is noted as 17:50
8:25 p. m. is noted as 20:25
10:45 p.m. is noted as 22:45
11:55 p.m. is noted as 23.55
12:00 a.m. is noted as 00:00

To read the 24 - hour clock keep in mind the starting point is 12 midnight (00:00) and thus all times from midnight to 12:59 p.m. are read as we read time in the United States. To read any time after 12:59, subtract 12 hours from the time to arrive at our time (p.m.). Study the following examples:

13:00 minus 12 = 1:00 p.m.
14:15 minus 12 = 2:15 p.m.
16:45 minus 12 = 4:45 p.m.
18:25 minus 12 = 6:25 p.m.
21:40 minus 12 = 9:40 p.m.
23:30 minus 12 = 11:30 p.m.

You will need to read the 24 hour clock when you go to France. State the following times as used in the 24 - hour clock in time as used in the United States. Convert only if necessary.

1. 04:00
2. 17:48
3. 12:25
4. 23:57
5. 09:05
6. 15:35
7. 20:16
8. 07:30
9. 19:14
10. 13:50
11. 22:38
12. 10:15

Exercice oral

Refer to the railroad schedule on page 303 to understand the answers given by Louis and M. Ploton as they read the time schedule for Jean et Marie.

1. **Jean:** A quelle heure part le train (#103) de Paris pour Lille?
   Louis: Le train pour Lille part à dix-sept heures dix-neuf.
   Jean: A quelle heure est-ce qu'il arrive à Lille?
   Louis: Le train arrive à Lille à dix-neuf heures quarante.

2. **Marie:** A quelle heure part le train (#522/3) de Longueau à Douai?
   M. Ploton: Le train pour Douai part à Dix-huit heures trente-cinq.
   Marie: A quelle heure est-ce qu'il arrive à Douai?
   M. Ploton: Le train arrive à Douai à dix neuf heures vingt-deux.

Paris-Nord ----Tourcoing

Numéro de train		2533	2033	2429	103	2235	76239	76239	522/3
Notes à consulter		1	2	3	4	5	6	7	8
					#				TGV
Paris-Nord	**D**		**17.02**	**17.02**	**17.19**	**17.19**			
Creil	D		|	|	|	|			
Longueau	**D**		|	**18.10**	**18.26**	**18.26**			**18.35**
Amiens	D	18.10	18.11	|	|	|	18.34	18.34	|
Albert	**A**	**18.32**		|	|	|	**19.06**	**19.06**	|
Arras	A	18.51		18.41	18.56	18.56		19.47	19.04
Douai	**A**	**19.09**			**19.15**	**19.17**			**19.22**
Lille	A	19.34			19.38	19.40			19.43
Croix-Wasquehal	**A**				**19.58**	**19.58**			
Roubaix	A				20.02	20.02			
Tourcoing	**A**				**20.07**	**20.07**			

Conversation

Peer partners ask one another at what time certain trains leave Paris for the destinations indicated and at what time they arrive. (The number in parentheses will give you the train to take.)

1. A quelle heure part le train (#615) de Paris à Lyon-Part-Dieu?
   A quelle heure est-ce qu'il arrive à Lyon-Part-Dieu?

2. A quelle heure part le train (#845) de Paris à Nice-ville?
   A quelle heure est-ce qu'il arrive à Nice-ville?

3. A quelle heure part le train (#865) de Paris à Avignon?
   A quelle heure est-ce qu'il arrive à Avignon?

4. A quelle heure part le train (#819) de Paris à Marseille-St Charles?
   A quelle heure est-ce qu'il arrive à Marseilles-St Charles?

5. A quelle heure part le train (#815) de Paris à Valence V?
   A quelle heure est-ce qu'il arrive à Valence V?

6. A quelle heure part le train (#845) de Paris à Antibes?
   A quelle heure est-ce qu'il arrive à Antibes?

Paris --- Nice-ville

Numéro de train		5089	845	615	815	865	449/8	6173/2	6173/2	617	5051	5049	5289	819
Notes à consulter		1	2	3	4	5	6	7	8	9	10	11	12	13
			TGV	TGV	TGV	TGV				TGV				TGV
Paris-Gare-de-Lyon	D		**10.41**	11.00	**11.40**	11.45				**12.00**				12.55
Dijon-Ville	A		|	|	|	|				|				|
Macon-Ville	A		|	|	|	|				|				|
Lyon-Part-Dieu	A		**12.45**	13.02	|	|		13.50	13.50	**14.02**	14.06	14.11		|
Lyon-Perrache	A	12.31	|	13.10	|	|		|	|	**14.10**	|	|		|
Valence V	A	13.49	|		**14.35**	14.43		14.49	14.49		15.07	15.07		15.48
Orange	A	14.46	|		|	|		15.39	15.39		|	|		|
Avignon	A	15.06	|		**15.30**	15.34		15.58	15.58		16.10	16.10	**16.25**	16.45
Arles	A	15.26	|		|			|	|		16.31	16.31	**17.20**	|
Marseille-St-Charles	A	16.11	|		**16.22**		**16.39**	16.55	17.04		17.25	17.25		17.39
Cannes	A		**17.10**				**18.39**		19.17		19.36	19.36		
Juan-les-Pins	A		|				|		19.29		19.48	19.48		
Antibes	A		**17.22**				**18.49**		19.34		19.53	19.53		
Cagnes-sur-Mer	A		|				|		|		20.02	20.02		
Nice-Ville	A		**17.38**				**19.05**		19.53		20.16	20.16		

Les trains circulant tous les jours ont leurs horaires indiqués en gras

Tous les trains offrent des places assises en 1re et 2e classe, sauf indication contraire dans les notes.

Exercice écrit

Write and answer the questions of the **Conversation**, numbers 1 - 6.

Vocabulaire

A quelle heure part le train? *At what time does the train leave?*
de ... à ... *from ... to ...*
A quelle heure est-ce qu'il arrive? *At what time does the train arrive?*
à ... *at ...*

Note culturelle

S.N.C.F., Society Nationale des Chemins de Fer Français, France's national railroad, provides service to all parts of France. Reservations are required for all long distance travel, but these and other tickets can be purchased up to five minutes before departure, provided seats are available. The trains have two classes, first and second, but in most of the intercity trains open-plan cars make up *Corail* trains, comfortable even in second class.

The fastest trains are the TVG which reach speeds of 160 to 190 miles per hour. These trains are extremely comfortable and cut rail travel time remarkably. Reservations should be in hand well before departure time. The slower trains (the slowest is the *omnibus)* often require overnight travel for long distances, and one might have to resort to expensive *wagons-lits* (sleeping cars). In general, the rail service is excellent and it is the most popular means of intercity transportation in France.

Lecture

Charles et sa soeur Françoise vont passer trois jours à Strasbourg, une jolie ville à l'est de la France et la capitale de l'Alsace. Charles décide de prendre l'autobus pour aller à la gare de l'Est où il va recontrer Françoise après sa classe.

1. **Charles:** Excusez-moi Monsieur! Comment est-ce que je peux aller à la gare de l'est s'il vous plaît?
2. **Le monsieur:** Voulez-vous prendre l'autobus ou le métro?
3. **Charles:** Je préfère prendre l'autobus parce que je sais déjà voyager par la métro.
4. **Le monsieur:** Bien. Il faut prendre l'autobus numéro 43.
5. **Charles:** Où est la station la plus proche?
6. **Le monsieur:** C'est au coin.
7. **Charles:** Combien coûte un ticket d'autobus?
8. **Le monsieur:** Le ticket coûte 10 francs.
9. **Charles:** Merci beaucoup. Vous êtes très aimable.
10. **Le monsieur:** De rien!

Il est trois heures moins le quart. Charles descend de l'autobus et entre dans la gare. Là, il demande à une dame.

11. **Charles:** Pouvez-vous me dire où sont les renseignements?
12. **La dame:** C'est à droite.
13. **Charles:** Merci. *(Il court aux renseignements.)* Françoise, depuis combien de temps est-ce que tu m'attends?
14. **Françoise:** Cela fait une demi heure que je t'attends.
15. **Charles:** Comme tu le sais, je ne vais pas perdre une occasion de pratiquer. A quelle heure part le prochain train pour Strasbourg?
16. **L'employé:** Le prochain train part à quinze heures dix. C'est un express.
17. **Charles:** Et à quelle heure est-ce qu'il arrive?
18. **L'employé:** Il arrive à dix-sept heures vingt-cinq. Voici les horaires pour votre prochain voyage.

Charles va à un guichet pour les voyages de longues distances.

19. **Charles:** Je voudrais deux billets pour Strasbourg s'il vous plaît.
20. **L'employé:** Première ou deuxième classe?
21. **Charles:** Deuxième classe. Combien coûte chaque billet?
22. **L'employé:** Cela coûte 112 Francs par billet.
23. **Charles:** Merci beaucoup monsieur.

Charles et Françoise marchent rapidement pour monter dans le train à temps. Tout à coup du haut parleur on entend: "Attention! Messieurs les voyageurs. Le train sur le quai numéro 3 direction Strasbourg va partir.

Compréhension de lecture:

1. Charles et sa soeur vont passer trois jours à **Tours.**
2. Il va **seul** à la gare de l'Est.
3. Il decide de prendre **le métro** pour aller à la gare de l'Est.
4. Charles **ne sait pas** voyager par le métro.
5. L'arrêt d'autobus le plus proche est **au coin.**
6. L'autobus coûte **plus cher** que le taxi.
7. Le prochain train part à **trois heures dix de l'après-midi.**
8. Charles achète **un billet** au guichet pour voyages de longues distances.
9. Ils vont voyager en **première classe.**
10. Le train arrive à Strasbourg **à dix-sept heures vingt-cinq minutes le soir.**

Vocabulaire de la lecture:

joli(e) *attractive* décider *to decide*
va rencontrer *is going to meet*
1: Comment est-ce que je peux aller ...? *How can I get to ...?*
*la gare *the railroad station*
2: Préférez-vous aller ...? *Do you prefer to go ...?*
3: Je préfère prendre ... *I prefer to take ...*
Je sais déjà voyager ... *I already know how to travel ...*
4: Il faut prendre ... *You have to take ...*
5: Où est l'arrêt le plus proche? *Where is the next stop?*
6: Continuez tout droit. *Continue straight ahead.*
C'est au coin. *It's on the corner.*
7: Combien coûte un ticket d'autobus?
10: De rien! *It's nothing!*
descendre *to get off* entrer *to enter*
11: Pouvez-vous me dire ... où sont les renseignements?
Can you tell me ... where Information is?
13: Depuis combien de temps est-ce que tu m'attends?
How long have you been waiting for me?
14: Cela fait une demi heure que je t'attends.
I have been waiting for you for half an hour.
15: Comme tu le sais ... *As you already know ...*
Je ne vais pas perdre une occasion
I'm not going to miss an opportunity ...
16: le prochain train *the next train*
20: Voici un horaire. *Here is a schedule.*
le guichet pour les voyages de longues distances
the ticket window for long distnce travel
20: en première classe *in first class* en seconde *in second ...*
21: Combien coûte chaque billet? *How much does each ticket cost?*
rapidement *rapidly* monter dans le train *to board the train*
à temps, à l'heure *on time*
monter dans l'autobus *to board the bus*
tout à coup *suddenly*
on entend *one hears*
le train sur le quai *the train situated on the track*
à destination de ... *whose destination is ...*
quai *platform* va partir *is going to leave*

***Note:** **la gare** is <u>always</u> the railroad station
la station is <u>always</u> the bus or *métro* station

Activité

A. The class is divided into groups of three. One student plays the role of the tourist, another plays the role of the resident of Paris who gives directions, and the third student plays the role of the ticket seller.

1. The tourist says "Excuse me." to a person on the street. He then asks him how he can get to the gare du Nord.
2. The person then asks if he prefers to go by bus or by *Métro.*
3. The tourist says that he prefers to go by bus.
4. The person states that he has to take bus number 64.
5. The tourist asks where the nearest stop is.
6. The person tells him to go straight ahead and that it is on the corner.
7. The tourist asks how much a bus ticket costs.
8. The person answers that it costs 10 francs.
9. The tourist thanks the person and says that he is very kind.
10. The person answers "You're welcome." and says that he hopes everything goes well.

(The tourist takes the bus to the gare du Nord and goes directly to the ticket window. It is now 2:00 in the afternoon.)

11. The tourist asks what time the next train leaves for Cannes.
12. The ticket seller tells him when the next train leaves for Cannes and the type of train it is. (Refer to the railroad schedule *"Paris-Nice-ville"*, page 303.)
13. The tourist says that he wants to buy one ticket to Cannes.
14. The ticket seller asks "In first or second class?"
15. The tourist answers "In first class" and then asks how much the ticket costs.
16. The ticket seller tells him what the ticket costs.
17. The tourist asks what time the train arrives at Cannes.
18. The ticket seller tells him when the train arrives at Cannes. (Refer to the train schedule.)
19. The tourist thanks him very much and tells him that he is very kind.

B. This activity can be repeated with students changing roles.

UNIT TWELVE

Les magasins

Mon quartier

Les métiers / Les professions

TOPIC

A. Stores and Specialty shops
B. The neighborhood/community D. Earning a living

SITUATION

Interaction with individual peers

FUNCTION

Providing and obtaining information about one's city and neighborhood
Providing and obtaining information about one's job or profession
Expressing personal feelings

PROFICIENCY

Can comprehend simple statements and questions
and can respond appropriately with possible need for repetition
Can ask questions appropriate to the communicative situation
Can understand some aspects of French culture

AIM I: Each student will be able to identify the stores found in any town or city in France

AIM II: Each student will be able to describe the neighborhood in which s/he lives including the principal stores, public services and recreational facilities

AIM IIIA: Each student will be able to identify some of the jobs and professions people have in the communicy

AIM IIIB: Each student will be able to recognize jobs and professions which are cognates
Each student will be able to ask a peer "What do you want to be and why?" and be able to answer the questions

Aim I: *Each student will be able to identify the stores found in any town or city in France.*

Exercice oral

Conversation

Partner A asks the questions in Column A. **Partner B** asks the questions in column B. ***Examples:***

A: Quand tu es en France, où achètes-tu les vêtements?
B: Quand je suis en France, j'achète les vêtements dans un magasin de vêtements.

B: Quand vous êtes en France, où achetez-vous les chaussures?
A: Quand je suis en France, j'achète les chaussures dans un magasin de chaussures.

Partner A

1. Quand tu es en France, où est-ce que tu achètes le pain?
2. Quand tu es en France, où est-ce que tu achètes les médicaments?
3. Quand tu es en France, où est-ce que tu achètes la viande?
4. Quand tu es en France, où est-ce que tu achètes les livres?
5. Quand tu es en France, où est-ce que tu achètes les fruits?
6. Quand tu es en France, où est-ce que tu achètes les timbres?

Partner B

1. Quand vous êtes en France, où achetez-vous les gâteaux?
2. Quand vous êtes en France, où achetez-vous les parfums?
3. Quand vous êtes en France, où achetez-vous le poisson?
4. Quand vous êtes en France, où achetez-vous les journaux et les revues?
5. Quand vous êtes en France, où achetez-vous la nourriture?

la Pâtisserie: The pastry shop sells cakes, pastries and sweets.

la Poissonnerie: This shop sells fish, shell fish, and fish products.

le Kiosque: The kiosk sells mainly newspapers and magazines. One can o find postcards and maps.

l'Epicerie: The grocery store sells everything from milk, cheese and ggs to oil, vegetables and fruits. In almost every neighborhood of towns and ties, you can find *le marché,* the market, a place that has under one roof all nds of specialty shops such as *le marchand de fruits, la charcuterie, la oissonnerie, etc.* Le marché is often in the open in the main plaza. In the last w years American-style supermarkets have also become fashionable in the ties.

le Magasin de vêtements: The clothing store sells ready made clothes. here are *tailleurs,* tailor shops, where mens' suits are made to order. Some omen have *une couturière,* a dressmaker, make their clothes.

le Marchand de chaussures: The shoe store sells all kinds of footwear nown as *les chaussures.* Bear in mind that the Metric system of measurement used in France. For men an American 7 is French size 40, an 8 is a 41, a 9 is a 2, etc. For women, an American 5 is a French size 37, a 6 is a 38, a 7 is a 39.

Les heures d'ouverture et de fermeture des magasins: Almost all ores in France are open from 9 a.m. to 12:30 p.m. and from 2:00 p.m. to 6:00 or 00 p.m. The exceptions are the large department stores which do not close in e afternoon.

1. State three differences between French and American stores. Give ecific examples.

Exercice écrit

Complete the following statements with the name of the store where one buys each product.

1. Robert achète les livres à la _____.
2. Mon amie achète les fruits chez le _____.
3. Monsieur Platon achète les journaux et les revues au _____.
4. Mademoiselle Vavasseur achète le pain chez le _____.
5. Madame Ramos achète la viande chez le _____.
6. La famille d'Hélène achète la nourriture chez l' _____.
7. Mon ami achète des chaussures chez le _____.
8. La tante de Jean achète les parfums à la _____.
9. La grand-mère de Robert achète le parfum à la _____.
10. La famille de Charles achète les vêtements dans_____.
11. Anne achète des gâteaux chez le _____.

Résumé

Fill in the blank with the appropriate item(s) sold in each store or shop.
Example:

Jean: Qu'est-ce qu'on vend à la librairie?
Anne: On vend des livres à la librairie.

1. Qu'est-ce qu'on vend à la boucherie?
   On vend _____ à la boucherie.

2. Qu'est-ce qu'on vend à la pâtisserie?
   On vend _____ à la pâtisserie.

3. Qu'est-ce qu'on vend chez le marchand de fruits?
   On vend _____ chez le marchand de fruits.

4. Qu'est-ce qu'on vend à la poissonnerie?
   On vend _____ à la poissonnerie.

5. Qu'est-ce qu'on vend à la pharmacie?
   On vend _____ à la pharmacie.

6. Qu'est-ce qu'on vend chez le marchand de chaussures?
   On vend _____ chez le marchand de chaussures.

7. Qu'est-ce qu'on vend au magasin de vêtements?
   On vend _____au magasin de vêtements.

8. Qu'est-ce qu'on vend dans le kiosque?
   On vend _____dans le kiosque.

9. Qu'est-ce qu'on vend à la librairie?
   On vend _____ à la librairie.

10. Qu'est-ce qu'on vend à la boulangerie?
    On vend _____ à la boulangerie.

11. Qu'est-ce qu'on vend à la pharmacie?
    On vend _____ à la pharmacie.

12. Qu'est-ce qu'on vend à l'épicerie?
    On vend _____ à l'épicerie.

Vocabulaire

Les magasins ***stores***

la boucherie *the butcher shop*
la pharmacie *the drugstore*
la parfumerie *perfume store*
le marchand de fruits *the fruit store*
la librairie *the book store*
la boulangerie *the bakery*
la pâtisserie *the pastry shop*
la poissonnerie *the fish store*
le kiosque *the newstand, kiosk*
la crèmerie *dairy store*

l'épicerie *the grocery*
le magasin de vêtements
the clothing store
le marchand de chaussures
the shoe store

la viande *meat*
les médicaments *medicines*
le parfum *perfume*
les fruits *fruits*
les livres *books*
le pain *bread*
la pâtisserie *pastry*
le poisson *fish*
les journaux *newspapers*
les revues *magazines*

la nourriture *food*

les vêtements *clothing*

les chaussures *shoes*

Quand tu es en France .../ Quand vous êtes en France...
When you are in France...
Quand je suis en France... *When I'm in France...*
Où achètes-tu.../ Où achetez-vous ...? *Where do you buy ...?*
Qu'est-ce qu'on vend ...? *What is sold in ...?*
On vend ... *... is sold*

Notes culturelles

Les Magasins

la Charcuterie: Sells a wide variety of patés, hams, chickens, cold cuts and cooked sausages. La charcuterie sells pork products and cold salads, but no beef products.

la Boucherie: Sells a variety of meats, including veal, lamb and beef.

la Parfumerie: You can buy a whole range of perfumes, cologne, and toilet items here, but not medicines.

la Pharmacie: The pharmacy is the place where you buy medicines. It can be identified by the sign bearing a green cross against a white background.

le Marchand de fruits et légumes: A wide variety of fruits and vegetables are available at the fruit store. These are abundant in France because it has a large and diverse agricultural production. Fresh produce arrives daily to all the fruit stores, markets and supermarkets of the country.

la Librairie: This is a bookstore, not a library.

la Boulangerie: Most bakeries sell only bread. The standard type of loaf is the *baguette*, an elongated loaf about two feet long. Bread is a staple in the French diet and is eaten, usually without butter, with ever
prefer to buy their bread fresh daily. Pre-packaged bread is nc

Aim II: *Each student will be able to describe the neighborhood in which s/he lives including the principal stores, public services, and recreational facilities*

Lecture

Il est deux heures de l'après-midi. Anne, Jacques, et quelques amis se retrouvent dans une caféteria du Boulevard Saint Michel, une rue renommée dans le quartier Latin (quartier des étudiants). Paul veut connaître la ville et le quartier où habite Anne.

1. **Jacques:** Anne, dans quelle ville habites-tu?
2. **Anne:** J'habite à New York.
3. **Jacques:** Comment est New York?
4. **Anne:** C'est une grande ville avec des bâtiments modernes, de grandes avenues et des rues larges.
5. **Jacques:** Combien est-ce qu'il y a d'habitants?
6. **Anne:** Il y a trois millions d'habitants.
7. **Jacques:** Et comment est le quartier où tu habites?
8. **Anne:** Mon quartier est joli et tranquille, mais tous les quartiers ne sont pas bons. Ma meilleure amie habite dans un quartier dangereux.
9. **Jacques:** Est-ce que tu habites près de ou loin des magasins?
10. **Anne:** J'habite près des magasins.
11. **Jacques:** Et quels sont-ils?
12. **Anne:** Il y a le supermarché, la boulangerie, trois magasins de vêtements, deux pizzérias et un restaurant chinois. Il y a aussi deux banques, la poste, la bibliothèque, l'église et la synagogue.
13. **Jacques:** A quels magasins est-ce que tu vas le plus souvent?
14. **Anne:** Je vais souvent dans les magasins de vêtements.
15. **Jacques:** Et avec qui est-ce que tu y vas?
16. **Anne:** Quelquefois j'y vais avec ma mère et quelquefois avec ma meilleure amie.
17. **Jacques:** Quels sont les endroits intéressants dans ta ville?
18. **Anne:** Il y a beaucoup de musées, de parcs, de cinémas, de discothèques et un stade pour les sports de baseball et football.
19. **Jacques:** Est-ce qu'il y a quelque chose d'historique?
20. **Anne:** Certainement! La Statue de la Liberté dans le port de New York un cadeau du gouvernement français aux Américains.

Compréhension de lecture:

If the statement is true, state *Vrai.* If the statement is false, state *Faux* and **correct the bold part.**

1. Il est **cinq heures et demie** de l'après-midi.
2. Jacques, Anne et des amis sont dans une **cafétéria**.
3. La ville de New York est très **petite**.
4. Les rues de la ville sont très **étroites**.
5. Le quartier d'Anne est **laid et bruyant**.
6. Anne habite **loin des** magasins.
7. Il y a trois **supermarchés** dans le quartier d'Anne.
8. Anne va **seule** dans les magasins de vêtements.
9. Il y a **beaucoup** d'endroits intéressants dans la ville de New York.
10. **Les Français** ont donné la Statue de la Liberté aux Américains.

Conversation

1. Est-ce que tu habites dans une ville? Un village?
2. Comment s'appelle la ville (ou le village) où tu habites?
3. Comment est la ville où tu habites?
4. Combien est-ce qu'il y a d'habitants?
5. Comment est le quartier où tu habites?
6. Est-ce que tu habites près ou loin des magasins?
7. Quels sont les magasins principaux de ta ville?
8. A quels magasins est-ce que tu vas le plus souvent?
9. Avec qui est-ce que tu vas dans les magasins?
10. Quels sont les endroits intéressants et où on peut s'amuser dans la ville?
11. Est-ce qu'il y a quelque chose d'historique dans ta ville? Qu'est-ce que c'est?

Résumé

Draw a map of your own neighborhood. Include and label in French the principal stores, public services and recreational facilities.

Vocabulaire

Il/elle veut savoir ... *he / she wants to know ...*
Dans quelle ville est-ce que tu habites? *In what city / town do you live?*
Dans quelle ville habites-tu? *In what city / town do you live?*

Comment est la ville? *What is the city like?*
grande *large* moyenne *medium* petite *small*
rues larges *wide streets* rues étroites *narrow streets*
le bâtiment *building*
Combien est-ce qu'il y a d'habitants? *How many inhabitants?*
Il y a...million d'habitants. *It has ... million inhabitants.*
Il y a...mille habitants. *It has ... thousand inhabitants.*

Comment est le quartier? *What's the neighborhood like?*
joli *pretty* tranquille *quiet*
laid *ugly* bruyant *noisy* dangereux *dangerous*
tous les quartiers ne sont pas ... *all the neighborhoods aren't ...*
près de *near* ou *or* loin de *far from*

Quels sont-ils? *What are they?*
le restaurant chinois *Chinese restaurant*
la synagogue *synagogue*
A quels magasins est-ce que tu vas le plus souvent? *What stores do you go to often?*
quelquefois *sometimes*
Avec qui est-ce que tu y vas? *With whom do you go?*
J'y vais avec... *I go with ...* Je vais seul(e). *I go alone.*

Quels sont les endroits intéressants et de récréation dans ta ville?
What places of interest and recreation are there in your city?
Est-ce qu'il y a quelque chose d'historique?
Is there anything of historic interest?
Certainement! / Bien sûr! *Of course!*
Il n'y a rien d'intérêt historique. *There is nothing of historical interest.*
la Statue de la Liberté *the Statue of Liberty*

Aim IIIA: *Each student will be able to identify some of the jobs and professions people have in the community*

Exercice oral 1

Quel métier / profession fait-il/elle? Il/elle est...

l'avocat | la maîtresse de maison | l'éboueur

le pompier | le boucher | le facteur

l'infirmière | le docteur | le boulanger

l'agent de police | le professeur | la programmeuse d'ordinateurs

Exercice oral 2

A. ***Personne:*** the name of the person who does certain work
B. ***Action:*** the action or type of work the person does
C. ***Produit ou personne:*** the product which is involved or the person who receives the service
D. ***L'endroit:*** the place where the person works

Your teacher will ask you questions such as the following:
Questions pour pratiquer: numéro 1

1a. Qui défend les clients au tribunal?
1b. Que fait l'avocat au tribunal?
1c. Qui est-ce que l'avocat défend?
1d. Où est-ce que l'avocat défend les clients?

A. Personne	B. Action	C. Produit ou personne	D. L'endroit
1. L'avocat(e)	défend	les clients	au tribunal.
2. La maîtresse de maison	s'occupe	des enfants	à la maison.
3. L'éboueur	ramasse	les ordures	dans les rues.
4. Le pompier	éteint	les feux	dans les bâtiments.
5. Le boucher	vend	la viande	dans la boucherie.
6. Le facteur	distribue	le courrier	dans les maisons.
7. L'infirmier	aide, soigne	les malades	à l'hôpital.
8. Le docteur La doctoresse	examine	les malades	dans le bureau. de consultation.
9. Le boulanger	vend	le pain	dans la boulangerie.
10. L'agent de police	aide	les gens	dans la rue.
11. Le professeur	enseigne	aux élèves	à l'école.
12. Le programmeur d'ordinateurs La programmeuse ...	écrit	des programmes	pour la compagnie.
13. Le vendeur La vendeuse	vend	des vêtements	dans le magasin de vêtements.

Conversation 1

Partner A asks his/her partner who does the particular job or work and then **Partner B** asks the questions. Partners reverse roles the second time. Partners answer the questions with a complete sentence. ***Example:***

Q: Qui vend les vêtements dans le magasin de vêtements?
A: La vendeuse vend les vêtements dans le magasin de vêtements.

Partner A

1. Qui enseigne aux élèves à l'école?
2. Qui vend la viande à la boucherie?
3. Qui aide les gens dans la rue?
4. Qui soigne les malades à l'hôpital?
5. Qui écrit les programmes pour la compagnie?
6. Qui ramasse les ordures dans la rue?

Partner B

7. Qui vend le pain dans la boulangerie?
8. Qui défend les clients au tribunal?
9. Qui examine les malades dans le bureau de consultation?
10. Qui distribue le courrier dans les maisons?
11. Qui s'occupe des enfants à la maison?
12. Qui éteint les feux dans les bâtiments?

Qui distribue le courrier dans les maisons?

Conversation 2

Partner A asks his/her partner where the person does a particular job or work and then **Partner B** asks the questions. Partners reverse roles the second time. Partners answer the questions with a complete sentence.

Partner A

1. Où est-ce que la maîtresse de maison s'occupe des enfants?
2. Où est-ce que le docteur examine les malades?
3. Où est-ce que le pompier éteint les feux?
4. Où est-ce que le boulanger vend le pain?
5. Où est-ce que le facteur distribue le courrier?
6. Où est-ce que l'avocat défend les clients?

Partner B

7. Où est-ce que l'infirmière soigne les malades?
8. Où est-ce que l'éboueur ramasse les ordures?
9. Où est-ce que la police aide les gens?
10. Où est-ce que le boucher vend la viande?
11. Où est-ce que la programmeuse écrit les programmes?
12. Où est-ce que le professeur enseigne aux élèves?

Où est-ce que le professeur enseigne aux élèves?

Exercice écrit

Write the questions and answers of the **Conversation 1,** numbers 1 - 6, and the **Conversation 2,** numbers 1 - 6.

Aim IIIB: *Each student will be able to recognize jobs and professions which are cognates*
Each student will be able to ask a peer "What do you want to be?" and "Why?" and be able to answer the questions

Exercice oral 1

un acteur
une actrice
un/une architecte
un/une astronaute
un/une bibliothécaire
un charpentier
un chauffeur d'autobus
un conducteur de train
un/une dentiste
un électricien
un/une photographe
un/une ingénieur
un mécanicien
un/une modèle
un musicien
un/une pédiatre
un pilote
un plombier
un/une politicien(ne)
un/une psychologue
un/une psychiatre
un/une secrétaire
un chauffeur de taxi
un/une vétérinaire

Exercice oral 2

1. **Jean:** Qu'est-ce que tu veux être?
   Marie: Je veux être comptable.
   Jean: Pourquoi?
   Marie: Parce que j'ai de bonnes notes en mathématiques et je veux gagner beaucoup d'argent.

2. **Charles:** Qu'est-ce que tu veux être?
   Catherine: Je veux être maîtresse.
   Charles: Pourquoi?
   Catherine: Parce que j'aime l'école et j'aime travailler avec les enfants.

3. **Pierre:** Qu'est ce que tu veux être?
   Hélène: Je veux être doctoresse.
   Pierre: Pourquoi?
   Hélène: Parce que j'aime la médecine et je veux aider les gens.

4. **Claude:** Qu'est-ce que tu veux être?
   Robert: Je ne sais pas ce que je veux être.
   Claude: Est-ce que tu aimerais être docteur?
   Robert: Non, je n'aimerais pas être docteur parce que je n'aime pas voir les personnes malades.

Conversation

1. Each student asks three classmates what s/he wants to be and why.

2. Peer partners ask each other the question and listen carefully to his/her partner's response. Then groups of 4 - 6 students are formed. Each member of the group then tells the other members what his/her partner wants to be and why. ***Examples:***

a. Marie veut être comptable parce qu'elle a de bonnes notes en mathématiques et elle veut gagner beaucoup d'argent.
b. Catherine veut être maîtresse parce qu'elle aime l'école et elle veut travailler avec les enfants.
c. Hélène veut être doctoresse parce qu'elle aime la médecine et elle veut aider les gens.
d. Robert ne sait pas ce qu'il veut être. Il n'aimerait pas être docteur parce qu'il n'aime pas voir les personnes malades.

Exercice écrit

Write the questions you would ask of a peer to find out what s/he wants to be and why. Then you answer the question.

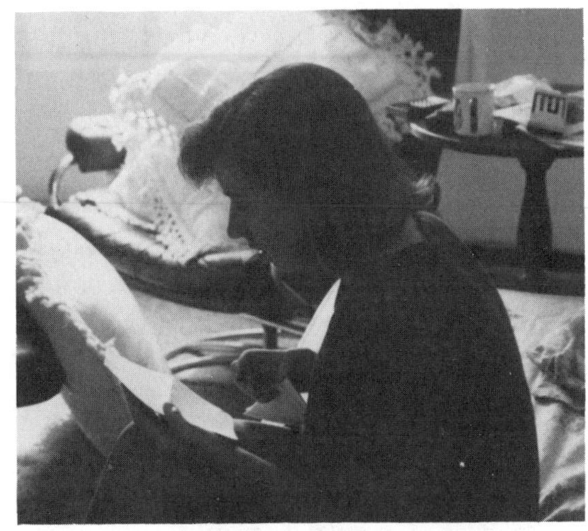

Je veut être psychologue.

Vocabulaire

1. **L'avocat** défend les clients au tribunal.
   The lawyer defends clients in court.
2. **La maîtresse de maison** s'occupe des enfants à la maison.
   The housewife takes care of the children at home.
3. **L'éboueur** ramasse les ordures dans la rue.
   The sanitation worker collects the garbage in the street.
4. **Le pompier** éteint les feux dans les bâtiments.
   The fireman extinguishes fires in buildings.
5. **Le boucher** vend la viande dans la boucherie.
   The butcher sells meat in the butcher shop.
6. **Le facteur** distribue le courrier dans les maisons.
   The mailman delivers letters to homes.

L'éboueur ramasse les ordures dans la rue.

7. **L'infirmière** soigne les malades à l'hôpital.
   The nurse helps sick people in the hospital.
8. **Le docteur** examine les malades dans le bureau de consultation.
   The doctor examines patients in the doctor's office.
9. **Le boulanger** vend le pain dans la boulangerie.
   The baker sells bread in the bakery.
10. **L'agent de police** aide les gens dans la rue.
    The policeman helps people in the street.
11. **Le professeur** enseigne aux élèves à l'école.
    The teacher teaches students in school.
12. **La programmeuse d'ordinateurs** écrit des programmes pour la compagnie.
    The computer programmer writes programs for the company.
13. **La vendeuse** vend des vêtements dans le magasin de vêtements.
    The saleswoman sells clothes in the clothing store.

Quel métier/profession fait-il/elle? *What work does he/she do?*
Qui ...? *Who ...?* Où ...? *Where ...?*
A qui ...? *Whom ...?* Que fait ...? *What does ... do?*
un bâtiment *a building*
Qu'est-ce que tu veux être? *What do you want to be?*
Je veux être comptable. *I want to be an accountant.*
Je ne sais pas ce que je veux être. *I don't know what I want to be.*
Pourquoi? *Why?*
... parce que je veux aider les gens.
... because I want to help people.
... parce que je veux travailler avec les enfants.
... because I want to work with children.
... parce que je veux gagner beaucoup d'argent.
... because I want to earn a lot of money.
... parce que je n'aime pas voir ...
... because I don't like to see ....
Est-ce que tu aimerais être ... *Would you like to be ...?*
J'aimerais être ... *I would like to be ....*
Je n'aimerais pas être ... *I wouldn't like to be ....*
Il/Elle n'aimerait pas être ...
He/she wouldn't like to be ....

Il/Elle veut être ... parce que ... *He/she wants to be ... because ...*
Il/Elle ne sait pas ce qu'il /elle veut être.
He/she doesn't know what he/she wants to be.

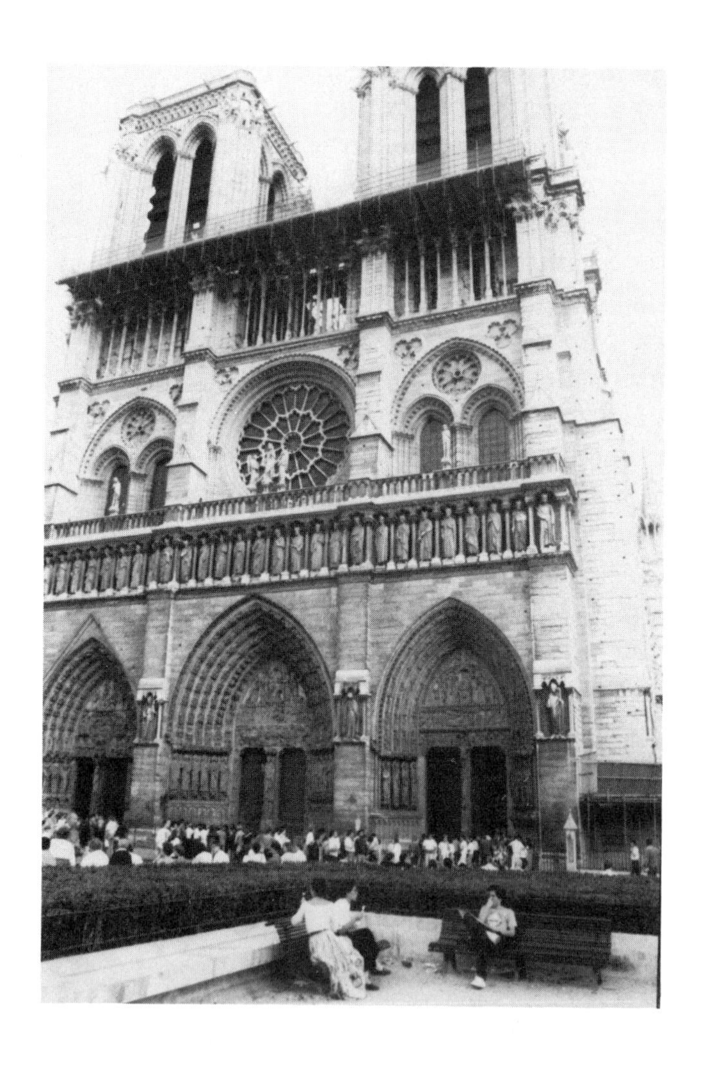

GLIMPSES OF FRANCE

VOCABULAIRE

français - anglais

Vocabulaire: français - anglais

Abbreviations: m.masculine f. feminine s. singular n. neuter pl. plural

A

à *to*
les achats *errands, shopping*
acheter *to buy*
l' activité *activity*
l' addition *restaurant check , addition*
l adresse *address*
l' aéroport *airport*
l' Afrique *Africa*
l' âge *age*
l' agent *agent*
agréable *agreeable*
l' aide *the help*
aider *to help*
l' aîné(e) *the eldest*
l' alentours *the surroundings*
l' algèbre *algebra*
aller *to go*
Je vais *I go*
Je vais au cinéma. *I go to the movies.*
Je vais bien. *I am fine. I am well.*
Je vais à la partie. *I am going to the party.*
aimable *kind, amiable*
aimer *to like, to love*
j'aime *I love, I like*
j'aime bien *I like better*
j'aime mieux *I like best*
Qu'est-ce que tu aimes?
Qu'est-ce que vous aimez?
What do you like?
Allo! *Hello!*
Américain(e) *American*
l' Amérique *America*
l' ami (m) *friend*
l' amie (f) *friend*
(s)' amuser *to have fun*
l' anglais *English*
les animaux *animals*
l' année *year*
l' anniversaire *birthday*
antipathique *repugnant*
août *August*
l' appartement *appartment*
appeler *to call*
je m'appelle *my name is*
l' appétit *appetite*
Bon appétit. *Good appetite! Enjoy!*
après *after*
l'après-midi *afternoon (part of the day)*
apporter *to bring*
apprendre *to learn*
l' art *art*
l' argent *money (silver)*
arrêter *to stop*
l' arrêt *a stop*
arriver *to arrive*
l' ascenseur *elevator*
l' aspirine *aspirin*
l' assiette *the plate*
assis *seated*
athlétique *athletic*
Atlantique Océan *Atlantic ocean*
attendre *to wait*
aujourd'hui *today*
au revoir *good bye*
aussi *also*
moi aussi *me too*
l' automne *autumn, fall*
l' autobus *bus*
autre *other*
l' autre the other
avant *before*
avec *with*
l' avenue *avenue*
avoir *to have*
j'ai *I have*
tu as *you have (inf.)*
avoir faim *to be hungry*
avoir soif *to be thirsty*
l' avocat *lawer*
avril *April*

B

la baignoire *bath tub*
le bain *bath*
la banque *bank*
le baseball *baseball*
le basketball *basketball*
le bâtiment *building*
bavarder *to chat*
beaucoup (de) *a lot, a lot of*
beau(m), belle(f) *beautiful, pretty*
il fait beau *the weather is nice*
la Belgique *Belgium*
le beurre *butter*
la bibliothèque *library*
la biologie *biology*
bien *good, well*
bien-sûr *of course*
bientôt *soon*
à bientôt *see you soon*
le bifteck *steak*
le billet *ticket*
blanc *white*
bleu *blue*
le blouson *sport jacket*
boire *to drink*
je bois *I drink*
vous buvez *you drink*
nous buvons *we drink*
la boisson *a drink*
le bois *wood*
bon(m) bonne(f) *good*
bonjour *hello*
bonsoir *hello after 6 p.m., goodbye or good night*
la bouche *mouth*
le boucher *butcher*
la boucherie *butcher shop*
le boudin *blood sausage*
le boulanger *baker*
la boulangerie *bread shop*
border *to border*
bordé *bordered*
les boules *bocci*
le bureau *office, desk*
le bureau du directeur *Principal's office*
le bras *arm*
bronzer *to tan (sun tan)*
le bruit *noise*
bruyant *noisy*
le bus *bus*

C

le cadeau *gift, present*
le café *coffee*
le café au lait *coffee with milk*
la cafétéria *cafeteria*
le cahier *notebook*
le Canada *Canada*
la carotte *carrot*
la carte de crédit *credit card*
le cassis *black currant*
la cathédrale *cathedral*
ce, cet, cette *this, that*
ces *those*
la ceinture *belt*
les céréales *cereals*
certainement *certainly*
C'est ça. *That's it.*
la chaine *chain*
la chaise *chair*
la chaleur *heat*
la chambre *the bedroom*
les champignons *mushrooms*
la chance *luck*
changer *to change*
chanter *to sing*
le chapeau *hat*
le charcutier *person who works in a deli*
la charcuterie *deli shop*
le château *castle*
chaud *hot*
Il fait chaud. *The weather is hot. It's hot.*
les chaussettes *socks*
les chaussures *shoes*
la chemise *shirt*
le chemisier *blouse*
cher(m)chère(f) *dear, expensive*
chercher *to look for*
les cheveux *hair*
la chimie *chemistry*
le chocolat *chocolate*
le chocolat chaud *hot chocolate*
choisir *to choose*
le choix *choice*
la chose *thing*
cinq *five*
cinquante *fifty*
cinquième *fifth*
le citron *lemon*

la classe *classroom*
le client *client*
le club *club*
comme ci, comme ça *so so*
commencer *to start*
combien *how many*
combien coûte *how much (cost)*
comment *how*
Comment ça va?
Comment allez-vous?
How are you?
Comment es-tu? *How are you?*
comment est *how is*
Comment t'appelles tu?
What's your name?
la commode *bureau*
comprendre *to understand*
la communauté *community*
la confiture *jam (preserves)*
confortable *comfortable*
connaître *to know*
je connais *I know*
content(e) *happy, contented*
la conversation *conversation*
la corbeille *basket*
la corbeille à papier *waste paper basket*
la correspondance *correspondence*
correspondre *to correspond*
la Corse *Corsica*
le côté *side*
à côté *near, next to*
le cou *neck*
couper *to cut*
le costume *suit*
la cour *yard, backyard*
courir *to run*
le cours (du soir) *course (evening classes)*
le couteau *knife*
coûter *to cost*
la coutume *custom*
le cousin(m) *la cousin*
la cousine(f) *cousin*
la craie *chalk*
la cravate *tie*
le crayon *pencil*
créatif(m), créative(f) *creative*
la crèmerie *dairy shop*
les crevettes *shrimp*
la cuisine *kitchen*
faire la cuisine *to cook*
le cuisinier(m) *cook*
la cuisinière(f) *cook, stove*

D

d'abord *first*
la dactylo *secretary*
la dame *woman*
dangereux(euse) *dangerous*
dans *in*
danser *to dance*
la date *date*
décembre *December*
décider *to decide*
le degré *degree (weather)*
le déjeuner *lunch*
délicieux *delicious*
demain *tomorrow*
à demain *see you tomorrow*
demander *to ask*
la demie *half*
la dent *tooth*
depuis *since*
derrière *behind*
descendre *to get off, to get down*
désirer *to desire, to want*
le dessert *dessert*
la destination *destination*
deux *two*
deuxième *second*
devant *in front, front*
devenir *to become*
devoir *to have to*
je dois *I must, I have to, I owe (money)*
les devoirs *homework*
différent(e) *different*
difficile *difficult*
dimanche *Sunday*
le dîner *dinner*
dîner *to dine*
la direction *direction*
la discothèque *disco*
le disque *record*
la distribution *distribution*
la distribution des prix
award ceremony
dix *ten*
dixième *tenth*
dix-sept *seventeen*
dix-huit *eighteen*
dix-neuf *nineteen*
le docteur(m), la doctoresse(f) *doctor*
le doigt *finger*
dormir *to sleep*

le dos *back*
douze *twelve*
douzième *twelfth*
dramatique *dramatic*
drôle *funny, fun*
la droite *the right*
droit *right*
tout droit *straight ahead*

E

l' eau *water*
l' éboueur *sanitation worker*
l' école *school*
l'école secondaire *secondary school*
l' économie *economy*
écouter *to listen*
écrire *to write*
j'écris *I write*
l' éducation *education*
l' éducation physique *physical education*
l élève *student, pupil*
elle, elles(pl) *she (they)*
embrasser *to kiss, to embrace*
je t'embrasse *I embrace you*
enchanté *glad to meet you*
l' endroit *place*
l' enfant *child*
les enfants *children*
ennuyeux (m), ennuyeuse(f) *boring*
enseigner *to teach*
ensuite *then, thus*
entier, entière *entire*
entrer *to enter*
entre *between*
l' entrée *entrance*
l' épicerie *grocery*
l' épicier *grocer*
l' éponge *eraser (blackboard)*
les époux *spouses*
l' Equateur *Equator*
l' équipe *team*
les escargots *snails*
l' espagnol *Spanish*
l' Espagne *Spain*
en espèces *cash*
payer en espèces *to pay cash*
espérer *to hope*
l' estomac *stomach*
essuyer *to dry*
j'essuie *I dry*
et *and*
l' étage *floor*
l' état *state*
les Etats-Unis *United States*
l' été *summer*
l' étudiant(e) student
étudier to study
être *to be*
je suis *I am*
étroit *(e)* *narrow, thin*
l' Europe *Europe*
l' examen *exam*
l' exercice *exercise*
faire des exercices
to exercise (as a sport)
excusez-moi (for.) *excuse me*
excuse-moi (inf.) *excuse me*

F

facile *easy*
la famille *family*
le facteur(m) le factrice(f) *mail carrier*
faible *weak*
la faim *hunger*
faire *to do, make*
je fais *I do, make*
Il fait beau. *The weather is nice.*
Il fait chaud. *The weather is hot.*
Il fait froid. *The weather is cold*
Il fait mauvais. *The weather is bad.*
(or, It's hot., etc.)
le froid *the cold*
fatigué(e) *tired*
le fauteuil *armchair*
le frère *brother*
la faveur *favor*
faire une faveur *to do a favor*
favori *favorite*
la femme *the woman*
la fenêtre *window*
la feuille *leaf, piece of paper*
février *February*
la fièvre *fever*
la fille *girl*
le fils *son (always with an "s")*
la fleur *flower*

le fleuve *river*
la fourchette *fork*
le fond *bottom*
le football *soccer*
le football Américain *football*
frais *cool*
la fraise *strawberry*
les fruits *fruit*
fort *strong*
fromage *cheese*

G

les gants *gloves*
le garçon *boy*
garder *to keep*
le garage *garage*
la gare *railroad station*
le gâteau *cake*
gauche *left*
à gauche *to the left*
gazeux(euse) *carbonated water*
non gazeux(euse) *non carbonated water*
généreux(euse) *generous*
le genre *the kind*
la glace *ice cream*
les gens *people*
Genève *Geneva*
la géométrie *geometry*
la gorge *throat*
le golf *golf*
la gomme *eraser*
grand(e) *big*
gris(e) *grey*
la Guadeloupe *Guadeloupe*
la grand-mère *grand mother*
le grand-père *grand father*
les grandparents *grand parents*
gros(sse) *fat, heavy*
la guitare *guitar*
le groupe *group*
la Guyane *Guyana*

H

habiter *to live*
le hamburger *hamburger*
les haricots (verts) *string beans*
l' heure *time*
Quelle heure est il? *What time is it?*
l' histoire *history*
historique *historical*
l' hiver *winter*
l' hôpital *hospital*
le hockey *hockey*
l' homme *man*
l' horaire *schedule*
les hors-d'oeuvre
appetizers (hors-d'oeuvres)

I

ici *here*
l' immeuble *building*
inconfortable *uncomfortable*
infirmier(e) *nurse*
intelligent(e) *intelligent*
l' informatique *computers*
intéressant(e) *interesting*
intérêt *interest*
inviter *to invite*
l' île *island*
l' Italien *Italian*
il y a *there is, there are*

J

la jambe *leg*
le jambon *ham*
la jaquette *jacket*
janvier *January*
jaune *yellow*
les jeans *jeans*
le jeu *game*
le jeu de vidéo *video game*
jeudi *Thursday*
jeune *young*
les jeunes *young people*
jetter *to throw*
jouer *to play*
joli(e) *pretty*
le jour *day*
le journal *newspaper*
les journaux *newspapers*
la journée *day*
juillet *July*
juin *June*
la jupe *skirt*
le jus *juice*
jusqu'à *until*

L

la *the*
le lac *lake*
laid(e) *ugly*
le lait *milk*
la laitue *lettuce*
la lampe *lamp*
le lavabo *bathroom sink*
laver *to wash*
le (s.) *the*
les (pl.) *the*
la leçon *lesson*
laver la vaisselle *to wash dishes*
les légumes *vegetables*
la lettre *letter*
la librairie *book store*
libre *free*
la ligne *line*
les lunettes *eyeglasses*
lire *to read*
je lis *I read*
le livre *book*
loin de *far from*
lundi *Monday*
le Luxembourg *Luxembourg*
le lycée *high school*

M

ma *my*
la machine *machine*
à calculer *calculator*
à laver *washing machine*
Madame (Mme) *Mrs.*
Mademoiselle (Mlle) *Miss*
le magasin *store*
magnifique *magnificent*
le magnétoscope *VCR*
mai *May*
maigre *slender*
maigrir *to loose weight*
le maïs *corn*
mal *bad*
avoir mal *to hurt*
le maillot *T-shirt*
le maillot de bain *bathing suit*
la main *hand*
la maison *house*
le maître *elementary or middle school teacher*
malade *sick*
Je suis malade. *I am sick.*
la Manche *English channel*
la manche *sleeve*
manger *to eat*
je mange *I eat*
nous mangeons *we eat*
manquer *to miss*
le manteau *coat*
le marchand(e) *merchant*
marcher *to walk*
mardi *Tuesday*
le mari *husband*
le mariage *marriage*
se marier *to get married*
le match *the match, game*
marron *brown*
mars *March*
le matin *morning*
la Martinique *Martinique*
les mathématiques *math*
mauvais(e) bad
il fait mauvais *the weather is bad*
le mécanicien *mechanic*
méchante *nasty*
Méditerranée *Mediterranean*
la même *same*
le melon *melon*
le médicament *medicine*
le meilleur(e) *the best*
le ménage *house cleaning*
faire le ménage *to clean house*
la mère *mother*
merci *thanks, thank you*
mercredi *Wednesday*
mes (pl.) *my*
la messe *mass*
le métro *subway*
le métier *manual job*
mille *thousand*
le mien(ne) *mine*
les miens, les miennes (pl.) *mine*
mince *thin*
minérale *mineral*
l' eau minérale *mineral water*
minute *minute*
Miquelon *Miquelon*
moderne *modern*
moi *I*
moi-même *myself*
moins *minus*
le mois *month*

mon *my*
la montre *wristwatch*
Monsieur (M.) *Mr., Sir*
le mouton *lamb*
le morceau *piece*
la mousse *whipped chocolate dessert*
moyen(ne) *average*
le mur *wall*
la musique *music*

N

nager *to swim*
nous nageons *we swim*
la natation *swimming*
naître *to be born*
je suis né(e) *I was born*
navré *sorry*
être navré *to be sorry*
je suis navré *I am sorry*
neiger *to snow*
il neige *it's snowing*
neuf *new, nine*
neuf-cents *nine hundred*
neuvième *ninth*
le neveu *nephew*
le nez *nose*
ni ... ni ... *neither ... nor ...*
la nièce *niece*
noir *black*
le nom *name*
nous *we, us*
non *no*
la note *grade*
la bonne note *the good grade*
la nourriture *food*
nuageux *cloudy*
Il fait nuageux. *It's cloudy.*
la nuit *night*
le numéro *number*
novembre *November*

O

obtenir *to obtain*
une occasion *an occasion*
l' océan *ocean*
octobre *October*
l' oeuf *egg*
les oeufs *eggs*
l' oeil *eye*
les yeux *eyes*
l' oignon *onion*
l' oncle *uncle*
onze *eleven*
onzième *eleventh*
une orange *orange*
l' oreille *ear*
l' ordinateur *computer*
l' ordre *order*
ou *or*
où *where*
où est *where is*
D'où es-tu? *Where are you from?*
l' ouest *west*
oui *yes*

P

Pacifique (l'océan) *Pacific Ocean*
le pain *bread*
le panier *basket*
le papa *papa*
le papier *paper*
le parapluie *umbrella*
parce que *because*
les parents *parents*
paresseux *lazy*
le parfum *perfume*
la parfumerie *perfume shop*
Paris *Paris*
parler *to talk*
participer *to participate*
la partie (le boum) *party*
partir *to leave, to go*
le passant *passer-by*
passer *to pass, to spend time*
passer un examen *to take a test*
la pâtisserie *bakery*
le pâtissier *baker*
pauvre *poor*
payer *to pay*
je paie *I pay*
le pays *country*
pendant *during*
petit(e) *small*
le petit déjeuner *breakfast*
les petits-enfants *grand children*
la petite-fille *grand daughter*
le petit-fils *grand son*
le père *father*
perdre *to lose*
personne *person*
la pièce *a room, a coin*

personnel(le) *personal*
le pied *foot*
à pied *by foot, on foot*
peu *little, few*
la pharmacie *drug store*
la physique *physics*
la pizza *pizza*
la plage *beach*
le plaisir *pleasure*
avec plaisir *with pleasure*
le plan (de métro) *subway map*
la pluie *rain*
Il pleut. *It's raining.*
plus-tard *later*
à plus-tard *see you later*
le porc *pork*
la poire *pear*
le poisson *fish store*
la poissonnerie *fish store*
la poitrine *chest, dresser*
le poivre *pepper*
le pôle *pole*
pôle nord *north pole*
la police *police*
la pomme *apple*
la pomme de terre *potato*
le pompier *fireman*
la porte *door*
porter *to carry*
la poste *post ofice*
la poubelle *garbage can*
le poulet *chicken*
pour *for*
le pourboire *tip*
pourquoi *why*
pouvoir *to be able to*
je peux *I can*
pratiquer *to practice*
premier *first*
premier janvier *January first*
préférer *to prefer*
prendre *to take*
je prends *I take*
presque *almost*
pressé(e) *hurried*
être pressé *to be in a hurry*
près de *near, close to*
le printemps *spring*
prochain(e) *next*
proche *near*
produire *to produce*
le professeur *professor*
le programme *program*
programmeur(m)
programmeuse(f)
computer programmer
la promenade *walk*
faire une promenade
to go for a walk
le pudding *pudding*
puissant(e) *powerful*
puisque *because, thus*
pull-over *sweater*
les Pyrénées *Pyrenees (mountains)*

Q

le quai *embankment*
le quartier *a district*
quand *when*
quarante *forty*
quatre *four*
quatrième *fourth*
quatre-vingts *eighty*
Le Québec *Quebec*
quel, quels (m) *which, what*
quel livre *which book*
quels livres *which books*
quelle, quelles (f) *which, what*
quelle robe *which dress*
quelles robes *which dresses*
quelque *some*
quelquefois *sometimes*
Qu'est-ce que c'est? *What is it?*
Qu'est-ce que tu fais?
What are you doing?
Qu'est-ce que vous faites?
What are you doing?
une question *a question*
poser une question
to ask a question
quinze *fifteen*
quinzième *fifteenth*
Quoi de neuf? *what's new?*

R

la radio *radio*
rapidement *quickly*
le raisin *grapes*
la raison *reason*
recevoir *to receive*
réfléchir *to think*
la receptioniste *receptionist*
la récréation *recreation*
le réfrigérateur *refrigerator*
regarder *to look*
regretter *to regret*
régulier *regular*
le relief *relief*
rencontrer *to met*
les renseignements *Information*
les repas *meal (always plural)*
répondre *to answer*
se reposer *to rest*
le restaurant *restaurant*
la Réunion *Reunion*
revenir *to come back*
la revue *magazine*
le rhume *(a) cold*
riche *rich*
être riche *to be rich*
le riz *rice*
la robe *dress*
romantique *romantic*
rouge *red*
le rosbif *roast beef*
rose *pink*
rôtir *to roast*
rôti *roasted*
la rue *street*
le rugby *rugby*

S

le sac *bag*
saignant *red(meat)*
la saison *season*
Saint Pierre *Saint Pierre*
la salade *salad*
la salle *room*
la salle de séjour, le salon *living room*
les sandales *sandals*
samedi *Saturday*
la sauce *sauce*
en sauce *in sauce*
la saucisse *sausage*
le saumon *salmon*
savoir *to know*
je sais *I know*
je ne sais pas *I don't know*
la science *science*
le sel *salt*
la semaine *week*
sentir *to feel*
séparer *to separate*
sept *seven*
septième *seventh*
septembre *September*
seul(e) *lonely, alone*
le serveur *waiter*
la serveuse *waitress*
la serviette *napkin, towel*
le short *shorts*
si *if (yes in response to a negative sentence)*
signe *sign*
s'il te plaît (inf.)
s'il vous plaît (for.)
please
simple *simple*
sincère *sincere*
six *six*
sixième *sixth*
skier *to ski*
le soda *soda*
la soeur *sister*
le sofa *sofa*
la soif *thirst*
avoir soif *to be thirsty*
j'ai soif *I am thirsty*
soixante *sixty*
soixante-dix *seventy*
les soldes *sales*
le soleil *sun*
Il fait du soleil. *It's sunny.*
la sortie *exit*
sortir *to exit, get out*
je sors *I get out, I leave*
la soupe *soup*
le sous-sol *basement*
souvent *often*

le sport sport
le stade *stadium*
la station *station (bus or subway)*
le stylo *ball point pen*
le sud *south*
le sujet *subject*
le supermarché *supermarket*
sur *on*
la Suisse *Switzerland*
sympathique *sympathetic*
la synagogue *synagogue*

T

la table *table*
le tableau *blackboard, painting*
la taille *size, waist*
la tante *aunt*
taper à la machine *typewriter*
la tarte *pie*
la tasse *cup*
le taxi *taxi*
la technologie *technology*
la température *temperature*
le temps *weather, time*
Quel temps fait-il?
What is the weather like?
le temps libre *free time*
le tennis *tennis*
les tennis *sneakers*
le téléphone *telephone*
téléphoner *to phone*
la télévision (la télé) *television*
la tête *head*
le thé *tea*
le théâtre *theater*
le thon *tuna*
la terrasse *terrace*
le ticket *ticket*
le timbre stamp
toi *you*
Et toi? *And you?*
les toilettes *bathrooms*
la tomate *tomato*
ton (m.) *your*
le tourisme *tourism*
le tourne-disque *record player*
tous(pl.) *all*
tous les jours *everyday*
tout(e) *all*
le train *train*
le transport *transport*
le travail *work*
travailler *to work*
traverser *to cross*
tranquille *quiet*
treize *thirteen*
treizième *thirteenth*
trente *thirty*
trentième *thirtieth*
très *very*
trois *three*
troisième *third*
tu (inf.) *you*

U

un (m.) *a*
une (f.) *a*

V

la vaisselle *dishes*
le veau *veal*
le vélo *bicycle*
vendre *to sell*
vendredi *Friday*
venir *to come*
le vent *wind*
Il fait du vent. *It's windy.*
vert *green*
le vêtement *clothing*
la viande *meat*
le vidéo *video*
la vie *life*
vieille(f.) *old*
vieux (m.) *old*
la ville *town*
vingt *twenty*
vingtième *twentieth*
la visite *visit*
visiter *to visit*
vivre *to live*
voici *here*
voilà *there*
voir *to see*
la voiture automobile

le volleyball *volleyball*
vouloir *to want*
voyager *to travel*

Z

zéro *zero*
le zoo *zoo*